Bob Dylan's Never Ending Tour

Published by Lasavia Publishing,

Auckland, New Zealand

www.lasaviapublishing.com

Copyright © Mike Johnson, 2025

Cover/Design: Daniela Gast

ISBN: 978-1-991083-34-0

Bob Dylan's
Never Ending Tour

Volume I

The Eighties and Nineties

Mike Johnson

LASAVIA
PUBLISHING

Acknowledgements

Thanks to Tony Attwood, for hosting this series on Untold Dylan, A special thanks to Rowan Sylva and Daniela Gast for their Herculean effort designing these volumes, and to Chris Griffin, my right-hand man when it came to locating and downloading concerts. Thanks also to Dylan scholar Jochen Markhorst for his comments and enthusiasm. My thanks To Janscie Sharplin for her poof-reading, comments and encouragement, and my family for their many years good natured tolerance of this Bobcat. Finally, a heartfelt thanks to the tapers and the bootleggers like Crystal Cat who made this series possible. As Dylan sang in Sugar Baby (2001) '*Some of these bootleggers, they make pretty good stuff.*'

Preface by Tony Attwood

In February 2020, Mike Johnson sent me an article which opened with the tentative statement that, "I begin this journey through thirty-two years (and counting) of Bob Dylan's Never Ending Tour with many fears and trepidations..." I was invited to consider publishing the series in the daily *Untold Dylan* blog.

Four years later I received the 144th and final article, "Virgil's farewell: It's not dark yet", and the most important and most informative series of articles on Bob Dylan it has ever been my honour to read, let alone publish, was complete.

Of course, as a blog publisher, one is used to series starting with trumpets blaring, and then faltering to an early conclusion, as the author realises just how much work it takes to write well-considered and historically accurate articles week after week. And so, sadly, more often than not, the great plans hatched in the imaginations of contributors quickly falter and fade, never reaching their promised conclusion.

Mike however is made of different stuff. He had, after all, already completed the "Master Harpist" series for the Untold Dylan website. I thought that was indeed a "masterful" series, but it was as nothing when compared with what was the follow.

144 episodes of insights and musical examples. It made *Untold Dylan* a force to be reckoned with, and leaves me eternally in Mike's debt. Indeed it was Mike's work that took us to over 4 million hits in one year for the first time. A publisher does not forget that.

Tony Attwood, publisher *Untold Dylan*.

Contents

Foreword by Jochen Markhorst

The Echo Man

In 1992, renowned, famously infamous East German Liedermacher and satirist Wolf Biermann is siting with his guitar on a stage in Vienna and freezes. Total black-out. For the love of God he cannot remember the first line, nor the melody or the chords of *"Die Ballade vom gut Kirschenessen"* – The Ballad Of Tangling Well:

> It lasted maybe a minute, which is an eternity in front of so many strangers who have paid for a ticket. Nothing tragic, I saved myself with the truth and stuttered: my head is cloudy from four days in the stench of the Stasi files.

(*Tiefer als unter die Haut* - Deeper than under the skin, *Spiegel,* 27 January 1992)

Biermann was exiled from the GDR as an enemy of the state in 1977. Two years after the fall of the Wall, he finds the courage to request the thousands and thousands of pages of his Stasi file. And then reads everything: which "friends" were actually in the service of the dreaded East German secret service, the Stasi, which neighbours betrayed him, the eavesdropping protocols, the plots to compromise him with drugs, with underage prostitutes, and whatnot, the attempts to seduce his wife or get him killed in a staged accident.

Four days he ploughs through the disgusting muck, the fifth day he has to performin Vienna. Understandably, his mind goes blank. After that interminable minute's silence and his apology, he recovers, plays his popular 1966 hit *"Populär-Ballade,"* but bursts into laughter after the first chorus, stops playing, grabs his notebook, and then reads "in original Stasi-prose" from a wiretapping protocol. Source: "the bug under my bed:"

Wolfgang Biermann had sexual intercourse with a woman. Later he asks if she is hungry. The lady states that she would like a Cognac. It is Eva

Hagen. Afterwards there is silence in the object.

Equally witty, slightly less wry but more cynical is the *"Echomann"* protocol he also discovered in the acts. While eavesdropping, the spies note down everything they can pick up from Biermann's home, including the new songs he rehearses. Ironically, also the new song in which he sings of his deep pity for the eavesdropping officials:

> *I feel humanly connected*
> *With the poor Stasi dogs*
> *Who in snow and downpours*
> *Have to watch out for me with difficulty*
> *Who installed a microphone*
> *To hear all the loud songs*
> *Jokes, quiet curses*
> *In the loo and in the kitchen*
> *Brothers from securityYou alone know all my suffering*
> *You alone can bear witness*
> *How all my human endeavour*
> *Passionate, tender and wild*
> *Is for our great cause*
> *Words that would otherwise have disappeared*
> *You capture them firmly on tape*
> *And I know that every now and then*
> *You sing my songs in bed*
> *Gratefully I give you credit:*
> *The Stasi is my Ecker-*
> *The Stasi is my Ecker-*
> *The Stasi is my Eckermann.*

Any German who paid attention in school knows who Johann Peter Eckermann was: Goethe's friend and unofficial secretary in the last nine years. Eckermann tirelessly listened and noted down everything Goethe spoke, sifting from his thousands of notes a wealth of pearls, wisdoms, aphorisms and observations, and after Goethe's death published *Gespräche mit Goethe in den letzten Jahren seines Lebens* ("Conversations with Goethe in the Last Years of His Life"), according to Nietzsche *"das beste deutsche Buch, das es giebt"* - the best German book there is.

But apparently the Stasi servants never heard of Eckermann. Contagiously ridiculing them, Biermann reads out what *the poor Stasi dogs* thought they understood:

> *The Stasi is my Echo--*
> *The Stasi is my Echo--*
> *The Stasi is my Echo-man*

About two hundred years later, the Goethe of our time is on stage. He never blacks out or freezes, he knows his songs well before he starts singin', and he has his own Eckermann. Fortunately not an uncultivated Stasi dog, but a real Eckermann. An Eckermann who, like Johann Peter at the time, has an uncanny ear for the remarkable, who has the vistas to put the remarkable into context and the writing skills to communicate it. Well, *more* than just communicating actually.

Mike Johnson, even more so than our Johann Peter, is blessed with poetic talent. "On this side of the gates we stand in the fallen, nightmarish world and face the ineffable, the mystery of mysteries, all that lies beyond our known world of pain and war, beyond the weary world of words. What lies behind the knowable?" asks Mike before letting us listen with new ears to Dylan's 31 October 1964 performance of *Gates Of Eden*.

"Note the extra chord between verses that Dylan was later to drop," Mike instructs us. And then slaloms past Hieronymus Bosch and Revelations, points out a missing harmonica, picks the finest 1965 performance, surprisingly finds a parallel with *Mr Tambourine Man* and, for dessert, serves up a fascinating, informal *Gates Of Eden* studio recording of Dylan and George Harrison.

"*Rollin and Tumblin'* was always meant to be a rough and rowdy, hard-edged basic blues. Another night of sweaty insomnia and anger, that hint of violence again," warns Mike before we press the play button to hear the Rothbury 2009 rendition. Or, equally poetic, analytical, and stimulating on a *John Brown* version that is "both simpler and more deadly."

Or almost philosophical about Dylan's harmonica playing in a *Tangled Up In Blue* performance: "Experience, as mediated through memory, becomes something not so much to be celebrated with wild sounds but gently probed. A whiff of sadness and nostalgia for times past can be heard in the opening and closing harp breaks."

For years and years, miner Mike Johnson hacked his way through mighty mountains of live performances, endlessly and tirelessly sifting through the ore, bringing out the precious stone to the surface, and crafting it into sparkling jewellery:

Mike Johnson is our Ecker-
Mike Johnson is our Ecker-
Mike Johnson is our Eckermann.
... writing perhaps *"das beste Dylanbuch das es gibe"*

Editor's note

Mike Johnson's epic three-volume work, *The Never Ending Tour* is adapted from his popular blog series of the same name, published on the Untold Dylan website. In adapting the blog series to a print book we opted for a minimal intervention approach, retaining the idiosyncrasies of the blog form. The small chapters, for example, still say by Kiwipoet at the top, Johnson's blogging name, and each chapter signs off with his trademark, until next time, Kia Ora. It also contains references to earlier blog posts.

The posts were written and published over a four-year period between 2020 and 2024, and while they cover thirty-two years of Bob Dylan's professional life they also reflect the changes in the world in which they were written. Earlier posts reference things such as Covid-19 while posts written after 2020 contain plenty of references to the Russian Ukraine war. Some stylistic issues also changed along the way. In the early posts, Johnson provided a title for the different years. In later posts he drops that, having a title for the chapters only.

The most challenging aspect of adapting the blog posts to a book form was how to deal the multi-media aspect. The posts essentially curated the best, or most interesting, performances from bootleg recording of each given year. Listening to the music was a key part of enjoying and understanding the posts. Unfortunately, that is something that the print book cannot on its own provide. Readers are thus encouraged to look up the relevant blog post and corresponding audio link on **bob-dylan.org. uk/never-ending-tour**.

Introduction, or, How To Use This Book

'I've been in trouble ever since I put my suitcase down.' (Bob Dylan, 'Mississippi')

What is known as The Never Ending Tour is a remarkable musical odyssey beginning in 1988 and effectively ending in 2019 when covid closed the venues, thirty-one years of continuous touring, averaging around a hundred concerts per year. It was not the end of Dylan's live concert career, however. In 2021 he hit the road again with his Rough and Rowdy Ways tour and, at 83, is still on the road even as I write.

It has been my job to act as your guide for those thirty-one years, but with some 3066 concerts in all, and with an average of nineteen songs per concert, we have over 58,000 performances, and while I have striven to find the best of these performances my selection has been inevitably personal.

Written over four years for the blog Untold Dylan, these articles have been a journey of exploration for me into the nature of this Nobel Prize winner's art. Themes emerged which I will not anticipate here except to say they relate to the dramatic nature of Dylan's performance art and the 'collage' like nature of his songwriting. One of the fascinations of this journey has been to accompany Dylan in his exploration of American music to its deepest roots.

It was also fascinating to watch the development of this artist who outgrew all the understanding or images we might have of him. By 2019 he had become something else, a Renaissance Man of music, somebody who could exemplify and encompass a huge and varied tradition, while at the same time making something new out of it.

This book is not just for Dylan aficionados but for all those interested in the history and development of modern music. At this point, no one has to argue Dylan's pivotal role in that history, and what we can witness in this book is how that played out onstage in the post-youthful phase of Dylan's career, for Dylan was forty-seven when he hit the road in 1988. For many he was already history. and that suited him fine, he had room to reshape himself. And shape the band that evolved with him over the years to become one of the finest bands to ever hit the stage. 'You may buy the ticket because it has Dylan's name on it; you will leave having seen one of the greatest bands you will ever see live.' Tim Sommer.

Hearing that band in action is one of the pleasures of this book.

To get the most out of this book you will need a device for accessing the internet and decent headphones or speakers. Headphones that muffle the sound, or have too much bass, don't do justice to these informal, raw audience recordings. I use HD 569 headphones which are not expensive and give a clear, crisp sound.

Each of the 144 chapters contains links to the website, Untold Dylan, where this series was first hosted and where you can listen to the songs discussed. The articles are there too, and at first I did not see the need for a book. There is a growing awareness, however, that most of us are more comfortable, and retain information better, reading off the page when it comes to longer texts, and of course a book offers freedom from endless scrolling, dealing with adverts etc. Flicking through a book is far more satisfying than scrolling and clicking.

My proof reader, Janscie Sharplin, helped convince me that the articles were worth preserving in a 'form that can be seen more as a whole work.' The reader can enter the book at any given year, it doesn't have to be read in sequence, but if it is read in sequence a narrative of that musical odyssey emerges. It's an exciting adventure if you want to follow it from the beginning.

With these raw recordings you will probably need to adjust your volume with each new song. The Mp3s do vary in quality somewhat, have different qualities of sound depending on the particular recording, I had to exclude some material as it was sonically inferior, but what is here are the best I could find.

Enjoy the experience. The pleasure of reading a book and listening to one of the greatest performing artists of our time.

Mike Johnson
Waiheke Island
April 2025

1987

NET: 1987 – Farewell to all that

By Mike Johnson (Kiwipoet)

'And I try to harmonize with songs the lonesome sparrow sings'
(Gates of Eden)

I begin this journey through thirty-two years (and counting) of Bob Dylan's Never Ending Tour with many fears and trepidations. I have to confess from the outset that I am no Dylan scholar; there are few Dylan books upon my shelf. Of Dylan's life I know very little. I got about half way through Clinton Heylin's compendious *Behind the Shades* but gave up on it. I'd rather spend the time I had listening to the songs.

That there might be something more to this than mere indifference only recently occurred to me when I encountered this quote from Jalāl ad-Dīn Muhammad Rūmī, a Persian poet from the Thirteenth Century:

> 'Study me as much as you like, you will never know me.
> For I differ a hundred ways from what you see me to be ...
> I have chosen to dwell in a place you can't see.'

Does this remind you of anybody we know? Wherever you think he is, he's not there. In a similar vein Dylan has said:

> 'I change during the course of a day. I wake and I'm one person, and when I go to sleep I know for certain I'm somebody else.'

Rather than study Dylan, I immerse myself in the songs, entering them as one might a warm bath. You don't study a warm bath, it might go cold on you; you just get into it. There may be hidden glimmerings of a life behind the songs, but it is through the songs themselves, and their various performances, that we come to know who 'Bob Dylan' is. And he is what he is in that moment of performance only. 'I'm only Bob Dylan when I have to be. Most of the time I'm just myself.' Most of the time.

So my journey through the NET will not become a biography, but rather move from performance to performance, the best performances of each year, at least those I can find. Unfortunately, I cannot date every performance, or move chronologically through each year, as my own records are patchy, and I sometimes didn't keep the date of the song, only the year.

I could go on with more fears and trepidations and confessions of unfitness for the task ahead, but now I'm impatient to get on with it.

The first concert of the NET was on June 7 1988, but the best place to start is the year before, so we can get a sense of where Dylan was before the tour kicked off.

The misleading popular press would have it that Dylan was 'in a sad place' in 1987, in the months leading up to the tour. We are led to believe that he was 'lost' and 'in search of directions.' Maybe so, but this is not reflected the performances of that year, which are full of power and vigour.

Dylan worked with two bands in 1987, Tom Petty's band and the

Grateful Dead. Dylan had been working with Petty's band since 1985, and by 1987 the performances were assured and confident. Dylan's voice was sharp and clear, but he'd developed a staccato vocal style, breaking up his longer lines into shorter bursts and even single words, and this would carry through into 1988.

You can hear this breaking up of the lines clearly in the following performance of 'Forever Young.' The simple, clichéd lyrics can hardly account for the power of this song, which I believe lies in the impossibility of its repeated injunction: 'may you stay forever young.' There's a heartbreak in here; we'd like to stay forever young, and our children too, but it is a forlorn yearning. Time will be time.

Of course we can stay young at heart, but even that doesn't last forever. The two versions of 'Forever Young' on the 1974 *Planet Waves* album point to the different ways of delivering this song, as an uplifting, upbeat celebration – or a dirge. The ninety-one year old Pete Seeger played it upbeat on the Dylan Amnesty tribute album, *Chimes of Freedom* (2012), but Dylan has almost always played it as a dirge, drawing out the essential pathos of the song. The slower the beat, the more drawn out and agonizing the main injunction becomes.

None more so than with this performance, London, November 17. Those who followed my Master Harpist series will be happy to note the thoughtful, gentle harp solo that introduces the song. The harp solo elaborates the theme of mortality, and improvises around the sad-making melody line with its doomed uplift.

[Forever Young]

Wonderful, to hear way the voices of the girl chorus come floating in as we reach the end of the verses. Although he'd been working with girl choruses since the 1978 tour, and they played a big role in the Gospel years, by 1987 Dylan was using them very discretely and with subtle effect. Enjoy them while you can as 1987 was the last year Dylan was to use them.

Wonderful too, to hear how Petty's pianist Beaumont Tench anchors the musical line with playing that is solid and inventive.

Tench's piano can also be heard to great effect on this haunting performance of 'John Brown', a little skipping riff that adds to the eeriness of the effect.

[John Brown]

'John Brown' is one of those songs never officially released but which crept up on us through performances. Like 'Masters of War', John Brown is seen as an anti-war, protest song. It is that, but the driving heart of the song is the dramatic confrontation between mother and son on the train platform, when John Brown 'comes home from the war.'
The first verses quickly take John Brown off to war and back again, and build up the mother's dewy-eyed patriotism and pride.

> 'She got a letter once in a while and her face broke into a smile
> As she showed them to the people from next door
> And she bragged about her son with his uniform and gun
> And these things she called a good old-fashioned war.'

Her illusions are shattered when her son returns, a broken man, to accuse her, and he finally 'dropped his medals down into her hand.' It is the bitterness of the young man, and the folly of his mother, that drives the narrative. At the same time, we get what is perhaps Dylan's most succinct attack on war, a telling observation that must surely resonate in our own age of perpetual war:

> "Oh, and I thought when I was there, God, what am I doing here?
> I'm a-tryin' to kill somebody or die tryin'.
> But the thing that scared me most
> was when my enemy came close
> And I saw that his face looked just like mine."

'Die trying' has entered our language as an expression of determination, but it is that identification of self with the hostile other that gives the song its touch of greatness. The songs on *John Wesely Harding* (1967) are shot through with moral paradoxes and mysteries. 'I dreamed I saw Saint Augustine', written twelve years before Dylan's conversion to Christianity, is steeped in religious feeling, a sense of spiritual despair. St Augustine is doomed to 'tear through these quarters', that is our world, 'searching for the very souls/ whom already have been sold.'
    At the end of the song we are confronted with the same realization that

we found in John Brown – we are our own enemies.

> I dreamed I saw St. Augustine
> Alive with fiery breath
> And I dreamed I was amongst the ones
> That put him out to death
> Oh, I awoke in anger
> So alone and terrified
> I put my fingers against the glass
> And bowed my head and cried

On the album, the song comes over as sad, and slow, but in performance, and these are quite rare, there is an added sense of anger and despair. In 1987, his 'cut up' vocals lends the song a strange edge, as if each word or phrase is being torn out of the melodic line, torn out of the singers throat. A wonderful, powerful performance, again anchored by Tench's piano.

[I thought I Saw St Augustine]

Another song from that album that Dylan began to feature that year is 'Wicked Messenger'. A mysterious narrative with religious overtones, I've always thought of it as a sister song to 'All along the watchtower' and it can be powerful in performance. It is, however, perhaps a little too mysterious, and without the apocalyptic subtext of 'Watchtower', although both songs appear to bring bad news.

I particularly like the sound the band achieves in this performance, a hard, rough and ready, minimal sound. Interesting, how Dylan was slowly shaping Petty's band, which can play loud and heavy, into this thin, sharp sound. It's beginning to sound more like he effect he will achieve in the first years of the NET.

[Wicked Messenger]

We will see this song emerge in the late 90s in powerful, upbeat forms, but I think it's the musical and vocal timing in this one that makes it one of my favourites.

'I and I', a gentle little song from the second side of *Infidels*, 1984, became a staple of the Petty years, often hard, bashing versions. By 1987 the sound was cut back to a crisp minimum. It's worth picking up on the song here, as it will re-emerge in the 90s in both hard rock and softer forms.

[I and I]

There's an apocryphal tale told about Dylan and Lenard Cohen having a conversion. Dylan expresses his admiration for Cohen's 'Halleluiah', and asks him how long it took to write. "Five years," Cohen replies, then expresses his admiration for 'I and I' and asks how long Dylan took to compose it. "Fifteen minutes," Dyan says. In terms of the lyrics, it's an offbeat, whimsical song, touched with fantasy, which seems to express our fundamental aloneness in the world, even from our lovers, although the thought of them might offer comfort. The song contains the genius line: 'Someone else is speaking with my mouth/but I'm listening only to my heart.'

And that wonderful chorus line:

'I and I, in creation where one's nature
neither honours nor forgives.'

Another hard, unremitting, Old Testament view of human nature.

A song that will also stick around well into the 90s is the apocalyptic, 'Senor', off the 1978 album *Street Legal*. There are some fine performances of this song during the Gospel years but here, in 1987, it gets a particularly passionate treatment. (I have written about this song in Master Harpist 3, and suggest the reader check out those comments). Tench and Dylan again work well, with a hard-edged but minimal rock sound.

[Senor]

What Dylan setlist would be complete without 'The Times They Are A-changing', the protest song that doesn't protest anything? It must be in the running for Dylan's most iconic song, and we'll see it going through its own changings. In 1987 he could still deliver it like the Dylan of old, as a challenge, and play discordant harp just like he used to. As he grows older, the stridency of the song will give way to more mellow, philosophical performances; like that other iconic protest song, 'Blowin in the wind', 'Times...' is more like a meditation on time than a call to arms.

[The Times They Are A-Changin']

The work Dylan did with the Grateful Dead has been pretty well documented. Like other Dylan commentators, I often find the results strangely lacking despite the obvious effort everyone is putting in. There are however some real gems. Among them is a rare performance of 'Under your spell', the final track on Knocked out loaded, 1986. It is a forlorn song indeed, straight from the dark night of the soul: 'I was knocked out and loaded in the naked night...'

The soul is in a piteous state, unable to connect emotionally or spiritually, facing death 'two feet from the well'; in other words, so close to salvation, yet so far away. I take the 'well' to imply the waters of life in the deserts of feeling. The last lines are pure Old Testament despair:

> 'Well the desert is hot, the mountain is cursed
> Pray that I don't die of thirst
> Baby, two feet from the well'
> Surely must be Dylan's most despairing last lines ever.
> To 'let the dead bury the dead' (Mathew 8: 22) suggests we put
> aside the past so we might be 'born again' into the future free
> of spirit. In this song, however, the spirit is heavily burdened by
> emotional stuff, intoxicated and unable to shake free.
> I'll see you later when I'm not so out of my head
> Maybe next time I'll let the dead bury the dead

[Under Your Spell]

Because of the poor recording, Dylan's voice sounds distant and wan – you have to strain to hear it - and this, more by accident than design I'm sure, fits in perfectly with songs ambience, its inherent pathos. A distant keening voice, almost extinguished. The thin sound of the harmonica picks up on that dreary mood and carries it to the end of the song. A mini masterpiece it seems to me.

'Idiot wind,' an acknowledged masterpiece, is difficult song to sustain in performance. It's long and angry and I imagine takes a considerable emotional effort. Yet it remains the greatest of Dylan's 'attack' songs, full of spite, anger, self-justification, smugness, pain and more pain – it's an emotional tour-de-force. In this performance with the Grateful Dead, Dylan gives it all he's got. Not an easy song to listen to, to see a soul laid bare in such a way. Magnificent.

[Idiot Wind]

As is this ripping performance of 'Ballad of a Thin Man', another song that we will often run into on our journey through the NET. I think it's about the soul's encounter with 'otherness' – the Other. In this age of multiple sexualities, this song seems to me to be more relevant than ever A carnival of the libido. These distorted carnival freaks reflect our own sexuality back to us, throw it in our faces, and when they're done they say – 'Here is your throat back, thanks for the loan.'

In carnival land, your power, status and literary pretentions mean nothing. Logic gives way to absurdity. Ego has nothing to cling to. You are in existential free fall crying 'Oh my God am I here all alone.' Riddled with sexual imagery, the song sounds best when it's given a sinister twist, as it is on the album Highway 61 Revisted, 1965. In this 1987 performance Dylan is in fine voice and there's some nice guitar work by Gerry Garcia.

[Ballad of a Thin Man]

If there is such a thing as definitive 'Knocking on Heaven's' door, then this epic performance must be it. He just keeps on knocking! Is that a newly made-up verse I hear towards the end? Yes, and it sounds good.

This is a song of farewell, the final farewell of all. Death looms over the sweetness of this song, and Garcia sounds inspired. It's Dylan's vocal however which commands attention. Anyone tells you Dylan can't sing, play them this one. Vibrant and passionate, full of promise. A perfect way to end this post.

[Knocking on Heavens Door]

See you next time for 1988, when the tour kicks off for real.

Kia Ora!

1988

NET 1988: Desperate stratagems, Part 1 - Heroes and Villains

By Mike Johnson (Kiwipoet)

'They say sing while you slave
and I just get bored' (Maggie's Farm)

When Bob Dylan appeared at Concord Pavilion on June 7 1988 for the first concert of a tour that was to last for the rest of his life, his line up was strictly minimal: lead guitar, bass and drums. With Dylan playing second or rhythm guitar. Gone were the big bands and girl choruses.

It was back to basics for Bob, with GE Smith on lead guitar, Kenny Aaronson on bass and Chris Parker on drums. But thanks to GE Smith's comprehensive guitar work, the band didn't sound too minimal. The pace was mostly fast and jangly. Often the guitars became a blurred, amorphous 'wall of sound' sound behind Dylan's voice.

Not all Dylan followers like the GE Smith period, which was to last until 1991, accusing him of pulverising Dylan's subtle melodies with his often shattering sound, but I don't think Smith was entirely responsible for that. Dylan himself seems, at times, to be assaulting his songs as much as singing them, rattling through them as if to get them out of the way, as if he's sick of them.

These 1988 performances create an ambivalent effect. On one hand Dylan's voice is as powerful and expressive as ever, on the other hand he seems to want to tear the heart out of the songs. His voice is a shock, too, for those used to his clear high mercurial tones; he grunts and snarls and vocalises in a hoarse, breathless, broken style like a man at the end of his tether. His frustration is palpable. You wanna hear this old song again? Well here it is, watch me rip it to pieces.

[Like A Rolling Stone]

An unsettling listening experience, I think you'll agree, but it's become my favourite because it's so unsettling. The gleeful triumph of the Sixties performances has given way to a muffled rage. Almost sounds like the Sex Pistols!

Such 'attack' songs have been criticised as being vindictive, and this performance might support that impression, but it's too easy to forget the influence of Existentialism in the 1960s when those songs were written. Everybody was reading Camus or a book by Colin Wilson called The Outsider. The idea is that most of us live in bad faith; we are not honest with ourselves or each other. We choose our blindness. We cling to precious illusions. What we need to do is live 'authentic' lives.

The girl accused in 'Like A Rolling Stone' is an example of the worst kind of bad faith – a wilful blindness built on snobbery. Ultimately, living inauthentically is not living at all. This same understanding animates other songs too, 'Ramona', 'She Belongs to Me', 'Positively Fourth Street.'

The shattering of pretensions, illusions and delusions lie behind such great songs as 'It's Alright, Ma...' and 'Gates of Eden'. In that song, political, religious and ontological delusions are mocked, made meaningless, by the mysterious gates. Only behind those gates is the source of authenticity to be found; the only source of truth.

> 'Sometimes I think there are no words
> But these to say what's true
> And there are no truths
> Outside the gates of Eden'

I love the softer, more spooky versions from the late 90s, which take advantage of the Celtic melody, but this angry, powerful version reminds us that this is a kind of protest song. The drums crash and roll; the guitars plunge through the chords. No surrender to melodic sweetness here. Some of the lines come to life with this rough treatment.

> 'The savage soldier sticks his head in sand
> and then complains...'

Wilful blindness again. The nightmare hallucinatory visions are thrown into stark relief by Dylan's emphatic 1988 style.

> 'The lamppost stands with folded arms
> its iron claws attached.'

[Gates of Eden]

The year, however, was not totally dominated by GE Smith's guitar. There were a few great acoustic moments we can't pass over. One is a strong rendition of 'With God on Our Side,' recorded in Oakland for TV (12/4), which accounts for its superior quality. You can still find this on You Tube. We could quibble that this song was recorded before the NET tour began, but I think it's too good to miss. I was reluctant to drop it on that technicality because Dylan adds a verse about the Vietnam war he doesn't use again. That war becomes included in the list of false histories learned at school.

> 'The names of the heroes
> I was made to memorise
> With guns in their hands
> And god on their side.'

Some things don't change much, it seems. This is one song that doesn't alter significantly in performance, although these performances are rare enough. This sounds pretty much as it will sound six years later at the Unplugged 1994 concert, just a bit rawer.

[God on Our Side]

Wonderful to hear Dylan play acoustic solo guitar. I think Dylan has a second guitar with him on this folk classic 'Barbara Allen', a rough-edged performance which, because it doesn't fall into a steady beat, sounds like a cross between a recitation and a song. A compelling performance. It's of special interest because of its mention of Scarlet Town and Sweet William, both of which will appear in Dylan's 2013 song 'Scarlet Town.' What a treasure this one is for those who love the folkie Dylan.

[Barbara Allen]

And while we're on the subject of acoustic performances, along comes 'The Times They Are A-Changing' again. I prefer this more intense, thoughtful version to the raucous, crowd-pleasing 1987 version, although I do miss Tench's piano. (See NET 1987) The song changes with the times and suits the 1988 minimal sound just as much as big, dramatic productions.

[Times They Are a-Changing]

The next offering is a real delight, capturing a rare performance of 'The Ballad of Frankie Lee and Judas Priest' from the 1967 album *John Wesley Harding*. Dylan tried a few talking songs during *The Basement Tapes* era that preceded the album, but this is one of the few to make it onto an album. I've never quite worked the song out, despite being apparently told the moral at the end. The so-called moral just increases our puzzlement. It's all about temptation and falling into illusion, but it's a lot less straightforward than it seems: nothing is revealed.

> 'No one tried to say a thing
> When they took him out in jest
> Except, of course, the little neighbour boy
> Who carried him to rest
> And he just walked along, alone
> With his guilt so well concealed
> And muttered underneath his breath
> Nothing is revealed'

It bounces along very nicely, however. GE Smith behaves himself and it makes for a lighter moment among some intense performances.

[Frankie Lee and Judas Priest]

At this stage, I think, we begin to notice something. Because Dylan almost never pulls out the harmonica, and because GE Smith often puts himself in the background, the whole weight of the performance falls on Dylan's voice. Despite GE Smith's ability to produce quite a racket, the performances have a minimalist feel. This gives 1988 its unique sound; that harried, hurried, somehow forced rush of a voice carries the show.
A more gentler song like 'Man in Me' from the 1970 *New Morning* album, however, takes on a sharper edge in the 1988 performances. Dylan's half-shouting vocal style brings the song to life. A sudden eruption of joyousness. When you stop hiding (from yourself and others) you can be your authentic self. 'Oh, what a wonderful feeling!'

[The Man in Me]

'Joey,' of the 1975 *Desire* album, has never been one of my favourite songs. I find that it drags, and I haven't often listened to it all the way through. Underneath it all, I think I am resistant to a celebration of a gangster's life. I can't help contrasting it to 'The Lonesome Death of Hattie Carrol' in which a poor, black working woman is randomly killed by a gangster who could have been Joey. If this is a protest song, it seems to miss the mark. I include it here, however, out of a sense of duty since it was very rarely performed, and this is a powerful performance, stronger than the album version I would say. The song benefits from Dylan's energetic, half shouting, 1988 style.

[Joey]

Arguably, 'Blonde on Blonde' is Dylan's greatest album. Dylan's adolescent, petulant whine and insinuating vocal style gives many of those songs something of a sinister edge that has never been duplicated in subsequent performances, at least for me. Dylan's voice keeps hinting at some subtext we have to keep reaching for, giving the songs a depth and mystery beyond their lyrics. 'Absolutely Sweet Marie' is a good example. All that brooding resentment and whining complaint perfectly delivered in Dylan's wah-wah Sixties-tones, the inimitable rise and fall of his voice.

> 'I waited for you
> when I was half-sick
> I waited for you
> When you hated me
> I waited for you
> Inside of the frozen traffic
> When you knew I had
> Some other place to be'

This tone doesn't come across in later performances. In 1988 we get the energy and the anger – and a bouncy rock song. It's a lively performance, and what it does do is remind us of the rock and roll roots of Dylan's music; it almost has a 50s feel, Buddy Holly like. Dylan snarls and jeers in fine 1988 style, and if you can forget about the album version, it's quite a lot of fun.

[Absolutely Sweet Marie]

I've reserved the last slot of Part 1 for a cover. Dylan does Lenard Cohen. Hallelujah! As well as Cohen's own loveable plodding version, and Jeff Buckley's soft and soulful version, we have some sixty other cover versions, most of them in the Buckley vein. Typical of Dylan's 1988 mood, that the song should be shouted out, the repeated 'Hallelujah!' more like a cry of agony than a shout of joy.

[Hallelujah]
We'll be back shortly with Part 2, 1988, for more of that year's rich and abrasive sounds.

Kia Ora!

NET 1988: Part 2 – the 1960s revisited

Check any setlist of Dylan's in 1988 and you'll find it weighted towards his sixties hits, his tried and true favourites. We have traditional folk songs, and 'Silvio' and 'Rank Strangers', not written by Dylan, from the album Down in the Groove released in May 1988, just before the NET began. I found one performance of 'Drifting too far from Shore' from Knocked Out Loaded, 1986, but the recording is too poor to include here.

The ten songs in this post, therefore, are from his early period, 1962 to 1966. What he appears to be doing is putting together a group of core songs, known to the audience, and popular songs on which his reputation was built. This group of songs, with variations, was to carry him through into the 2000s when a lot of new songs would come on stream, and the sixties material would begin to take a back seat. He wanted durable songs that would keep him going night after night. And there were plenty to find.

Songs like 'Just Like Tom Thumb Blues', the junky's lament. He delivers the song in a brisk four and half minutes here. It's pretty up-tempo, which may not appeal to everybody. The song may better suit the world-weary, druggy slowness you find on the album version. The backing is mediocre, but, as in all these 1988 performances, Dylan's voice, right up front, pushes the song right into your face.

[Just like Tom Thumb's Blues]

We heard John Brown powerfully delivered in 1987, and this 1988 version is hardly less powerful, although I do miss Baumont Tench's nifty piano riff (see NET, part 1, 1987). The pace is a little slower, Dylan's vocal delivery more emphatic than the 1987 performance, and GE Smith's sharp, twangy sound fits well with the hard-edged drama that takes place between the returning soldier and his mother.

[John Brown]

For the fan of the old acoustic Dylan, however, it is Dylan's acoustic performances of 1988 that must stand out. Dylan continued to perform solo acoustic guitar with his songs until 1993, so while this version of his 1964 classic 'Love Minus Zero/No Limit' is to be surpassed in later, more sumptuous versions, this 'primitive' simple solo strumming takes us right back to the old Dylan, the tousled haired kid who charmed us with his poetry.

This song happily idolises his love without the awful sting in the tail we get with songs like 'She Belongs to Me.' There's a tenderness and beauty that even the gruff 1988 Dylan can't hide. This song is tribute to his love. There is a touch of the divine to this figure, who, possessed by a deep wisdom, seems to rise above the everyday aspects of life.

> 'The cloak and dagger dangles
> Madams light the candles
> In ceremonies of the horsemen
> Even the pawn must hold a grudge
> Statues made of matchsticks
> Crumble into one another
> My love winks, she does not bother
> She knows too much to argue or to judge'

[Love Minus Zero]

Similarly, 'A Hard Rain's A-Gonna Fall' sounds pretty much the way Dylan first sang it, way back in 1962. Perhaps his greatest protest song, a surreal nightmare of what life might be like in an apocalypse. Surely this song must ring a bell in a world right now suffering it own viral apocalypse. These images are terrifying and universal, images of a dying world which speak just as clearly to us now as they did when they were written. The harsh, urgent, 1988 voice suits the song perfectly.

[Hard rain]

Written in 1967, thirteen years before Dylan's Christian period, 'I shall be released' expresses the desire of the soul for liberation, for release. Release from being hemmed in, trapped and isolated in 'this lonely crowd'. We find this theme in 'All Along the Watchtower,' and still going strong in 'Mississippi,' in 2001, where the soul is 'all boxed in no room to escape.' In 'I Shall be Released' we find: 'So, I swear I see my reflection/Somewhere inside these walls.'

I bet that pretty much describes a lot of us right now living in lockdown. The raucous versions from The Rolling Thunder Tour, with The Band singing along, do not, to my mind, serve this rather delicate, oblique little song that well; it suits a quieter, more acoustic sound. We don't get that exactly with GE Smith in the background, but it's great to hear Dylan singing solo on the choruses, and, sounding raw, this is as affecting as any performance you might hear.

[I Shall be Released]

There are some songs that remind us of Dylan's rock/blues roots, and 'It takes a lot to laugh, it takes a train to cry' (1965), is one of those. On the album, *Highway 61 Revisited* (1965), it takes the form of a gentle, lyrical, bluesy ballad, somewhat on the melancholy side.

> 'Now, the wintertime is comin', the windows are filled with frost
> I went to tell everybody but I could not get across
> Well, I want to be your lover, baby, I don't want to be your boss
> Don't say I never warned you when your train gets lost.'

It has the feel of country blues about it with simple strumming and minimal backing. In performance it became something else, a heavier and more urban blues, a rollicking rocker. It stays that way, with variations right up to the present time. You can find a heavy, crashing version on YouTube from 2018. Meanwhile, here's how it sounds in 1988.

[It Takes a Lot to laugh]

Along with 'Hard Rain', 'Masters of War' is associated with Bob Dylan the protest singer, the one who is 'young and unlearned' but knows the truth anyway, the truth that can't be hidden. Stripped of any Dylanesque ambiguities, the song hits hard at the real war criminals, the arms manufacturers. (I've written about this song in the post Masters of War and Extinction Rebellion.) It's a song that suits both acoustic and electric treatment. Here it gets a hard-edged treatment, courtesy of GE Smith's guitar and Dylan's punchy voice.

[Master of War]

'Maggies Farm' from the 1964 album *Bringing It All Back Home* typifies the defiance and rebellion that marked Dylan's early image. Maggies farm, the place, is another closed-in space to be broken out of, a place full of lies, hypocrisy, slavery and general paranoia – 'his bedroom window is made out of bricks...' The farm is the absurdist face of modern American culture, represented as the mad, dysfunctional family. Who wouldn't want to make their escape? The implicit anger in these 1988 performances finds a perfect vehicle here. Dylan's voice is dripped with fury and contempt.

[Maggies Farm]

And a touch of that same contempt suits the psychology of 'She Belongs to Me'. She doesn't belong to anybody, and is the much revered and hated mistress of his soul. She is sarcastically described as a 'hypnotist collector' a 'walking antique' but on the other hand she has him down on his knees peeking through keyholes. Like 'Romana', it sounds like a love song, like an intention towards a love song, but it isn't. The love, hate and humiliation are all there, given powerful voice. What this performance may lack in smoothness and some of the more rounded versions we hear later, it makes up for in raw, rough power. Interestingly, 'She Belongs to Me' would last all the way through the NET, even through the Frank Sinatra years from 2014 to 2017 and undergo many transformations.

[She Belong to Me]

'All along the Watchtower' from *John Wesley Harding* was to become the standard rocker with which to end shows – to go out with an apocalyptic roar. GE Smith is only too happy to oblige. But once more, the presentation is minimal; packed into four minutes, it makes its statement and gets out with none of the wild improvisations we're going to find further down the track. This is the unadorned core of the song, and as such is typical of these 1988 performances.

[All along the Watchtower]

That's it for Part 2 of our tour through 1988. Next post will be Part 3, finishing off 1988 with a few choice performances.

See you then, and in the meantime, stay safe.

Kia Ora

NET 1988: Part 3-
Absolutely still on the road

We finished Part 2 of our tour of the first year of Dylan's Never Ending Tour with 'All along the Watchtower,' a song that would remain embedded in Dylan's setlist for many years. We begin Part 3 with Tangled Up In Blue (from *Blood on the Tracks*, 1974) another perennial.

I have traced one thread of this song's remarkable history in the Master Harpist epilogue, Tangled up in Harmonicas Part 1 and Tangled up in Harmonicas Part 2

And while this song did become a showcase for Dylan's virtuoso harmonica playing, this is not the case in 1988 where, true to that year's form, there is no harmonica, the song bustles along with a bit of jingle-jangle from guitarist GE Smith, and is all over in six minutes.

However, Dylan is right on top of the vocals, in full mastery of the song, and gives us a clear, up front performance, using his 1988 abrasiveness to put a sheen of irony on the lyrics. This is not an exercise in nostalgia for times lost past, as the song can sometimes be, but a wry, hard-bitten look at what we call 'experience.'

[Tangled Up In Blue]

Another song of love and regret from *Blood on the Tracks*, 'You're a Big Girl Now
doesn't last the course the way Tangled does in terms of Dylan repertoire but can carry a strong emotional punch when performed. The bitterness underpinning the repeated '..you're a big girl now,' is not softened in this 1988 performance; there's no attempt to ease the pain, or let the melancholy of the melody take over. Those who like that album for its raw edge might well enjoy this.

[You're a Big Girl Now]

'Rank Strangers' isn't a Dylan song but it could be. Like 'Silvio', 'Rank Strangers' is one of those songs he has made his own, all the more as its sentiment is very Dylan like – that sense of estrangement or alienation from the world. This 1988 version is a very solid performance indeed, with the full power of Dylan's voice evident, enough to blow you out of your seat. And the performance is not rushed, with some thoughtfulness in the backing that will become a feature of 1989.

[Rank Strangers]

A traditional song that Dylan also made his own is 'Man of Constant Sorrow.' He sang it often in the early 1960s, and it was to appear again in a completely transformed version in 2005. Being a 'man of constant sorrow' was a part of

Dylan's image, always leaving town, always on the dark side of the road burdened with a broken heart. What I find interesting is how this archetype of the alienated outsider that comes through so much of the old, country-and-western and cowboy music was absorbed into Dylan's persona, and reflected in his lyrics. He became the archetype.

[Man of Constant Sorrow]

Dylan would never perform 'Gotta Serve Somebody' with the same fervour as during the gospel years, 1979 – 1981, and this is not a particularly distinguished performance, so why place it at the end of my tour of 1988? Because, rough-and-ready as it is, it comes with a completely new set of lyrics, and I can't know this for sure of course, but it sounds as if he's improvising, making up new verses as he goes. In other words, just having fun, which is not the feeling we get from most 1988 performances, which are tightly constrained.

In this respect it points forward to later years, when improvisation will play a greater role. And the new lyrics, as far as I can make them out, are also fun and cheeky, suggesting that Dylan hasn't entirely lost his sense of humour.

[Gotta Serve Somebody]

So how are we to regard the performances during the first year of the Never Ending Tour? They seem rushed and abrasive. Call it a garage band roughness. Dylan's voice often sounds forced and hoarse, with a throw-away feel you can hear most strongly in the first song of this study 'Like A Rolling Stone' (See NET, 1988 Part 1). He sounds impatient, tearing through his old songs and spitting them out as fast as he can. It's all pretty tightly controlled.

These are Dylan songs stripped down to their bare essentials, to the core of each song. There is nothing relaxed or expansive here, the performances are driven, often seemingly torn from the singer's will. There's no lack of passion, and some of the performances are masterful – 'Gates of Eden' is one of my favourites. (See NET, 1988 Part 1) Dylan's voice is always upfront, the words in our faces.

It is a little too easy to overlook these early NET performances, as there were greater things to come, and sometimes I have returned to them and been surprised and gratified by their direct and unadorned force.

There is something deeper here too. I called this year 'Desperate Stratagems', not quite sure why. Now I think it has to do with an underlying claustrophobia evident in the performances; there's an almost breathless desperation here. A flailing against invisible walls. This is the sound of a soul paying its dues, as it were, on the treadmill of song, and he will never sound quite like this again.

See you next time for a four part look at 1989.

Stay alert, stay alive!

Kia Ora

1989

Dylan's NET, 1989: Part 1 - The Piercing Edge

By Mike Johnson (kiwipoet)

> 'and I'm just like that bird
> singing just for you'

Coming from the tightly controlled performances of 1988, we find lots that's new and different in 1989, despite the same line up: lead guitar, second guitar, base guitar and drums. There is a looser, more expansive feel; it's not all so locked down. And Dylan rediscovers his harmonica as a lead instrument, taking the pressure off his voice as the main focus.

There are other changes too. On June 10, Dylan was joined by a new, young bass player, Tony Garnier, who is to stay with Dylan for the next thirty years, becoming the backbone of Dylan's sound. Always there, steady as a rock. Together Garnier and GE Smith, who's had a year now to settle in with Dylan, provide a sensitive and sometimes imaginative backing for Dylan's songs. For my money, 1989 is GE Smith's best year with Dylan.

At the same time, the recordings from that year all have a metallic quality not evident in 1988. At first I thought it might be the recordings themselves, but now I think that the sharp, piercing sound is what Dylan wanted. On the 18th of September, 1989, Dylan released the album, *Oh Mercy*. It was Dylan's 26th studio album, and hailed by the critics as being his best since *Blood on the Tracks* fifteen years earlier. Dylan didn't swamp his set list with *Oh Mercy* songs, however, as he was equally interested in dusting off some songs seldom performed. The 1989 performance of 'Queen Jane Approximately' in this post is probably the best he ever did of that song.

One of the highlights of *Oh Mercy*, is 'Most of the Time'. It's brilliant the way the refrain 'most of the time' undercuts all the bold posturing in the song. All the bravado and protestations are shown up, at the end of every verse, to be hollow.

> 'I can smile in the face
> of mankind
> don't even remember
> what her lips felt like on mine
> .... most of the time'

The almost whispered performance on the album, with its swampy background, is fully expressive, almost revelling in the emotional paradoxes of the song. The sarcastic edge is softened by the whispered voice and Laniot's spooky musical backdrop.

In the following performance (10-29-89), we get a very different sense of the song. These quiet and hollow self-reassurances become shouted defiances. The undercutting 'most of the time' comes slashing in with rage and confusion. It starts quietly enough, but the vocals soon begin to build. Building a song to a vocal climax is something Dylan is just starting to feel out. Of special note is the way the ending is staged, moving from restraint to pogoing its way to a shrieking conclusion.

[Most of the Time]

'What good am I' must be one of Dylan's quietest and most reflective songs. It captures those self-doubting moments we all have when we wonder if we've done enough for others and the world. Moments when we're forced to face our uselessness. A song with a different sentiment, but which matches its humble mood might be 'What Can I do for You' (1981). Gentle as it is, it holds the soul to task. In the age of the Covid 19 plague in which I'm writing, and as the daily death count gets higher, I can't help noticing these lines. (I've broken the lines here to try to match how Dylan sings them)

> 'If I just turn my back
> while you silently die
> what good
> am I?'

In this 1989 performance (11-02), it remains slow and thoughtful but there is a sharp edge to the music, and the vocal build up veers towards self-accusation rather than self-reflection.

[What good am I?]

My personal favourite from *Oh Mercy* would have to be 'Man in the Long Black Coat.' There is an urban legend that the Devil will hang around dance halls looking for easy prey – innocent young females. After one dance, the Devil would spirit the innocent girl to hell; having danced with the devil she was no longer innocent. This story was probably told to said innocent girls to scare them off dances and keep them at home at night doing their homework and other innocent things.

In Dylan's hands it becomes a tale of temptation and fate, sinister and ghostly. Dylan was to come back to this song many times in the 1990s, but here's how it sounds given his 1989 whiplash treatment.

[Man in the Long Black Coat]

Like 'What Good am I?' 'The Disease of Conceit', is a quiet, reflective song from *Oh Mercy*. The sentiment seems obvious until you reflect on the huge damage done by egotism. Like many of the human failings and crimes Dylan writes about, conceit is blind, and such blindness will lead to delusion and death.

> 'Give you delusions of grandeur
> and an evil eye
> Give you the idea that you're too good to die
> Then they bury you from head
> to your feet
> From the disease of conceit'

As with 'What Good Am I' the performed version is harder and sharper than the album version. Dylan takes to the piano for this one. Dylan playing keyboard on stage is still a rarity at this point in the NET.

[The Disease of Conceit]

There is a continuity of message from Dylan's early protest songs, a warning about the false nature of modern materialism:

> 'Advertising signs they con you
> into thinking you're the one
> that can do what's never been done
> that can win what's never been won'
> 'It's all right Ma (I'm only bleeding)'

Other songs from *Oh Mercy* would have to wait their turn. Dylan had begun to get interested in how he could not only adapt his early songs for the rock stadium stage, but reinterpret those songs, give them something new in performance. In the case of 'Queen Jane Approximately', the 1989 live performance here (date not known), with its thoughtful, gentle harmonica opening, reaches for an emotional range that the album version doesn't quite achieve.

The tiredness of the album version is attractive, but this vibrant performance seems to touch the core of hurt that lies at the heart of the song. The song is an appeal. When all the false appearances and expectations of this world have fallen away, then come and see me. Again, Dylan experiments with an extended ending, using the harmonica to wring the last ounces of feeling from the situation. It all sounds a bit unrehearsed but all the better for that spontaneous feel. And GE Smith has moments of inspiration.

[Queen Jane Approximately]

After the end of the gospel tour in 1981, Dylan seldom revisited his Christian songs. 'Gotta Serve Somebody' appears now and again, and Dylan has had an ongoing interest in 'When You Gonna Wake Up,' from *Slow Train Coming*, 1979. In the 21st Century, this song would reappear with a whole new set of lyrics. Here, in 1989 (10-20), he has fun with the song, experimenting with his 'primitive' 1930s, staccato piano style.

[When You Gonna Wake Up]

'Ballad of a Thin Man' gets a nice quiet intro with harmonica. Dylan's vocal is clear and powerful. Dylan returns to the harp for a final solo with some whimsical work by GE Smith. This song, an encounter with the stranger regions of our psyche, sounds good spooky, as it is on the album, and it makes for a good crashing rocker, but I like this version for its cutting feel, and edgy sharpness.

[Ballad of a Thin Man]

We have been following Dylan's wonderful protest song, John Brown, now since 1987, all wonderful performances. I have written about this song in those previous posts, and how the song is driven by the dramatic encounter between mother and son on the train station after John Brown got 'home from the war.'

It now occurs to me that this song puts its finger on the generational divide that became so evident in the sixties. The young anti-war boomers turned on their parents who could still talk in terms of 'a good old fashioned war.' There is no such thing. The dropping of his medals into his mother's hand at the end is a gesture of contempt, and a rejection of the values of the 'older generation.' It is for songs like this that Dylan is known as a 'spokesman for his generation,' a label Dylan has always rejected.

[John Brown]

In 1989, Tangled Up In Blue begins to emerge as the crowd pleasing, foot-stomper it will become in the 1990s. At this stage, however, it is still pretty tightly controlled, and Dylan bustles through it at a fair pace. We could almost be back in 1988, except for the extended harp break at the end. This harmonica break is pretty tentative compared to the glories to come in the nineties (see the Master Harpist series), but the pattern is laid down here, a willingness to use the catchy, precipitous rhythm of the song for extended instrumental breaks. A strong vocal performance.

[Tangled Up In Blue]

We can look forward to some exciting stuff in the next post, which will feature some of Dylan's quieter, more acoustic moments in 1989.

Stay safe

Kia Ora

NET 1989: Part 2 – A fire in the sun

By Mike Johnson (Kiwipoet)

I'm very excited about the set of performances in this post. Not only some of the finest for 1989, but some 'best ever' or at least 'very hard to beat' performances of these 1960s favourites. I've learned my lesson when it comes to proclaiming a 'definitive' performance of any song, not just because someone will come up with a better one, but because the performances change from year to year and you can't compare chalk with cheese. Nevertheless, if you can point me to a better performance of 'The Ballad of Hollis Brown' (10-31-89) please do – maybe 1974, with the Band?

[The Ballad of Hollis Brown]

And while you're enjoying the crisp, kick-arse vocals, and GE Smith's scratchy little riff, take a moment to admire this elegant piece of storytelling. With its roots in the dustbowl poverty that Woody Guthrie sang about, this deadly, driving blues adroitly takes us through the stages of mind that lead Hollis Brown to murder his children and himself. One moment the shotgun is 'hangin' on the wall' and the next it is in his hands. It's narrated in the second person (you), rare in story telling, most opting for he/she or I. This 'you' brings us right into Hollis's state of being; we're right there standing in his shoes:

> 'Well your brain is a-bleeding
> and your legs can't seem to stand...'

Interestingly, neither the first person (I), or the third person (he/she) would work here.

Is there anything to match that? Well, I think there is, in a gentler, more acoustic vein. 'Love Minus Zero/No Limit' has, for me, remained a mystery wrapped in an enigma, just like the subject of the song herself, the silent, all knowing one. And yes, it is a love song, and a very tender one, but what are we to make of these two verses?

> 'The cloak and dagger dangles
> Madams light the candles
> In ceremonies of the horsemen
> Even the pawn must hold a grudge.
> Statues made of matchsticks
> Crumble into one another
> My love winks, she does not bother
> She knows too much to argue or to judge.
>
> The bridge at midnight trembles
> The country doctor rambles
> Bankers' nieces seek perfection
> Expecting all the gifts that wise men bring.
> The wind howls like a hammer
> The night blows cold and rainy
> My love she's like some raven
> At my window with a broken wing.'

I could write ten thousand words and still be no closer to understanding these lyrics. Since they are resistant to interpretation, they keep their mystery. In performance, combined with the music and vocalisation, they seem to fit perfectly. Dylan has said that we can enjoy a song without understanding it. He's right. The question is, not what do these words mean, but rather how do they fit in with the feeling-tone of the song. This is Dylan at his best – specific yet elusive, restrained yet passionate. Enjoy!

[Love Minus Zero]

It's all over in 2mins 53 seconds, the length of a pop song. Could be a no-frills 1988 performance. At the end of the song we get some twangy guitar playing that is not GE Smith. That's Dylan, an early emergence of Dylan as second lead guitar. I'll have more to say about Dylan's guitar playing later, but it's enough at this point to note it, and the dissonant effect it creates.

People are heard to complain, 'Why doesn't Dylan sound like the old

Dylan?' Well, because he was so much younger then, but also there are times when he does. This 'Mr Tambourine Man' takes us right back to the 1966 performances, right down to the swooping harmonica break. Actually, this performance, direct and forthright, reminds me of the Concert for Bangladesh sound (1969). Dylan in full voice. Like many of Dylan's sixties songs, Mr Tambourine Man' expresses a yearning to escape, escape those 'ancient empty streets too dead for dreaming' and to get 'far from the twisted reach of crazy sorrow.' If you wonder why Dylan is celebrated as a poet, wrap your ears around this.

[Mr Tambourine Man]

One of simplest and most affecting love songs Dylan wrote is 'One too many mornings.' On the album the song takes a mere 2.45 seconds, but its brevity is matched by its profundity. The ache of loneliness we might feel after a night of love making, the alienation and distance from our own feelings.

> 'From the crossroads of my doorstep
> My eyes they start to fade
> And I turn my head back to the room
> Where my love and I have laid
> An' I gaze back to the street
> The sidewalk and the sign
> And I'm one too many mornings
> An' a thousand miles behind'

Add to that the despair the artist might feel, the hopelessness of the quest for meaning.

> 'It's a restless hungry feeling
> That don't mean no one no good
> When ev'rything I'm a-sayin'
> You can say it just as good
> You're right from your side
> I'm right from mine'

Note the consummate clumsiness of the lines, the Okie grammar, rhyming good with itself, all to emphasise the artist's confessed unfitness for the task. He don't mean it folks – he can say it gooder. In this 1989 performance he doubles the length of the song, but doesn't sacrifice brevity as he works through the verses in about 2.30 minutes and spends the next 3 minutes in guitar work, repeating a verse, and ending by trying to capture the exquisite nostalgia of the song in the frail tones of his harp.

[One Too Many Mornings]

We mustn't be fooled by 'Ramona', (*Another Side of Bob Dylan*, 1964). It may sound like a love song, waltz like a love song, assume an intimacy like a love song – but it is not that. Yes, it is a farewell song, but it is more than that. Like 'Like A Rolling Stone', which it prefigures, 'Ramona' is an attack on false values, on living unauthentically, blinded by all the bullshit:

> 'I see that your head
> has been twisted and fed
> with meaningless foam from the mouth...'

The music may sound gentle, but the attack is relentless, an expose of sorts of the subject's underlying drive to conform. To be what others want you to be and not yourself is a grievous sin in Dylan's moral universe. Peer pressure, we call it nowadays.

> 'From fixtures and forces and friends
> Your sorrow does stem
> That hype you and type you
> Making you feel
> That you gotta' be just like them...'

This, raw, acoustic 1989 performance doesn't spare anyone's feelings, but there's a certain compassion evident in the timbre of Dylan's voice. This is no victory song.

[Ramona]

Another farewell song from the same era, 'It's All Over Now, Baby Blue' gets the same raw, acoustic treatment. I noticed that the harmonica break at the end progresses to higher and higher notes until he seems to be squeezing out the highest notes, as if in search of a sound beyond audial range. I have written about the emotion behind this song in Master Harpist 2, in relation to a 1995 performance, and described it as love's last song. The issue is not so much living falsely, as in Ramona, but suffering the pain of a disappointed love:

> 'the lover who's just walked out your door
> has taken all his blankets from the floor.'

But lurking behind this pain, there's a sense of the greater moral emptiness and confusion of the great hippy, free-love movement.

> 'The empty handed painter from your street
> Is drawing crazy patterns on your sheet.'

And always we are haunted by our vagabond past.

> 'the vagabond who's rapping at your door
> is standing in the clothes that you once wore'

Despite the pain, we have to get up and get on with our lives. Strike another match. A very common saying, used to wonderful effect here, at the end of the song.

[It's All Over Now, Baby Blue]

'Knockin' On Heaven's door' is another kind of farewell song. We heard a very intense vocal on this one in 1987, with the Grateful Dead, (See Net 1987), and this is a lot rougher but no less intense. Dylan tears out the lyrics. Especially recommended is Dylan's high-pitched squeaky harp work so typical of 1989. Quite jazzy and experimental; he seems to want to push the little instrument to its very limits. The combination of Dylan on the acoustic guitar and GE Smith playing electric works well in this case. A knock-out version.
[Knockin' On Heaven's door]

This performance may not match the most magnificent 1988 'Gates of Eden' (See NET 1988), but the problem is mostly with the rowdy audience. I nearly excluded it on those grounds, but in the end Dylan's vibrant vocal proved too persuasive. If you can listen through the idiotic chatter, you'll hear genius at work, filling these mysterious lyrics with an equally mysterious passion.

[Gates of Eden]

In NET 1988 part 2, I called 'I shall be released' a rather delicate, oblique little song. None of us are to blame, of course, we've all been framed. We cry out loud for salvation. You'll have to decide how this one stacks up beside the 1988 performance. A little lyrical sweetness from GE Smith's guitar.

[I Shall Be Released]

The template for this fast-paced 'It's alright Ma...' (1964) was created during the Tom Petty years in the mid eighties and has changed little since. It is Dylan's most comprehensive protest song, an all-out assault on everything false and phony, the great rip-off machine. It's his last blast at the world before departing the protest scene.
In the light of Dylan's later development, and conversion to Christianity, consider the terms of his attack.

> 'Disillusioned words like bullets bark
> As human gods aim for their mark
> Made everything from toy guns that spark
> To flesh-colored Christs that glow in the dark
> It's easy to see without looking too far
> That not much is really sacred.'

The real crime is the desacralisation of culture from religion to sex. We are ruled by Mammon, the god of money, and he blasphemes: 'money doesn't talk it swears...' And yet the song does not despair; it has a message of resilience, because all this crap getting thrown at us is just 'life and life only.' And we 'can make it.'

Do the words just come pouring out! I loved the flat, nasal delivery of the mid-sixties, which constrained the passion of the song, and the 1974 howling version, but have grown to enjoy these hard-out fast versions. This one doesn't spark the way the 1990 performance will, but it gives us something to look forward to.

[It's Alright, Ma.]

So that's it for part 2 of 1989. I'll be back shortly with part 3, and we'll keep on rocking.

Kia Ora

NET 1989: Part 3 - Blown out on the trail

By Mike Johnson (Kiwipoet)

In Part 1, 1989, we considered new songs from *Oh Mercy*, with a few performances from older songs. In Part 2 we looked at Dylan's continuing love affair with his sixties songs. Today we we look at a spread of songs with a focus on the 1970s. Before we get there though, let's pause to listen to two traditional songs given wonderful voice here in 1989. I doubt you could find a more passionate rendition of 'The Water is Wide.' This is not just the best vocal performance of the year, or getting there, but one of Dylan's best ever. An NET standout. Kick back and enjoy.

[The Water is Wide]

The official Bob Dylan website claims 'Trail of Buffalo' as a Dylan song, but it is not. Wikepedia says: 'According to extensive research carried out by Jürgen Kloss in 2010-2012, this song is one of the many variants of John B Freeman's "The Buffalo Song". Dylan was continuing to do what he'd always done – immersing himself in the flow of traditional songs. There are many variants to the lyrics, also. At heart, it's a cowboy story of betrayal and murder. Familiar Dylan territory.

[Trail of the Buffalo]

Ah! Forever Young! We can't escape it. In 1974 Dylan is still pretty young himself; there is the ache of youth in his voice, but in 1989, with Dylan a couple of years off fifty, there's a sharp edge of anguish in the performance, and an extra edge of wistfulness in the extended harp break at the end. It's wonderful the way the song is built up; from acoustic roots it grows into a rich, full bodied rock song. His voice is raw and unaccompanied, and the song, with its impossible injuction to stay 'forever young' has seldom sounded so heartfelt.

[Forever Young]

Just as Dylan developed a core of sixties songs he could use night after night, in the grind of constant performance, so he did with the 1970's, mainly concentrating on *Blood on the Tracks*, with a nod to *Planet Waves* and *New Morning*. Only 'Senor' survives into performance from the powerful *Street Legal*.

Next to 'Tangled Up In Blue' we have 'Simple Twist of Fate', a song which is to be become a fixture on the setlists. Switching the pronouns in the song gives rise to different stories. If, at the end, she 'hunts him down by the water-front docks/where the sailors all come in' he is likely to be a sailor and the girl a maybe one time lover. However, if he hunts her down by the water-front docks etc, she is likely to be a prostitute scoring from the sailors. Either way. It's a one night stand or a short, intense affair that leaves a lingering taste of something that might have been – but there is no outguessing fate.

[Simple Twist of Fate]

'Shelter from the Storm' is still going strong, and will also stay the course through the years. It starts with the best lines Dylan ever wrote, surely.

> 'Twas in another lifetime, one of toil and blood
> When blackness was a virtue the road was full of mud
> I came in from the wilderness, a creature void of form
> Come in, she said I'll give ya
> shelter from the storm'

'A creature void of form'? How good can lyrics get? This godess gives shape to him. The song is the emotional counterpart of 'She Belongs to Me.' That song gives a warning about putting one's love on a pedestal, and the humiliation that follows. In Shelter from the storm, 'she' is not just on a pedestal but touched by divinity, one who can save him from his myarterdom:

> 'She came up to me so gracefully
> and took my crown of thorns...'

In performance, the song can be given a hard, driving rhythm, as in the 1976 Rolling Thunder tour. Here it is given an almost cowboy upflift. This most mystical of songs is given a jaunty treatment. Of interest is a joyful sense of experiment here. Dylan plays with a half-spoken style of vocal, puctuated by his harmonica in squeaky sixties style. Then he slows down the song for a few lines before picking up the rhythm again. The whole performance stays interesting right to the end. Don't miss the slow, quiet harp break that finishes the song. A gem this one.

[Shelter from the Storm]

How does it feel to be in the last stages of a relationship you suddenly don't want to lose? Pretty abject. You're on your knees pleading, making all kinds of promises about changing your lowdown ways. You do lots of crying, but it's all to no avail because... she's a big girl now.

[You're a Big Girl Now]

Note how he sings most of the song through before an extended musical break. Dylan again squeezes some high-pitched shrills from his harp and GE Smith scales the heights. I think the bitter-sweetness of the song suits the 1989, sharp-edged Dylan. We have to feel that 'corkscrew to the heart'.

'Man of Peace' (1984) is one song that clearly signals Dylan's withdrawal from certain kinds of Christian certainties. If Satan can come as a man of peace, then who can we trust? Even Jesus might have been Satan in disguise. Even the devil can quote scriptures. Dylan had this insight before. ('Slow Train Coming')

> 'But the enemy I see wears a cloak of decency
> All non-believers and men-stealers talkin' in the name of religion.'

Now we get a clearer picture what this 'Satan' looks like:

> 'Well, first he's in the background,
> and then he's in the front
> Both eyes are looking like they're on a rabbit hunt'

And what about these marvelous lines:
'Well, he can be fascinating, he can be dull
He can ride down Niagara Falls
in the barrels of your skull
I can smell something cooking
I can tell there's going to be a feast'

I don't know if this song has ever fully realized its potential in performance. The power of the words tends to get lost in the chuggy beat. Sometimes I wonder what it might have sounded like slowed right down.

[Man of Peace]

Talk of album's rarely visited, Empire Burlesque (1985) is a case in point. 'Seeing the Real You at Last' is the exception. You can see why; it's good old beaty rocker. Check out the lyrics to this song; there's lines from different movies. Tony Attwood does a great job of unpicking some of these lines. This is approaching a cut-up method of song writing, where lines are lifted from various sources and juxdiposed in interesting ways. Fascinating, in the light of Dylan's recent epic 'Murder Most Foul' where this cut-up method is used extensively. My favourite lines?

'I don't mind a reasonable amount of trouble
trouble always comes to pass'

A whiff of Humphrey Bogart in there.

[Seeing the Real You at Last]

That's for 'Blown out on the trail.' I'll be back shortly with the fourth and final part of this tour through Dylan's 1989 performances.

Kia Ora

NET 1989: Part 4 – Hanging in the Balance

You might say that I saved the best till last, once you hear the first couple of performances, but it was not deliberate! The pattern of these posts is starting to come clear to me. I use part 1 to introduce new songs, rare or unusual, and the part 2 and 3 to catch up with Dylan's new approach to old favourites. This last part is a safety net of sorts, to catch any performances that had slipped by me.

So I've got a couple of absolute beauties to kick this off. First up. 'She Belongs to Me', that hymn to the superior female, the girl who belongs to no one, probably the kind of woman your mother forgot to warn you about. Beware, lovers, put her on a pedestal and she'll have you grovelling. We have met this song before and will do so again, but never this way, just Bob on acoustic guitar and harmonica. For lovers of Dylan's acoustic sound, and his squealing 1989 harmonica style, this is an absolute gem. Classic performance coming up!

[She belongs to Me]

Just as you're sighing with satisfaction from listening to that, consider the next performance 'Every Grain of Sand'. Most Dylan followers agree that this is one of his greatest songs. There's a magic in it that goes beyond the lyrics. In Master Harpist 3 I wrote about the song, and how Dylan seemed to be able to make some fairly corny lines sound wonderful. Many lovers of the song prefer the demo version he did at home on the piano, to the lush, swept-up version on the album (*Shot of Love* 1981). Like me you might have wondered what it would sound like if Dylan just played it alone, on the acoustic guitar, like it was a folk song. Well...wonder no longer. Here it is, the gems of gems, the discovery of discoveries.

[Every Grain of Sand]

Around the time of the harmonica break in the middle of the song, a second guitar joins. GE Smith, I suspect, doing some very discreet work, harmonising beautifully and unobtrusively with Dylan, relatively rare to hear them working so closely together like this.

'Deadman,' also off *Shot of Love*, has always intrigued me because of its ambivalence. Presumably the 'deadman' is a man unredeemed, who'd never accepted the word of god. Reprobates. But the descriptions suggest Dylan could be talking about the very crowd he'd fallen in with – the Pentecostals.

> 'What are you tryin' to overpower me with,
> the doctrine or the gun?
> My back is already to the wall
> where can I run?
> The tuxedo that you're wearin'
> the flower in your lapel,
> Ooh, I can't stand it, I can't stand it,
> You want to take me down to hell.'

When he sings 'Do you have any faith at all/do you have any love to share?' he's most likely singing about those who claim to have faith and love, not the unconverted sinner. The deadman's sin is worse as it is rooted in hypocrisy and Dylan's old foe, godless materialism:

> 'The glamor and the bright lights
> and the politics of sin,
> The ghetto you build for me
> is the one you end up in.'

[Deadman]

Dylan's voice here is deeper and darker than it was in 1981, and we get a nice sinister feel from this performance, with some great opening work from GE Smith. The problem here is that GE Smith doesn't know when to end the song, which peters out after a couple of aimless choruses. It sounds to me as if Smith is expecting Dylan to round it off with another verse, or a harp break, and nothing happens. There are lot of these, shall we say 'unrehearsed' endings in 1989. Nobody quite sure what will happen next.

At the Toronto concert in 1980, his almost hysterical assertion of his faith in that powerful love song, 'I believe in You' might well be Dylan's greatest vocal ever. Any subsequent performances of the song have to suffer comparison with that superlative moment. I wasn't expecting too much, therefore, and was pleasantly surprised. The 1980 sound is big and warm and rich. Here, nine years later, it is hard and spare, with that sharp metallic edge we have come to associate with 1989. Dylan's performance is quite ragged, he messes up the lines a bit, but warms to the song as it goes. I find GE Smith's guitar work quite intrusive on this one, but we get some nice plaintive harmonica work at the beginning and end.

[I Believe in You]

'I dreamed I saw St Augustine,' although written twelve years before 'I Believe in You', fits in well with the religious theme here. I wrote about this song when we looked at 1988, and the sense of quiet despair that fills this little ballad. In the later, gospel songs, salvation is at hand, but in 'I dreamed I saw St Augustine,' salvation is nowhere to be found. On the album it's a slow, gentle acoustic song but here it turns up with a solid rock base, medium tempo, sounding good. Sometimes I wonder if Dylan's 'folk songs' are not rock songs in disguise.

Again we hear Dylan building the song up from a quiet, vocally understated beginning to the loud confessional climax: 'I put my hands against the glass/and bowed my head and cried.'

[I Dreamed I Saw St Augustine]

I have to admit to an ongoing fascination with 'Tears of Rage' (1967). Again, this religious undertone. Again, lyrics that seem to lie just beyond our ability to comprehend them. Perhaps the song is not written to a person but to America. Perhaps that 'false instruction' is the kind of materialism that turns a 'heart into a purse.' It's all perhaps perhaps, while the song continues to exert a mysterious power with a hint of grandeur. Dylan's declamatory vocal style suits the song well as a form of rhetoric – 'Oh what kind of love is this/which goes from bad to worse?'

[Tears of Rage]

Every concert, like every album, needs a fast, hard rocker or two to remind us that rock is one of Dylan's first loves, even before he became a folk singing icon. The fast, hard and irreverent 'Highway 61 Revisited' (on the album version, Dylan blows a police whistle) sounds frivolous, with throw-away lyrics, but that is far from the case. The first verse, however casual the language, catches the Biblical Abraham as he was about to sacrifice his son, Isaac. God holds Abraham back, an act of divine mercy.

The answer to all earthly woes is 'Highway 61'. Back in the druggy days of the sixties, junkies called their veins 'highways', but there's no need to get snagged by that interpretation, despite the allusion to some sinister ritual or other:

> Now, the fifth daughter on the twelfth night
> told the first father that things weren't right
> "'My complexion," she says, "is much too white"
> He said, "Come here and step into the light"
> He said, "Hmm, you're right,
> let me tell the second mother this has been done"
> But the second mother was with the seventh son
> And they were both out on Highway 61'

Highway 61 is a place where you can abdicate all responsibility and allow evil things to happen, even a 'next world war.' Have a think about all this serious stuff while you rock along!

[Highway 61 Revisited]

The accepted narrative is that Bob Dylan stopped writing protest songs and started writing 'surrealist' or 'symbolist' songs. That's so hardly true, it's false. Dylan stopped writing topical songs, like 'Oxford Town', 'The Lonesome Death of Hattie Caroll' and 'Who Killed Davey Moore?' but a song like 'Highway 61 Revisited' takes protest to another level – a zany, madcap level. Humour and satire are the weapons here. As Dylan was to write many years later, 'People are crazy and times are strange.'

'It Takes a Lot to Laugh, It Takes a Train to Cry,' off the same album, has quite a different intent. While Dylan never wanted to become trapped by the blues, he likes to put at least one twelve-bar blues on every album. I think it's his way of acknowledging the importance of the blues in his music. Blues singers were writing strange lyrics long before Bob, and of course the structure of the blues underlies a lot of rock music. On the album, it's a gentle rollicking love song with some impeccable verses, but in performance it tends to heavy up. It's easy for something that starts with the flavour of country blues to slip into a surging, urban blues.

[It Takes a Lot to Laugh]

To finish off this post, and the year of 1989, we come to 'Visions of Johanna', and I lose all objectivity and even-handedness as a commentator. For me, 'Visions' is a lot more than a song. To listen to the studio version (*Blonde on Blonde*, 1966), or the live acoustic performances of that year, is to enter another medium, like stepping into another world. It's like trying to stand underwater; it makes you feel queasy. You reach for the bottom but there is no bottom – you just keep falling. It's like being in somebody's bad trip. There are strange people in this world, which is a very claustrophobic place, and they plumb the depth of cynicism:

> 'The peddler now speaks to the Countess
> Who's pretending to care for him
> Saying, name me someone who's not a parasite
> And I'll go out and say a prayer for him.'

'Visions' is a nightmare of Dantesque proportions. The question it generates is, why does the poet's conscience 'explode' at the end of the song? Because sinister and unconscionable things have been going on, unsavoury rituals only hinted at. Everybody seems seriously fucked up.

> The jelly-faced women all sneeze
> And the one with the moustache says 'Jeez
> I can't find my knees.'

You find yourself in receding hallways of echoing voices, haunted by the absence of a certain Johanna. The phantasmagoric world around us becomes an 'empty cage' which we see 'corrode'. There is no salvation here, merely the echo of it. The song ends with the vanishing sound of harmonicas in the rain. It's a crepuscular song, a consummate mood piece... at least, that's how it sounded in 1966. After all this raving about it, I think we need to hear what I'm talking about. This is 'Visions of Johanna,' Sheffield, 1966.

[Visions of Johanna, 1966]

A voice like a fallen angel! Tony Attwood has posted Dylan's Australian performance from that year, one of delightful weariness. This is peak Dylan. These performances are unmatchable. Subsequent performances of the song just don't seem to cut the mustard. The lyrics are there, but the fast beat means he has to rush through them, almost throwing them away. He doesn't savour the lines, those magnificent lines, rolling them around in the echo chambers of his mind. The spookiness has gone, and the hints of depravity somehow don't resonate. But here it is, 'Visions' 1989 style. Just another song.

[Visions of Johanna 1989]

That brings to a close this article and the series 'The Piercing Edge' in which I looked at some highlights from Dylan's 1989 NET. What can we say about 1989? The effect is looser and less locked-down than 1988. Dylan's prepared to sing the song through, then allow time for improvisation, either GE Smith on the guitar or Dylan on the harp.

As I have commented, there is a sharp, metallic sound to most of these performances, reinforced by Dylan's piercing edge harmonica. He's beginning to work his songs from quiet beginnings, often acoustic, to a pounding climax. As in 1988, his voice is strong and to the fore and there are some passionate performances to be found.

I'll be back shortly with the next round, 1990 – a new decade. Take care out there, in the cities of the plague.

Kia Ora

1990

The Never Ending Tour 1990:
Part 1 – Vomiting fire

By Mike Johnson (Kiwipoet)

'I am the enemy of the unlived meaningless life.'
(Dylan: False Prophet)

The transition from 1989 to 1990 was a smooth one in that his line up didn't change and there was no significant change of musical direction and orientation. Just as towards the end of 1989 Dylan released a new album *Oh Mercy*, so towards the end of 1989 another new album appeared *Under the Red Sky*. So I had all my tracks lined up, according to the pattern

I established for the 1989 study, and was about to spin the first public performance of the title track of that album, when I remembered my father who, when teaching us how to play cards, would always say, 'lead with your longest and strongest' or 'lead 'em like you got 'em,' and my plan went out the window. I had an ace; I was dying to play it.

The performance I keep coming back to is that protest song to end all protest songs 'It's Alright, Ma.' Not only the best of 1990, but maybe the best performance of this song since the flat, hard-driving 1964 performances. We have the swirling performances from the Rolling Thunder Tour, and the fast and furious versions from the Tom Petty years. Dylan stayed with this fast and furious version through the early years of the NET, and you won't find a better performance of it than this one (02-07):

[It's Alright, Ma]

I have described this song as a wholesale attack on all things false and phony, which is why it sounds so up to date. The false and the phony still rule. If we want to know what he means when, in his new song 'False Prophet,' he sings that he is the 'enemy of the unlived meaningless life,' we just have to listen to 'It's Alight, Ma.'

The root of this 'unlived meaningless life' is the rank and godless materialism lambasted in 'It's Alright, Ma.' And while we are assaulted by lies, deceptions, false judgments and tyranny, we 'can make it', we have the insight and the courage to survive because it's 'life and life only'. This grim vision of a spiritually empty life turns out to be an inspirational song at heart.

'It's Alright, Ma' is not the only song that brings a true and horrifying report of the state of the world from a young person back to the mother. 'A Hard Rain's A-Gonna Fall' is built around the same motif. And it's the 1990 performance of that song which is the second ace in the hole. While I love the smooth gospel, 1981 version, and the hard, clanging Rolling Thunder version, this performance takes us back to the acoustic, 1960s Dylan, but not so plodding. And, I have to say Dylan's vocal expression is richer and more varied than his sixties performances. The emphatic vocal style of these early NET years, with broken up lines, suits this song particularly well as it emphasizes the fragmentary nature of the visions.

[Hard Rain]

(I can't be the only one to notice the importance of the mother, 'Ma' or 'Mama', in Dylan's early songs. And because 'mama' can also refer to a girlfriend ('mama you've been on my mind'), there is larger female presence at work here.)

As I've suggested before, in my view Dylan didn't stop writing protest songs, he simply extended the range of his attack on the false and the phony to his personal life, himself and those around him. In that respect 'Ramona' is just as much a protest song as 'Hard Rain' in its portrayal of someone who has fallen into the false and phony, distorted by propaganda.

> 'I see that your head
> has been twisted and fed
> with meaningless foam from the mouth'

Here is the 'unlived meaningless life' right in front of us.

> 'And it grieves my heart love
> to see you trying to be part of
> a world that just don't exist.'

False worlds full of false prophets. I have to say, when I look at my selection, I do favour the acoustic Dylan. A passionate, vibrant rendition of Ramona coming up.

[Ramona]

Before leaving the sixties behind, at least for the moment, this seems like a good place to slip in a rare and very well received 'Oxford Town', with its scene of racial violence. This is from *The Freewheelin' Bob Dylan*, 1962, and only occasionally performed. One thing to note, however, a certain scratchiness is evident in Dylan's voice, a lack of timbre noticeable here, which will become more accentuated in the following year, 1991. Dylan's voice is starting to go.

[Oxford Town]

So now I deal myself a new hand and pick up the story with some songs from Under a Red Sky (1990). This album lies very much in the shadow of the successful *Oh Mercy* (1989), and its hard, abrasive tones contrast sharply to the lush, swampy sounds of the earlier album. Nobody much liked Under the Red Sky. And yet, when we look at these two albums from the point of view of the NET, we can see that *Red Sky* is much more closely aligned to the sounds Dylan was producing onstage than *Oh Mercy*. Dylan didn't attempt to produce that swampy sound onstage.

There are, however, a couple of very strong songs on the album. 'Unbelievable' is a lyrical masterpiece hidden beneath the frenetic beat. It will be a couple of years before Dylan will try this song onstage. The title track, 'Under the Red Sky', with its obvious pathos and appeal to the world of fairy tales, is more immediately palatable.

I'm not sure why critics reacted so negatively to Dylan's use of childhood themes and motifs on this album. 'Man gave name to all the animals' from 1980 is a little theology in the guise of a children's song. 'Under the Red Sky' uses the same guise to explore adult themes. Perhaps listeners were a bit shocked at the casual way he sings, 'One day the little girl and the little boy were both baked in a pie.' Cooking and eating children? Where's Mr Tambourine Man when you need him? There was the feeling that the whole song was a bit off.

[Under the Red Sky]

The last lines of the song, however, gave me a chill when I first heard them, because it seemed to me that the song was a lament for the loss of the creative flow – fatal for any artist. It was as if he was telling us it was all over.

> 'Let the bird sing, let the bird fly
> One day the man in the moon went home
> and the river ran dry'

That magical, creative time of our childhood doesn't last. The 'little boy and the little girl', the divine twins (the eternal syzygy), source of the universal creative drive, are destroyed. As it turned out, my premonition was a true one, and it would be a long seven years before the next album.

But it was the first track of the album, 'Wiggle Wiggle', that caused the most consternation. After the sweeping grandeur of 'Most of the Time' and 'Man in the Long Black Coat', we get… 'Wiggle Wiggle'? Surely Dylan's most despised song. At the time it was held up as the ultimate proof that the master had lost his mojo – oh how the mighty have fallen, they cried. Perhaps this negative reaction is because the song is so good in its vicious, uncompromising attack on the sexual act. The mindless simplicity of the song mimics the mindless simplicity of sex.

> 'Wiggle till you're high
> Wiggle till you're higher
> Wiggle till you vomit fire'

Vomit fire? A powerful and disturbing image for orgasm. According to Collins dictionary, 'if it wiggles, it moves up and down or from side to side', unlike wriggling which contains a greater range of movements.

> 'Wiggle till it whispers, wiggle till it hums
> Wiggle till it answers, wiggle till it comes'

The only other Dylan song that expresses such a powerful revulsion to the sexual act that springs to mind is 'Yonder Comes Sin.' (1981)

> 'Look at your feet, see where they've been to.
> Look at your hands, see what they've been into…'

I think we don't like the song because Dylan is taking the piss out of our precious sexuality. The simple, childlike language, as if it were a children's rhyme, makes us even more uncomfortable.

> 'Wiggle, wiggle, wiggle, rattle and shake
> Wiggle like a big fat snake.'

Oh Lordy – well, here it is, rough as hell, with pretty much a completely new set of lyrics! The whole performance sounds pretty improvised to me, including the lyrics. Those incomparable lyrics and he doesn't sing them! Sounds like he's making it up as he goes along, and in some cases, just making Dylan-like noises that are not actually words…? (see what you can make of it)

[Wiggle Wiggle]

'TV Talking Song' might be described as a forgotten song on a forgotten album, but it recalls the madcap, fast-paced, early Dylan talking songs like 'Talking World War 3 Blues' or 'John Birch Society Blues.' Rambling comic monologues with a satirical edge. Lovely twist in the last line. I think this qualifies as a rare performance.

[TV Talking Song]

Dylan doesn't delve deep into Under the Red Sky. In later years 'Cat's in the Well' gets a good airing, and only much later in the nineties does he try to perform the powerful 'Born in Time.' He does, however, continue to explore material from the previous album, *Oh Mercy*. 'Where teardrops fall' is a wistful, sad song about a love that might be re-kindled, and this is one case where GE Smith's hard-edged guitar sound can't do justice to the, quieter, soft edges of the song. Dylan's voice sounds good but there's too much jingle-jangle from the guitar.

[Where Teardrops Fall]

The official narrative has Dylan deserting 'protest' songs in the sixties. And yet we have two hard-out protest songs on *Oh Mercy*, 'Political World' and 'Everything Is Broken.' In this fallen world of ours we can't escape politics.

> 'We live in a political world
> Under the microscope
> You can travel anywhere
> And hang yourself there
> You always got more than enough rope'

'Everything Is Broken' extends the attack from politics to our more common, unlived and meaningless lives.

> 'Broken hands on broken ploughs,
> Broken treaties, broken vows,

Broken pipes, broken tools,
People bending broken rules...'

It's a 1990s update on Subterranean Homesick Blues. It's a political world, and it's a broken world, and looking around us now, who could argue? As always Dylan's vision stays true.

[Political World]

[Everything Is broken]

Stay centered and keep safe, and we'll be back soon for the next installment.

Kia Ora

The NET 1990: Part 2 – Songs of love, songs of betrayal

By Mike Johnson (Kiwipoet)

We can already sense that Dylan's setlist is shifting towards new material, and he likes to throw in a wild card here and there, but we also find him cultivating his classics. The songs he sings and will go on singing night after night, year after year. The fascination for us will be to hear them growing and changing, staying alive or falling flat. So this post will mostly be dedicated to some of those old favourites, the songs that won't go away, songs that in themselves never seem to tire even if the singer sometimes might. It is after all through the songs that he lives, and what better song to kick off with than one of his very greatest, 'Desolation Row', and I'm very glad he kept it in his stable. We mustn't let it grow so familiar to us that we lose our sense of wonder at the huge canvas he's created with this song.

Like its great sister song, 'Visions of Johanna', 'Desolation Row' is a mood song, yet not as murky and dark as 'Visions'. The experience of an intense and melancholy alienation lies at the heart of both songs, but 'Desolation Row' is lit by the garish lights of the circus. Seems like everybody's in drag, and nobody is who they quite seem to be:

> Einstein disguised as Robin Hood
> With his memories in a trunk
> Passed this way an hour ago
> With his friend, some jealous monk

The darkness of the mood is ameliorated by the gentle beauty of the melodic line. This 1990 performance is exciting and fast paced. Worth noting is how well Dylan and GE Smith work together when playing acoustically. After all it's a long song and not that easy to carry, but to keep it brisk, Dylan sacrifices two verses, with the loss of incomparable lines. I always loved the line 'The Titanic sails at dawn' and always miss it when it's not there.

[Desolation Row]

Same goes for 'Tangled Up In Blue'. The loss of verses compromises the epic sweep of the song. The problem for Dylan with these long, complex songs is adapting them to a performance environment increasingly dominated by big stadium rock. Many of Dylan's songs seem made for small, intimate performance venues, so they have to be cut to fit the stadium rock experience. Still, you can't kill a good song like 'Tangled' and Dylan gives a spirited acoustic performance. Note the loose, jazzy feel that enters the music during Dylan's final harp break – this is a harbinger of things to come.

[Tangled Up In Blue]

We come once more to 'She Belongs to Me', that warning to all who might put their love on a pedestal. Later Dylan was to slow the pace of this song, but here he gives it the brisk 1990 treatment, pushing it along acoustically, with a harp solo that recalls the sixties rather than the squealing edge we got in 1989. Unadorned and vibrant, another acoustic gem from this year.

[She Belongs to Me]

'One Too Many Mornings' is one of Dylan's earliest songs. During Dylan's 1966 tour and Rolling Thunder Tour this edgy little ballad got the full band treatment but here it is restored to its acoustic setting – but what a wild and passionate vocal treatment! The faded world weariness of the album version has been replaced by an anguished desperation. Once more Dylan and GE Smith duet excitingly on their guitars and Dylan's harp work is rich and full of expression.

[One To Many Mornings]

Perhaps there will never be a performance of 'Knockin' On Heaven's Door' as sublime as the ecstatic 1987 version (See NET 1987), and anyone comparing the two performances can see how Dylan's vocal range has become constricted and his voice scratchy in the three years of touring and singing with the Travelling Wilburys. We'll face this again, even more so, when we come to 1991. But it builds up well from a lonely acoustic beginning to a thundering end. It is spirited rather than inspiring.

[Knocking On Heavens Door]

On another old favourite, the protest song 'The Ballad of Hollis Brown' Dylan drops to a lower register to accommodate his compromised voice, and so delivers a dark, threatening performance, using vibrato at the end of the lines, as with a lot of 1990 performances. That bit of vibrato makes it sound like he's really singing! The problem with this performance is that he misses out the second to last verse, and so ruins a wonderful piece of storytelling, as we don't get those shots ringing out 'like the ocean's pounding roar.'

People have rightly commented on what an incredible memory Dylan must have to recall all of those songs with their complex lyrics, and that's true – but he does mess up quite often. We'll come across this again later with that other great piece of story telling, 'John Brown.'

[The Ballad of Hollis Brown]

In Part 1 of this review of 1990 we saw several new songs from *Oh Mercy* enter the setlists, but he picked up on two he'd introduced in 1989, 'The Man in the Long Black Coat' and 'The Disease of Conceit,' for further development. (See NET 1989 Part 1)

'Man with the long Black Coat' is a spooky song, which would not fully come into its own until 1995, and in Part 1 of my 1989 study I mentioned a possible urban legend link to the story behind the song. In the 1990 version the gentle, strumming intro is augmented by a heavy, dark, fuzzy guitar from GE Smith, capturing something of the song's spookiness. The brief harmonica solo at the end is a brilliant return to 1989 form, high-pitched and, in the lyrical context, screeching with fear.

[Man in the Long Black Coat]

As in 1989, Dylan is back on the piano again for his *Oh Mercy* song 'Disease of Conceit.' 'Man in the Long Black Coat' shows Dylan working to create a mysterious subtext through a subtle build up of imagery. In 'Disease' he apparently gives up that artfulness and ability to be elusive to speak directly and plainly about conceit. I say 'apparently' because once more, as with 'one too many mornings' Dylan can hide his art behind his artlessness. The long, clumsy, prosy lines take us into a sermon. However, each verse begins with two long lines, followed by three or four narrowing lines with intensifying imagery. Consider the last verse:

> There's a whole lot of people in trouble tonight
> from the disease of conceit
> Whole lot of people seeing trouble tonight
> from the disease of conceit
> Give you delusions of grandeur and an evil eye
> Give you the idea that you're too good to die
> Then bury you from your head to your feet
> From the disease of conceit

There's nothing too discreet about the song, or how Dylan flaunts his sometimes clumsy sounding rhymes, and I wonder if behind all this overt preaching he may be hinting that he too is suffering from that same disease.

> 'Ain't nothing too discreet
> about the disease of conceit.'

This 1990 performance is a little smoother than the year before, and GE Smith surpasses himself in bringing the song to a rousing conclusion, even if we don't really need one.

[Disease of Conceit]

It would be a shame to finish our survey of this year without including 'You Angel You' from *Planet Waves*, 1974. In a setlist of darker, more serious songs, it's refreshing to come across this happy, rather goofy love song, and to catch a smile:

'The way you walk and the way you talk
I feel I could almost sing'

It's refreshing too, to hear a song that captures those first, carefree, intoxicated moments of love rather than the endless farewells that haunt Dylan's songs. It's too easy to see it as a throw-away song, but only because it captures those heady moments so exactly. Dylan hasn't performed this song very often, to our loss.

[You Angel You]

Nothing can ameliorate the pain in 'You're a Big Girl now' however. The pain of loss and betrayal. There seem to be two tendencies at work in Dylan's writing, the extravagant, surreal lyrical density we find on songs like 'Visions of Johanna' and 'Where are You Tonight' – 'Journey Through Dark Heat', and the sharp, pared down simplicity of some *Blood on the Tracks* songs. Look at these lyrics:

'Oh, I know where I can find you, oh
In somebody's room
It's a price I have to pay
You're a big girl all the way'

Nothing too elusive or symbolist here, at least until we get to the 'corkscrew to the heart', and that hurts.

[You're a Big Girl Now]

Interesting how this version is bracketed by the harmonica, in addition to a harp break before the last verse, and how jazzy the harp sounds. That jazzy whimsicality lifts the performance out of the heartbreak of the lyrics into some more resilient place.

I thought I'd finish this post, and our tour of the year with a lovely vocal performance – 'Tonight I'll Be Staying Here With You.' The last song on *Nashville Skyline*, 1969, it happily anticipates a night to be spent with a lover, happy to let the rest of the world go by. After all that love and betrayal. Looks like that ol' hell bound train will be leaving town without

Bob tonight.

[Tonight I'll Be Staying Here With You]

That finishes this post, and this brief trip through 1990. Mostly, it is a continuation of 1989, with a good sprinkling of acoustic songs and the mostly rapid performances we have seen since 1988. There are a couple of outstanding performances, 'It's alright, Ma' (see Part 1) and 'The Man in the Long Black Coat'. And while Dylan's voice got scratchier, his vocal performances are still full of power. A 'broken voice' suits some of these songs.

The overall sound is still metallic, and somehow without body, despite the hard work done by GE Smith to make all the backing sounds except drums and bass. Much of the harshness of the sounds from 1989 to 1990 are due to Smith's sharp and edgy guitar.

My next post will shift to 1991, the most difficult and perhaps most disastrous year of the whole NET.

Glad to have had you along for the ride. Take care!

Kia Ora

1991

NET 1991: Hidden Gems in a Train Wreck: Part 1 – The Undesirables

By Mike Johnson (Kiwipoet)

'And when it all came crashing down
I became withdrawn'

On a freezing night that January, the traffic locked solid on the snowbound London streets, we shuffled back to the Hammersmith Odeon to see the latest episode of the saga. Dylan came on wearing a strange boxy plaid jacket that looked as though it belonged to someone else, and performed with a sort of wilful lethargy, constantly picking up the wrong harmonicas, forgetting words, leaving out entire verses of Desolation Row... As he mangled some old favourite, reducing a fine melody and incomparable lyric to an indecipherable racket, I turned to the occupant in the next seat. "Well," I said, "I suppose they're his songs, and he can do what he likes with them." "Yes," she replied, "That seems to be his idea too."

Richard Williams, Bob Dylan, A Man Called Alias

My readers will be aware that I try to steer clear of commentaries and commentators in favour of looking at the performances themselves, and 1991 should be no exception. But there is pretty much a universal consensus that the NET crashed in that year, particularly the summer tour of Europe. Performances were messy and shambolic. Dylan's voice was scratchy and brittle, his new band raw and unrehearsed. It was hard to recognise the songs. And so on. Looked like Bob had had his day!

The bad reputation that the NET gained in the popular press was mostly due to some dismal performances in that year. The band began to call themselves The Undesirables because of their negative reception. The cracks were starting to show in 1990, with Dylan performing in a hoodie to hide his face, presumably, and covering his face while going through airports looking pretty wasted. Those wedded to referring everything he does back to Dylan's personal life have had a field day, blaming his abrupt decline on all kinds of things from the break up of his second marriage to too much of a good time with his Traveling Wilburys mates.

Gossip is a poor substitute for critical appreciation. And, being an avid listener to Dylan's performances, I have my own sense of what might have happened here, especially to Dylan's voice. We need look no further than the previous three years in which, as I observed from time to time, Dylan seems to be tearing the hell out of his voice. Remember those rough, forced performances in 1988, seeming to come from the back of his throat (see NET 1988, all parts). And those screaming-edge performances in 1989 and 1990. Not helped, perhaps, by having to compete with GE Smith's metallic guitar sound.

This might have been Dylan's attempt to re-create his 'high, wild, mercury sound', but my sense is that he did his voice in, simple as that. Three years of punishment, and he paid the price. It wouldn't be until 1994 that Dylan recovered the luminous clarity of his voice.

And yet ...and yet, if Dylan's voice is so shot, how come he can sing the way he does on some of these songs, such as 'The Man in Me'. Even given that he chooses the lower registers, mostly, the performances are passionate and his use of a low vibrato (to replace his high keening) makes it sound like he's really singing.

The issue as to what extent Dylan's voice really is shot, and to what extent he's forcing that scratchiness to give feeling to the songs (just as, in the early sixties, he tried to sound older than he was) is a moot one. Or is this all too complicated, and what we're hearing is just the natural ageing of his voice and the strategies he's using to deal with that? You'll have to be the judge.

There were other changes too that made for a messy year. GE Smith did his last concert with Dylan in October 1990, and guitarists auditioning with Dylan would find themselves onstage playing a concert. For the first 21 concerts of that European leg of the tour, Dylan added an extra guitar to the mix with John Jackson replacing GE Smith and Cesar Dias playing back up. After those first 21 concerts Dias dropped out, leaving the backing band as John Johnson, Ian Wallace on drums, and Tony Garnier on bass. It wouldn't be until the following year, 1992, with the arrival of the dobro, that Dylan began to forge the sound that would take him through the Nineties. In 2004 Dylan made an interesting comment about these early NET years.

> In the early 90's, the media lost track of me, and that was the best thing that could happen. It was crucial, because you can't achieve greatness under media scrutiny. You're never allowed to be less than your legend. When the media picked up on me again five or six years later, I'd fully developed into the performer I needed to be and was in a good position to go any which way I wanted. The media will never catch up again. Once they let you go, they cannot get you back. It's metaphysical. And it's not good enough to retreat. You have to be considered irrelevant.

Interview with Edna Gunderson

I can't help putting this quote from Dylan alongside the Richard Williams quote above and wonder if that 'indecipherable racket' Williams talks about isn't Dylan deliberately being 'less than his legend', crashing that legend so he can start again. But then I'd be doing what I criticise others for doing – reading motives into Dylan's behaviour. Sigh! After all, no performer willingly performs badly, surely? Still, by the end of 1991 there were lots of people writing Dylan off as irrelevant, past his best etc, giving him the camouflage he needed to forge his sound, so who knows?

So I approached this year with some trepidation, thinking I'd have nothing much to offer you but a bunch of botched performances. To my surprise I found all kinds of strange fruit – hidden gems and oddities, especially in that disastrous summer tour. It suddenly became an exciting adventure. Dylan was on a new path, the very beginning. His audiences would change. He would lose some, those who just wanted to see the legend; he wasn't playing for them. And he would gain some, those who wanted to follow a new musical direction. Those who could leave Bob Dylan behind.

So let's start with one. First blood, as it were. A messy, improved 'New Morning' from the summer tour but unrecognisable from the jaunty first song off that album. At first I thought the track had been misnamed as it sounds like a jam session, then Dylan starts to sing, some chords emerge, and low and behold! 'New Morning'.
Remarkable for its harmonica solo (how did I miss it for my Master Harpist series? I ask myself) and Dylan's free flowing piano work. Suddenly this is jazz. We're in another world. Dylan wouldn't take to the keyboards until 2002. And moving from harp to piano would come much later also. This is a special recording I would say, and shows Dylan willing to explore, improvise and re-arrange his songs. It is indeed a new morning.

[New Morning]

[Acoustic Jam]

In the same exploratory vein, we have this unnamed acoustic jam. It might have turned into a song but didn't. Another from that dreaded summer tour. The Undesirables having fun. When you've nothing, you've got nothing to lose. It just bounces along and then stops.

[Man Gave Names]

Now here's an oddity from that dreaded summer tour. 'Man gave Names to all the Animals.' A rarity enough in itself, and far from typical of his gospel songs, but here it gets a spirited airing. And the lyrics... not sure if he remembers them very well, and he mumbles over a few lines, and doesn't end the song properly, allowing it to peter out, but who cares?

[Bob Dylan's Dream]

Hidden away on the second side of *The Freewheelin' Bob Dylan* (1962) is a powerful piece of nostalgia, 'Bob Dylan's Dream,' – yet another neglected masterpiece, I suspect, since it's written from the point of view of someone much older than its 21 year old composer.

> Now, many a year has passed and gone.
> Many a gamble has been lost and won
> And many a road taken by many a first friend
> And each one I've never seen again

The song was justly praised for its extraordinary emotional maturity. It captures that sadness we feel when we look back at the friends of our youth, and the wonderful illusions we laboured under. And here's our protest singer showing an acute awareness of the complexity of things two years before 'I was so much older then,' which is often taken as his first indication that he was tuning out of the protest movement.

> As easy it was to tell black from white
> It was all that easy to tell wrong from right
> And our choices they were few so the thought never hit
> That the one road we traveled would ever shatter and split

What a pity Dylan didn't cultivate this song for his performances. I'm not pretending that this rare 1991 performance packs the same emotional wallop as the original, but in this rough, scratchy version, the age at least sounds about right.

[The Man in Me]

The next song, again from the summer tour, 'The Man in Me' from the *New Morning* album, is notable in several respects. Dylan's voice sounds just fine if a little reedy; we could almost be back with the voice he used on *Infidels* in 1984. There's a lot more than 'wilful lethargy' here.

Listen to the guitar break that begins around 2.25 seconds into the song and you hear Dylan on his Stratocaster. It may be difficult at first to distinguish Dylan's guitar from Jackson and Diaz, but it has a distinctive, wiry sound that dominates the music until the harp break begins around 4.25 seconds. This heralds the arrived of Mr Guitar Man, whose sound will dominate the electric sets until 2002, when Dylan will take to the piano. There is much to be said about Mr Guitar Man, but I'll leave that for a later date.

[It's All Over Now, Baby Blue (A)]

I want to finish this first part of The Undesirables with two takes on 'It's All Over Now, Baby Blue.' I have discussed this song previously, most fully in my Master Harpist series, when I presented Dylan's wonderful 1995 performance of the song (see Master Harpist part 2: performances you will simply not believe.), and refer my reader to that post.

The first take here is from the summer tour we have been dipping into. The emphasis is on crafting an effective vocal line for the song. It is all in the voice, which is close and intimate, and those sublime lyrics. Only the last sixty seconds are left for some sweet harmonica and guitar work, weaving in and out. It's tentative, but fresh and interesting.

[It's All Over Now, Baby Blue (B)]

The second take is from the later, fall tour of the US, as the band began to leave The Undesirables behind. Here Dylan slows the tempo, and while the last verse finishes at 4.20 secs, we have three more minutes of improvisation, both guitar and harp. While the harp break at the end cannot match the soaring grief of the 1995 performance, we can hear it taking shape, thoughtful, contemplative and sad.

That's it for now. I'll be back soon for the next instalment of this puzzling and provocative year – 1991.

Kia ora

NET 1991: Part 2 – Feet Walking By Themselves

Back to the most difficult yet fascinating year of the NET, the year of Undesirables, as the band called themselves. 1991, the year of botched performances and strange fruit. The year of hidden gems. The more I listen to these 1991 performances, the more I begin to wonder if there ever was any train wreck. What we are hearing, perhaps, are more like rehearsals, a new band finding its groove. Dylan reaching for a new sound. Feeling his way into the songs once more. As with the bit of jazzy undertow we find in this 'What Good Am I?' from *Oh Mercy*.

[What Good Am I?]

In an article in the New York Times, just published (2020), Dylan is asked what role improvisation plays in his music. This is his answer:

> None at all. There's no way you can change the nature of a song once you've invented it. You can set different guitar or piano patterns upon the structural lines and go from there, but that's not improvisation. Improvisation leaves you open to good or bad performances and the idea is to stay consistent. You basically play the same thing time after time in the most perfect way you can.

This is a bit trickier than it sounds, and it sounds like Plato. Somewhere, in the sphere of perfection, there is a perfect performance of the song, and no earthly performance can match its perfect form, merely approximate it. But you can play 'the same thing' many different ways, and notions of perfection might change over the years.

Perhaps improvisation is the wrong word for what Dylan is doing, say on a performance like this one of 'You're a Big Girl Now' from 1974. From the opening harp break, he's feeling his way into the 'structural lines' of the song in a sad, whimsical mood, rather than the prowling anger of the 1978 performances, or the howling grief of the 1976 performances. Those 'structures' are pretty open ended in terms of the 'patterns' that can be set on them. And sometimes those patterns seem ... well, improvised.

[You're A Big Girl Now]

And Dylan is not asked about vocal improvisation, ways of singing within the structures of the song that give it variation. Structurally, 'Blowin' in the Wind' must be one of Dylan's simplest songs, based as it is on the repetitive 'No More Auction Blocks.' But the vocal line can be quite complex in the way in which the voice can seek to link images and ideas. This performance, again from the much maligned summer tour, reminds me of Dylan's vocal work in 1981, extending across lines, rather than breaking them up, seeking variation within the set structure.

[Blowin' in the Wind]

New to Dylan's repertoire for 1991 is 'Shooting Star' from *Oh Mercy*. While everybody is naturally drawn to the magnificent 'Man in the Long Black Coat', and the dramatic 'Most of the Time', 'Shooting Star', with its powerful sense of lost possibilities, is hard to overlook. It could be treated as a straight love song, but for that middle section:

> Listen to the engine
> Listen to the bells
> As the last fire truck from hell
> Goes rolling by
> All the people are praying
>
> It's the last temptation
> The last account
> The last time you'll hear
> The sermon on the mount
> The last radio playing

As in medieval times, the shooting star may be a harbinger of doom, even the end of the world. This puts a different light on the rest of the lyrics. It's 'too late', not just to make up with lost loves, but to catch salvation. Too late to save the world. Our opportunities for reconciliation with God 'slip away' just like lost loves and loves that never were but could have been. Hard to find a better live performance of the song than this one – and his voice doesn't sound quite so wrecked all of a sudden, does it? In fact he's in fine voice.

[Shooting Star]

Those who have enjoyed Dylan's 'uncovers' of old Frank Sinatra and American Songbook songs will enjoy this next item, 'Lucky Old Sun'. It gets the acoustic treatment, sung with force and feeling. It's fascinating to compare this to performances he did of this song from 2015 – 2018.

[Lucky Old Sun]

In his book, Why Dylan Matters, Richard F Thomas cites, 'When I Paint my Masterpiece' as one of the earliest of Dylan's songs to show a strong connection with the classical world. Even the lines about following 'a pack of wild geese' should not be taken biographically, but refer to the sacred geese from the Roman goddess Juno who warned the Romans that invading tribesmen from Gaul were attacking. (see Thomas p79) Dylan seems to agree. When asked about the song in that same New York Times interview, Dylan says:

> It's grown on me as well. I think this song has something to do with the classical world, something that's out of reach. Someplace you'd like to be beyond your experience. Something that is so supreme and first rate that you could never come back down from the mountain. That you've achieved the unthinkable. That's what the song tries to say, and you'd have to put it in that context.

In other words, the Platonist's dream. The perfect song, or work of art. This is by no means a perfect performance. In fact it's pretty rough, and so is the audience. But my ol' harp-lovin heart is a sucker for the bluesy-jazz harp breaks at the beginning and end, and the song kicks along at a nice easy pace.

[When I Paint My Masterpiece]

Talk of masterpieces, and along comes 'Every Grain of Sand'. I've written about this song in previous NET posts, and in Master Harpist 4, about the alchemy that brings the elements of the song together in a way that moves us deeply, even when some of the lyrics may seem cliché. There's a vulnerability in this ragged-voiced version. This is far from the slick, accomplished album version. The beat is gentle, and once more Dylan's wirey, contentious guitar is evident, as is the constriction of his voice. It starts to sound pretty strained.

[Every Grain of Sand]

I'm not sure what he does with that last verse, and it all gets a bit shaky towards the end. This might be the most forlorn performance of the song I've heard.

And a song that could be forlorn, but isn't, at least here, is 'Girl from the North Country', another song from Dylan's stable of sixties favourites. By increasing the tempo and livening it up with a peppery harmonica, it escapes any tendency to wallow in nostalgia – that tendency had its full expression in the maudlin duet Dylan did with Johnny Cash back in 1970. Dylan was to develop this upbeat pattern for the song over the years, and we'll hear a sublime version of it when we get to 2000, but it starts here, rough and ready.

[Girl from the North Country]

Another sad number from the same era, and another from Dylan's sixties stable, is 'One Too Many Mornings.' Some of the pathos of the original, album version has been replaced with a feeling more gentle and resigned. Again, that easy, foot-tapping rhythm carries us along. We're back in Master Harpist territory with the exploratory harp work that brackets the vocals. It's not a dramatic, knock your eye out performance, but again we hear Dylan reaching for the structure of the song within a new tempo and mood.

[One Too Many Mornings]

We have been following 'Gates of Eden', one of the most mysterious songs in Dylan's sixties stable, and while I still go back to the stunning 1988 performance (See NET 1988, part 1), this more up tempo treatment does the song no injustice. Dylan's voice is reedier, but clear and sharp. Dylan has often been credited with bringing French Symbolism into modern American music in the style of Verlaine and Rimbaud, and the song certainly does that. But there is a strong echo of Ginsberg and the beat poets too:

> The motorcycle, black madonna
> two wheeled gypsy queen
> And her silver-studded phantom cause
> The gray flannel dwarf to scream

[Gates of Eden]

Dylan never lets us forget, for too long at least, that he is a rocker at heart. There is the feel of the fifties in this performance of 'Watching the River Flow.' This 1971 song, that seems to celebrate the values of relaxation and just kicking back, was not released on an album, but appeared on Bob Dylan's greatest hits Vol 2 in that year. In spirit, however, it belongs to *New Morning* and the bucolic Dylan from that era. It's a bit too kick-arse, however, to be really relaxed. That old 'midnight café' is a place for black coffee and brooding. I don't think Dylan hangs out much the way this song suggests. This is a gutsy, raw performance, from the summer tour of Europe.

[Watching the River Flow]

That's it for part 2 of our tour of that fascinating year, 1991. I'll be back shortly with the continuation.

Stay safe and Kia Ora

NET 1991: Part 3 – King of the Unsteady

By Mike Johnson (Kiwipoet)

By listening to the performances, we are starting to get a feel for that difficult and contentious year, 1991. Not quite the train wreck that the commentators claim, the year comes across to me more like a year of on-stage rehearsals, with Dylan trying out new arrangements and new musicians in front of audiences. This attempt to make old songs new again would not fully pay off until later years. Here we see them in their raw state, and the results are more gritty than pretty.

There is something of a deconstructive urge at work that I detected in the 1988 performances. The results can sound quite harsh and uncompromising. The tendency to flatten the melodic line with his scratchy voice, and so leach much of the drama from the songs, is evident in this performance of his 1966 epic 'Visions of Johanna'. Lacking the soaring spookiness of his 1966 live performances, or the midnight sinuousness of the album version, this 1991 performance lacks atmosphere, despite some energetic acoustic guitar. And, at least to my mind, the up tempo versions of the song fail to capture it in all its glory. He rattles through it well enough, but often those incomparable lyrics get blurred or rushed over. Verses get dropped out, and although he works the song up to a strong ending, the ultimate result is less than electrifying.

[Visions of Johanna]

We get a better result with 'Simple Twist of Fate'. He keeps the tempo slow and takes his time with the lyrics. The vocal works okay, with some interesting lyrical variations, but there is some dissonant guitar work from Dylan that puts us on edge. A trenchant harp break helps give the song some push, but the overall effect is of a sound that hasn't quite jelled. And I'm not sure about that 'trick ending' as Dylan describes it to the audience at the end of the song. It sounds to me as if he didn't quite know when and where to end it.

[Simple Twist of Fate]

That other classic from *Blood on the Tracks*, 'Shelter from the Storm' does not fare so well, although the vocal is not rushed and there's some nice jazzy harp. The real issue is with the overall sound and the general messiness of it. And we have to finally ask if Dylan is playing in the same key as everybody else. His tendency to play under the note, and to give even these semi-acoustic performances a punk like sound, makes for uneasy listening.

It seems that whatever the key of the song, Dylan always plays in the key of D – that is, the key of Dylan. The presence of Dylan as Mr Guitar Man is only just beginning to assert itself, and will become an increasing factor in the following years. A movement is taking place from Dylan as purely rhythm guitar, chord keeper, to Dylan the lead or assistant lead guitar. The results, particularly in 1991, are not easy on the ear.

[Shelter from the Storm]

On the other hand, the other guitarist, I assume it's John Johnson, doesn't help much either, with some odd tuning to his own guitar. Whoever it is, the overall effect is scrappy.

You notice some difference when Dylan is not playing the guitar, as on this rough and ready but serviceable performance of 'Under the Red Sky'. Dylan is on the electric piano, although not obtrusively, and although we have that scratchy voice to deal with, the performance carries us along okay. We are reminded once more of how good this droll song is.

[Under the Red Sky]

Dylan's 1984 'Man of Peace' gets a nice nineties chuggy beat (where have I heard that beat before?) and works well with Dylan on piano once more. It's a foot-tapper, but doesn't really take off. You can hear Dylan trying hard with that voice, but again, the strain is evident. The song doesn't have such a great reputation, but I think it sums up well his post Christian doubt.

[Man of Peace]

'Knockin' On Heaven's Door' is one of Dylan's most famous songs, and he has never let it drift too far from his setlist. This semi-acoustic version builds well, Dylan again on electric piano, with a lovely, free flowing break. Again, however, I'm less impressed with the guitar work. The vocal is up front, and while that same strain is evident, we can hear Dylan reaching for a new vocal line and not falling back on old tried and true formulations. It's not my favourite version, but it has a certain raw authenticity to it. It struggles rather than soars, but that fits the song too.

[Knocking on Heavens Door]

Then, out of these dusty corners there rolls another gem, Dylan's gospel classic from 1980, 'I Believe in You'. The pure, bluesy, opening harp break would alone justify its inclusion here, and once more I wonder where this song was hiding when I did my Master Harpist series. And while Dylan's washed-out voice doesn't have the richness of the 1980 Toronto performances, he takes to the song with a will, and all goes well until he flubs the lyrics, mixes the lines, and can't seem to recover the momentum of the song. For all that, however, it's a spirited performance well worth the listen.

[I Believe in You]

'Just like a Woman' has never been my favourite Dylan song, and this not my favourite performance of it. Nevertheless it is a sustained performance, with an intensification of the vocal towards the end. The tender vulnerability of the album version is lost, however, and the music meanders on for a few choruses after the verses to little effect. Just marking time, it seems to me.

[Just Like A Woman]

We can, however, quite safely kick our shoes off and do a little soft-shoe shuffle to 'I'll be your Baby Tonight'. It all seems to come together. Dylan sings with plenty of verve and imagination. The band seems to settle in too. You sense Dylan and the band are having the kind of good time the song promises as they chug along. It's about as laid back as Dylan gets. The jazzy harp sets it up nicely at the beginning, and finishes it off nicely at the end. Only towards the end of the song do we hear Dylan's dissonant Stratocaster messing with our heads. This is another from the summer tour.

[I'll Be Your Baby Tonight]

'Senor' is another regular to Dylan's set list. It's a great vocal, but he misses out the crucial last verse and the song chugs along for another two minutes without much happening. The sense of oppression this song can build up, and the drama of it, are largely lost here, not so much because of Dylan's vocal but because the looser chuggier beat doesn't suit the song, which Dylan will later learn how to build into a crescendo.

[Senor]

Songs like 'Senor' and 'Visions of Johanna' are mood songs – as is 'Man in the Long Black Coat'. But while the former two songs lost much of their atmosphere, 'Man in the Long Black Coat' must be one of the strongest performances of the year. Despite the tendency to flatten the melody somewhat, Dylan delivers a pungent, emotional performance, his voice once again seeking new ways through the melodic line. This performance has none of the polished grandeur of the 1995 Prague performance (see Master Harpist 1), but, in keeping with the year, it has a harsh, raw power.

[Man in the Long Black Coat]

That brings to an end our tour of Dylan's 1991 performances, and what a difficult and puzzling year it is to come to grips with. Not quite the train wreck of reputation, but things weren't right much of the time with the Undesirables. The band never really jelled. Painful when you compare it to the precision machine Dylan now has, evident on *Tempest* and *Rough and Rowdy Ways*. The overall sound was often discordant and sharp, especially when Dylan began to test his Mr Guitar Man fingers.

And there was a certain amount of deliberate jettisoning of the legend, and the image of the legend. Dylan's approach to the vocals was spirited, but he often elided words or forgot them, or left off verses. And there were unrehearsed and inconclusive endings to some of the songs. Messy endings. Yet there was a spirit of innovation in the air. Dylan playing electric piano. Dylan playing increasingly jazzy harp breaks, sounding thin and mercurial. Dylan stretching his often strained voice in new directions, seeking new ways of resonating with the songs. All this shemozzle would start to pay off in 1992. There was nowhere left to go but up.

Kia Ora, and see you next time.

1992

NET 1992: Heading for the Promised Land

By Mike Johnson (kiwipoet)

> Watch out, Lester
> Take it, Lou
> Join the monks
> The C.I.O
> Tell 'em all that Tiny Montgomery says hello

The Promised Land in Sight

Going from 1991 to 1992 is a bit like going from the desert to the Promised Land. We find a cornucopia of riches. At least a first sight. We have a lot to look forward to in the next few posts.

Dylan expanded the band by adding multi-guitarist Bucky Baxter and having two drummers, Charlie Quintana and Winton Watson. That duo lasted from April until September when Quintana left the band. With the slide guitar and dobro (Hawaiian guitar), Baxter would soften the sound of the band, but also add a richer, 'orchestral' effect which won't come fully into play until 1994/5.

Dylan's voice hasn't improved much, if at all, but the band is on fire. I could hardly credit that the jazz guitarist that comes racing out in some of these tracks is the same John Jackson who blundered along with Dylan in 1991. This jazzy turn sees the band kicking along in a way we've never heard before. It certainly gives a boost to the great apocalyptic 'All along the Watchtower'.

Within that jazzy framework, Dylan's harmonica too becomes more adventurous, more open and free. No other year quite captures that emergent spirit, the sense of joyful innovation. (Readers of my Master Harpist Series will recognise this track from Part 1 of that series)

[Watchtower]

Same goes for Dylan's great seventies epic 'Tangled Up In Blue'. This broken, fragmentary narrative, as the singer faces his painful, confused and confusing past, gets full epic treatment here. At nearly eleven minutes, with a medium tempo beat, this is the first in a long line of epic performances of this song. But Dylan's interest here is not so much in story telling, as he drops out the third verse anyway, but in musical exploration – Dylan taking long guitar and harp breaks.

[Tangled Up In Blue]

At this stage the guitar breaks are quite tentative (they will fully come into their own in 1993) compared to the confident, high flying harmonica. Baroque musical extensions work okay with songs like 'Watchtower' and 'Tangled,' which have an inherently Baroque reach, but what about the more minimalist songs?

'I and I' started life as a sweet/bitter little ballad on *Infidels* (1984) and became a loud, thumping crowd pleaser during the Tom Petty years. It resurfaces here as an eight minute epic with its own apocalyptic subtext to the fore. Dylan scratches away at the lyric as best he can with that sandpaper voice, showing his voice no mercy 'in creation where one's nature neither honours nor forgives'. It turns into a powerful vocal performance, scratch and all.

The bulk of the performance, however, is taken up with Dylan and John Jackson working with, and sometimes against, the textures Bucky Baxter is creating with those long, drawn out notes. This collaboration won't fully pay off until the following year for this song. But it's Dylan's musical development, in particular developing his own unique approach to the guitar, that is his main focus here. More Baroque developments to come.

[I and I]

Dylan might have stopped writing topical protest songs in the mid sixties, but I have argued that he extended the range of his social critique with so-called attack songs like 'Like A Rolling Stone', 'Ramona', and 'Just Like a Woman' to include living blindly and in bad faith – those 'unlived meaningless lives' (False Prophet). But he also continued to write politically, and one of his most political songs is 'Union Sundown', also from *Infidels*, a song attacking the loss of US productive capacity. An early insight into the pitfalls of globalization.

> When it costs too much to build it at home
> You just build it cheaper someplace else

But it aroused the antagonism of Dylan's more left wing audience, as it seems to blame the greedy unions and government regulations for America's decline.

> I can see a time coming when even your home garden
> is gonna be against the law

However, these sentiments are balanced with a deeper dig into what's going on politically. The last verse is as succinct and sharp as anything Dylan's written in terms of direct social commentary. The rhythms wouldn't fit, but the sentiment could have come from 'It's Alright, Ma' back in 1964.

Democracy don't rule the world
You better get that in your head
This world is ruled by violence
But I guess that's better left unsaid
From Broadway to the Milky Way
That's a lot of territory indeed
And a man's gonna do what he has to do
When he's got a hungry mouth to feed

The song has only rarely been performed. This is the only recording of it that I have, although others may exist. But is this 'Union Sundown' at all? I can't match any of the words except the chorus, at least those words I can make out. Is this another off the cuff performance, or has Dylan rewritten the song? I'd love to see a transcript of this, although I don't have the ear or the patience to do it. The song rocks along and the band is pretty tight, but Dylan's vocal delivery gets messy. I feel like I'm back in 1991, with a shambles just around the corner.

[Union Sundown]

'Cat's in the Well' from *Under the Red Sky* (1991) is another very political song, but the politics of Under the Red Sky are very different from *Infidels*. 'Unbelievable', off the latter album, delivers swift judgment on what might have happened to the Promised Land.

Once it was a land of milk and honey
now they say it's a land of money
who'd ever thought, they could make that stick
it's unbelievable, you can get this rich this quick.

'Cat's in the Well' puts the critique on a different level by using animals from fables. A menacing air is created at the beginning of the song.

Cat's in the well and the wolf is looking down
he got his big bushy tail dragging all over the ground

A cat in a well of course is a desperate creature. That same desperation lies behind our polite facades.

> The cat's in the well
> and the servant is at the door.
> The drinks are ready
> and the dogs are going to war.

Dylan's outrage at the state of the world is no less than it was, back in the early sixties, in his protest day.

> The cat's in the well and grief is showing its face
> The world's being slaughtered and it's such a bloody disgrace.

Dylan was often to use this song as a rocker to close gigs, and it was often rushed through or turned into a guitar fest, but this is a pretty clean performance.

[Cat's in the Well]

While on the subject of Under the Red Sky and Dylan's ongoing political commentary, we find a little song called '2 by 2'. In their eagerness to dismiss the album, and write off '2 by 2' as song writing by numbers, the commentators miss once more the engagement with social issues of these songs.

> How many paths did they try and fail?
> How many of their brothers and sisters lingered in jail?
> How much poison did they inhale?
> How many black cats crossed their trail?

It has a catchy melody and beat, but the song never quite came over, and Dylan rarely performed it. In this performance he misses out the chorus I've quoted in favour of repeating the last chorus twice, which is somewhat more generalised in terms of social critique.

> How many tomorrows have they given away?
> How many compared to yesterday?

How many more without any reward?
How many more can they afford?

Listen out for Bucky Baxter's nice slide guitar work, and an arresting ending to the song. No spoilers!

[2 by 2]

We can't leave Under the Red Sky without that much despised song 'Wiggle Wiggle.' I offered some defence for that song when looking at 1991 (See NET 1991 Part One), suggesting that it was a deliberate and provocative attack on human sexuality, and as such, a powerful song. So powerful it got everybody offended and up in arms. They came to see 'Blowin' in the Wind' and got 'Wiggle Wiggle'. Quite an effective way to destroy your legend. Here it is, with the lyrics restored. There's some pretty fancy guitar work here by John Jackson. This jazzy extension seems to be what interests the musicians. The audience seem to get it, and have a good time. 'Wiggle you can raise the dead!' Oh Lordy.

[Wiggle Wiggle]

Well, I'm going to wiggle right out of here and prepare the next post, which will check in on how the *Oh Mercy* songs are developing, plus some other goodies.

Be well

Kia Ora

NET 1992: Part 2 – What Good Am I?

By Mike Johnson (Kiwipoet)

We finished Part 1 of this tour through some of Dylan's 1992 performances by considering some of the songs from Under the Red Sky (1990) on his setlist that year. Now we turn to his previous album, *Oh Mercy* (1989), and catch up with some of those performances.

The four *Oh Mercy* songs Dylan presents this year were all first performed in 1990 and 1991. Two of these songs, 'Man in the Long Black Coat' and 'What good am I?' would stick around, and would be further developed, whereas 'Most of the Time' and 'Everything Is Broken' would fade away.

That makes the performances of the latter two songs all the more precious, especially 'Most of the Time', as it is a masterpiece of ironical undercutting. In 1990 we heard a passionate presentation of the song which was anything but reconciled to the song's contradictions.

This 1992 version creates a mixed impression. The sound is richer and more laid back, with Bucky Baxter again creating some fine musical textures. It all sounds pretty good. Then Dylan starts to sing and the whole thing becomes a lot more fraught. It's a strange, almost strangled performance, full of odd timing, moments of bitterness – and maybe he's not quite remembering the lyrics, the order of the verses. It's all pretty hair-raising, and far from the triumphant 1990 performance.

It's a pity that the harp break at the end is not better articulated. It strikes me that Dylan is just not able to find his way into this song in terms of performance, and it is perhaps not surprising that he drops it from his setlists.

[Most Of The Time]

'Everything Is Broken' fares much better. The band sounds good and strong with a rocking beat. Dylan sounds a little diffident at the beginning but soon warms to the vocals. Like a lot of Dylan's protest songs, this one is couched in terms which manage to be both specific and general.

Broken cutters, broken saws,
Broken buckles, broken laws,
Broken bodies, broken bones,
Broken voices on broken phones
Take a deep breath, feel like you're chokin',
Everything is broken

I quote these particular lines because they could have been written yesterday – or tomorrow. That 'feel like you're chokin' reminds me of 'I can't breathe' which has become the rallying cry of the Black Lives Matter movement. By these mysterious means Dylan songs stay relevant. When I hear 'broken laws/ broken bodies, broken bones' I see scenes of police violence in the streets of American cities right now.

[Everything Is Broken]

'What good am I?' is a song full of self doubt, often performed with Dylan on the piano. Not in this case, however. A soft easy rhythm is established against which Dylan delivers a passionate, quivering vocal. As I suggested when looking at the 1990 performance, I find this song seems to gain in contemporary relevance as the years roll on, and all those things we might turn a blind eye to have just grown worse. The question 'what good am I?' confronts us in the face of growing injustices, social and environmental.

[What Good Am I?]

Arguably 'Man in the Long Black Coat' is the jewel in the *Oh Mercy* crown, and Dylan worked hard at developing the song over the years. The direction of that development is towards great grandiosity, as the drama enacted in the song evolves from the swampy horror story of Lanois' album production into a cosmic tragedy – the seduction of innocence on a grand scale. Moral doubt and self-reflection play a large part in the album, including, 'What Good am I?', 'The Disease of Conceit', 'What was it you wanted?', and 'Shooting Star'. This shows up in '...Black Coat', in lines that cast doubt on the function of our consciences:

Preacher was talking there's a sermon he gave
He said every man's conscience is vile and depraved
You cannot depend on it to be your guide
When it's you who must keep it satisfied

This is the human paradox; morally, we can't trust ourselves. This is a shot across the bows of anybody who appeals to their own conscience alone as justification for their actions. That twisted sanctimoniousness that would take the word of scripture and turn it to evil purposes.

Somebody said from the bible he'd quote
There was dust on the man in the long black coat

Perhaps what makes this song special in the Dylan canon is that the devil himself puts in an appearance, sinister and dramatic. I can't think of any other Dylan song, even from his gospel period (1979 -1981), that so vividly personifies the seductive power of the devil.

This 1992 performance is certainly the best so far, with a sharp, telling harp break at the end, doing what Dylan's harp does best, elaborating and exploring the emotional valences made possible by the song. It's a wonderful performance, and a stepping stone to even greater performances in 1995

[Man in the Long Black Coat]

We move the clock back now to *Blood on the Tracks* (1974), and catch up with how Dylan has been working with those songs. We heard a scintillating performance of 'Tangled Up In Blue' in Part 1, 1992, and we now turn to those other perennials, 'Simple Twist of Fate' and 'You're a Big Girl Now', songs Dylan has been cultivating since they were written.

'Simple Twist of Fate', with its famously shifting pronouns is a quiet reflective song, and the effectiveness of Bucky Baxter's dobro in creating long sustained sounds behind the verses is evident. I nearly dropped this song out because of the rowdy audience. The background noise is frustrating, especially at the beginning when a quiet, melancholy mood is being set, but things quieten down somewhat after a while and Dylan delivers a moody, if scratchy vocal. The expression 'ships that pass in the night' is what passes through my mind when I think about this song. A connection made, but only just. A one night stand that turns sad with the dawn. A memory that will never fade. The one that got away will always haunt.

> He woke up, the room was bare
> He didn't see her anywhere
> He told himself he didn't care
> Pushed the window open wide
> Felt an emptiness inside

Except in this variation Dylan sings:

> He told himself he didn't care
> But he pushed back the blinds
> Found a note she'd left behind
> To which he just could not relate
> Any more than that simple twist of fate

[A Simple Twist of Fate]

There is a gorgeous harmonica break, sweet and sensitive, against the rolling thunder of the drums, but audience noise once more distracts us from the beautiful quiet ending.

More darkly driven than 'Simple Twist of Fate', 'You're a Big Girl Now' registers the anguish we might all feel when someone grows away from us, grows out of us as if we were clothes that had grown too small. The one that got away is the one most bitterly regretted.

> Oh, I know where I can find you, oh
> In somebody's room
> It's a price I have to pay
> You're a big girl all the way

Dylan's in fine voice for this performance, and once again we hear how this band can create quiet, more intimate music without having to be acoustic. Baxter again creating a rich, 'orchestral' texture. Dylan can go softly with the voice or hard; give it a harsh edge, or sound thin and vulnerable.

[You're a Big Girl Now]

As far as I know, 1992 was the last year Dylan attempted to perform that great splenetic masterpiece 'Idiot Wind' on stage. It must be a hell of a song to sustain, all that outrage and anger, over so many verses. And it's not the kind of song that offers alternatives in terms of musical interpretation or reworking. It flashes like fire or not at all. It can't be tamed. There is no sweetening the bitter pill. It is an aggrieved beast. I think the 1976 Rolling Thunder versions are probably the best in performance terms, but Dylan gives this 1992 performance his all, using 'upsinging' (raising his voice at the end of every line) to keep it rolling. The harp break keeps up the brittle edge of the song, but, perhaps in the final analysis, Dylan's voice, although he's trying hard, just isn't quite up to it – it's your call.

[Idiot Wind]

I'm going to finish this post with a song that doesn't quite fit anywhere else, 'Seeing the Real You at Last'. Off the 1985 album, Empire Burlesque, it's one of the new songs from that album that Dylan keeps coming back to from time to time. In one performance he had the stage lights directed at the audience when he hit the chorus line, suggesting that it might be us he's singing about. We, the audience, lurk behind the figure of the girl, but eventually we are exposed for what we are. Or again, the woman in the song could be a personification of America, the promised land which doesn't turn out to be quite what was promised but just a set of filmic projections.

> I'm hungry and irritable
> And I'm tired of this bag of tricks
> At one time there was nothing wrong with me
> That you could not fix.
>
> Well, I sailed through the storm
> Strapped to the mast
> Oh, but our time has come
> And I'm seeing the real you at last.

The strapped to the mast reference is to Odysseus, who straps himself to the mast so he can hear the song of the sirens and not be lured to his death, as the travellers pass that island.But there is no escaping paradox:

> From now on I'll be busy
> Ain't going nowhere fast

When I take a look around me, I see a whole world busy going nowhere fast. Maybe we are all seeing the 'real you' at long last – and it's not a pleasant sight.

[Seeing the Real You at Last]

Take care and stay wise. I'll be back soon to look at some of Dylan's acoustic performances in 1992

Kia Ora

NET 1992: Part 3 – All the Friends I Ever Had are Gone

By Mike Johnson (Kiwipoet)

At the end of 1992 Dylan released *Good as I Been to You*, an album of mostly traditional folk songs. The album was well received, better than *Under the Red Sky*, and he was to follow up in 1993 with *World Gone Wrong*. These were both solo acoustic albums, and were generally viewed as Dylan returning to his roots, searching for inspiration as the commentators saw it.

One of Dylan's favourite songs from these albums is 'Delia', from *World Gone Wrong*. 'Delia' is one of those songs which seems just made for Dylan; it sounds like a Dylan song, which goes to show how close much of Dylan's work is to that tradition.

Although it didn't come out until the following year, Dylan was trying it out in 1992, not as a solo acoustic, but a gently paced full-band ballad. It's a little gem, this one, with Dylan fully committed to the vocal.

[Delia]

However, 1992 did see some incomparable solo acoustic performances; the last year, I believe, when Dylan appeared on stage alone with guitar and harmonica. These following acoustic performances are all the more precious for that, but this wasn't just a last hurrah for the legend; these performances are superlative. He's not just dusting off his old material but re-exploring it with a passion, feeling his way into the songs as if he'd just written them, trying them out in different ways from one performance to the next.

Let's start with that mysterious love song 'Love minus Zero/No Limit'. The vocal is so upfront and clear that it sounds like a soundboard, rather than an audience, recording. This one is from the 24th of March. In this case the ragged edge to Dylan's voice works perfectly. This one is surely a candidate for one of the NET's finest moments – at least to date.

[Love Minus Zero(A)]

In other performances he brings in the harmonica. Hard to kill a legend when offering such legendary performances. Hard to escape a twinge of nostalgia when that harp begins to blow. Masterful vocal. Wonderful to sense a respectful audience. Sorry don't have the date for this one.

[Love Minus Zero (B)]

And, just in case you haven't had enough of that classic song, here's another knockout performance, this one from the 15th of March.

[Love Minus Zero (C)]

Sigh! Sometimes it's great when Dylan just plays Dylan, no tricks, no great baroque extensions. Just Bob and his genius. Blink for a moment and you're back in the 1960s. Here's 'Blowin' in the Wind' just like it ever was, except that exquisite vocal timing makes it lighter and more peppy than the sixties performances. And that dancing, peppering harmonica!

> How many years must some people exist?
> Before they're allowed to be free?
> And how many times can a man turn his head
> And pretend that he just doesn't see?

Perhaps we have become so familiar with these lyrics that we can't hear them anymore, but these rhetorical questions still cut to the heart of the human condition. The quoted lines take us right out onto the streets of our contemporary world where the Black Lives Matter demonstrations are happening. Perhaps it takes such a fresh performance to remind us. Simple it may appear, its questions unanswerable, 'Blowin' remains one of Dylan's greatest songs. And this must be one of his greatest performances of it.

[Blowin' in the Wind]

Listening to Dylan's wonderful acoustic guitar work as he accompanies himself, it occurs to me that we are reaping the benefits of those long hours he was putting in recording 'Good as I been to You', alone in his garage.

Discovering the guitar parts for those traditional songs seems to have lead to a rediscovery of his own songs and the joys of acoustic performance.

And while deep in the nostalgia of acoustic Legendland, we just can't afford to get any older without listening to this brisk but cutting performance of 'Ramona'. Perhaps behind this 'attack' song there is a plea for us to live more aware lives, to be aware of the 'fixtures and forces' that govern our lives and bring us to grief. Lovers of Dylan the Master Harpist will be in ecstasies over the last minute or so of this performance. Enough said!

[Ramona]

Ah, very nice, but there is more to come in this acoustic promised land. Like this tender version of 'Boots of Spanish Leather', one of Dylan's earliest separation songs. The song is remarkable for its dialogue, a score for two voices, and the build up of pathos. We feel that the lover will never return, at least not as a lover, and the singer will never get his boots of Spanish leather. Once more, note the gorgeous harp solo, reminiscent of, but more sophisticated than his sixties playing. Don't the audience just love this! No wonder, it's a treat.

[Boots of Spanish Leather]

We are so deep in our nostalgia trip now that there is no stopping us. The gentle, intimate and reflective Dylan is irresistible. So there's nowhere to go but to the equally tender and reflective 'Girl from the North Country'. I have described this song as one of Dylan's most pure love songs, as it is free of bitterness and without any ambiguous edges. The song is in itself an exercise in nostalgia, that place beyond tears where we can fondly remember old loves. So once more Dylan throws aside the stadium rocker, which he plays so well, to be his old folkie self again, and deliver this subtle, understated performance.

[Girl from the North Country]

Of course, the acoustic performance lies at the heart of early sixties protest songs, even songs like 'John Brown' which we have only heard in rock versions, probably because it makes such a good rocker. Think back to the 1987 performance with Tom Petty's band, one of the best ever (see NET 1987), or the version with GE Smith in 1990, another kick-arse rocker. But now we hear it as the acoustic song it must have started as. And what a powerful performance, with the song building to a climax as Dylan wrings everything he can from his sandpaper voice.

[John Brown]

'John Brown' takes us into the world of Dylan's early sixties protest songs, and perhaps the greatest of those songs, 'A Hard Rain's A-Gonna Fall'. This nightmare/hallucination still haunts after all these years, and Dylan certainly hasn't tired of it yet. Lines that seem so contemporary still jump out at us:

> I saw a white man who walked a black dog.

This performance is close to the tempo of the original, perhaps a little faster, and there is some fine acoustic guitar work. Dylan stretches his voice to deliver a performance with more vocal variation than we're accustomed to with this song. The challenge for many of these long, repetitive songs is to keep up the interest, to build, vocally and musically to that stunning final verse.

> I'm a-going back out 'fore the rain starts a-falling
> I'll walk to the depths of the deepest dark forest
> Where the people are many and their hands are all empty
> Where the pellets of poison are flooding their waters
> Where the home in the valley meets the damp dirty prison
> And the executioner's face is always well hidden
> Where hunger is ugly, where the souls are forgotten
> Where black is the color, where none is the number
> And I'll tell it, and speak it, and think it, and breathe it
> And reflect from the mountain so all souls can see it
> Then I'll stand on the ocean until I start sinking
> But I'll know my song well before I start singing

I quote these lines in full to remind us of just how good they are, in case we start taking the song for granted. These last lines demonstrate what dramatists call 'rising action' – a build towards a final climax, a lyrical momentum that gathers pace as the images flash by. This helps to mitigate the somewhat plodding nature of the original, which might have worked fine in the summer of 1962, when the song was written, but not so well thirty years later. This is a spirited vocal – just a pity he had to leave off those last two lines, suggesting that he didn't know his song so well before he started singing.

[Hard Rain]

Note that while this is acoustic, it is not Dylan alone onstage. I think I can detect two other guitars at work. It starts off sounding solo, but it isn't, not quite.

The same applies to that other iconic song, that ode to escapism, 'Mr Tambourine Man', which remains acoustic but slowly brings in the rest of the band, drums and all. This performance clips along a little too fast for me, but the extra pace makes for some nifty guitar work and a suitably squeaky harp break. Pity about the loudmouth in the audience who comes so close to wrecking the experience of the song that I almost left it out. Still, part of the experience of listening to these audience recordings is hearing the response of the audience, in this case a little too positive. Much depends on who was near the recorder at the time.

[Mr Tambourine Man]

Another track from side B of *Bringing It All Back Home* (1964) that we have been closely following is 'Gates of Eden', that classic symbolist song that never seems to lose its mystery. We have heard some very fine performances of this song, particularly the 1988 version (See NET 1988, part 1). This performance is not likely to go down as anyone's favourite owing to Dylan's scratchy, nasal performance, but the rapid strumming and faster pace, which seems to be a feature of 1992, keeps it interesting.

[Gates of Eden]

I'd like to pause for a moment here to note that both these songs offer some picture of their creator. In Mr Tambourine Man we find this:

> And if you hear vague traces of skipping reels of rhyme
> To your tambourine in time
> It's just a ragged clown behind
> I wouldn't pay it any mind
> It's just a shadow you're seeing that he's chasing

The 'ragged clown', I would suggest, is a perfect image for the Dylan who wrote this song. Those skipping reels of rhyme aptly describe the song itself. Those critics of Dylan's shift from his 'protest songs' to his 'symbolist songs' might well agree that the man had given up the good fight in favour of chasing shadows. In Gates of Eden we get a different formulation:

> And I try to harmonise with songs
> the lonesome sparrow sings

'The lonesome sparrow', I would suggest, is a perfect image for the Dylan who wrote 'Gates of Eden', as it is more cryptic and Zen-like than the 'Tambourine' quote. And 'Gates' ends on a suitably cryptic, Zen-like note:

> Sometimes I think there are no words
> But these to say what's true...

These lines should be my cue to exit this post, as I've hit the word limit, but I still have a couple of these acoustic performances to go. So, I'm going to unceremoniously jam them in at the end here. They are both songs we will return to. Guitar driven performances of 'Desolation Row' and 'It Ain't Me, Babe.'

[Desolation Row]

[It Ain't Me, Babe]

Stay safe from the ravaging plague, and I'll be back soon with the final part of this survey of the NET, 1992.

Kia Ora

NET 1992: Part 4 –
The usual suspects

By Mike Johnson (Kiwipoet)

As we have seen, 1992 was a big year for Dylan in terms of the development of the NET. He continued to cultivate songs from his two most recent albums, Most of the Time and Under the Red Sky (See NET 1992, parts 1 and 2); presented a strong acoustic set of his early pre-electric songs (See NET, 1992, part 3) as well as developing the electric side with some of his old favourites from the post electric 1960s – the usual suspects.

Another trend that developed in 1992 was the advent of what I call 'quiet electric'. It sounds almost acoustic. A gentle sound which gives Dylan room to be more intimate, not having to shred his voice against the scream of guitars – although that happens too! This recording of 'She Belongs to Me' (which I have re-named She belongs to Herself) is so close and quiet I thought for a moment that it was acoustic. The closeness of vocal suggests it's a soundboard rather than an audience recording.

[She Belongs to Me]

What a quiet, deadly, droll little gem. This song can sound laid-back, but it can never be laid back because of the warning it contains to all foolish lovers not to be deceived by flashy appearances. She may wear an Egyptian ring that 'sparkles before she speaks', but:

> You wind up peeking through a keyhole
> Down upon your knees

With Dylan, where there is love, humiliation is never far away. It's worth reminding ourselves that this song will stick around, will become a regular feature during the Sinatra years (2014 – 2017), and will undergo many changes and transformations. I think the seed of the much later approach to the song lies in this little performance. It has the right beat.

The same quiet approach marks this powerful performance of 'I Dreamed I saw St Augustine', although the music builds up as the song progresses, with Bucky Baxter to the fore on his dobro and Dylan powering up the vocal. Enjoy this while you can, as the song is fast disappearing from Dylan's setlists. Like 'What Good am I?', the song captures Dylan in a more humble, self-doubting mood. The extended quiet ending brings the song back to its acoustic roots. There's a subdued despair here, and a surrender to that despair not quite matched in any other Dylan song.

[I dreamed I Saw St Augustine]

There's gentleness too in 'If Not for You', although Dylan discovered that it could be given a driving beat that made it into a nice foot-tapper. This song is from the *New Morning* album, 1970, and is a refreshingly straightforward love song, even if it does focus on the negative consequences of not having love. Interesting, how Dylan experimented with this song during 1992, trying out different keys and tempos in his restless search for the perfect performance. This one from the April 15 Sydney concert features harmonica and a somewhat sweet delivery.

[If Not for You (A)]

By October the harp has gone and the delivery is a bit harsher. Notably this performance features some clever guitar work by John Jackson. Each version has its own listening pleasure.

[If Not for You (B)]

Apparently 'Lay Lady Lay' is the only song Dylan wrote in 1969, and of course went on to become one of his most famous love songs. I loved the modest seductiveness of the album version (*Nashville Skyline*, 1969), although I didn't relate quite so well to the raucous Rolling Thunder Tour performances which seemed to lose that seductiveness. This 1992 performance goes a long way to recapturing the more intimate aspect of the song. There is, however, a more forlorn feel to the song than previous versions – a little edge of desperation? The night will not be still ahead forever.

[Lay Lady Lay]

I have commented before, particularly in relation to that 1966 masterpiece 'Visions of Johanna', that the tone and general feeling of that album, *Blonde on Blonde*, seem to have been the most difficult to translate onto the stage, at least post 1960s. I think it was Dylan's leering, sneering vocal performance on that album that did the trick, filling the lines with all kinds of implications. Dylan at his note bending best. Later performances of these songs seem to lose the patina of magic we get on the album.

'Just like a Woman' is a good case in point. The leering/sneering vocal has gone, and Dylan avoids the melody line in favour of a high monotone delivery. This turns it from an 'attack' song to something quite different – a confession of vulnerability. It becomes clear that this song is about being pretentious and pretending, with the singer doing as much pretending as the girl in question.

Feminists found the album performance distasteful, and an attack on womankind. In her performance of the song, Nina Simone refused to sing the last line – 'you break just like a little girl' – and made a point of it. The trendy theory when the album came out was that the song was written to a man. Maybe one of those 'old queens' Dylan refers to in 'I contain multitudes' (2020). I think we need to pick up on the tenderness inherent in the song. For all its backbiting, there is a tenderness in Dylan's portrayal of the woman which comes across in this hard-edged performance. I note the emotional harp beak.

[Just Like a Woman]

On the album, 'Rainy Day Woman' is full of gloating insouciance. In this up tempo performance, the insouciance has gone, to be replaced by a raw insistence. Roll on rock and roll boogie. The band has fun and the audience does too, joining in on that provocative line 'everybody must get stoned'. Great to hear some bluesy blasts from Dylan on the harp, and nobody has to think too much about that sandpaper voice.

[Rainy Day Woman]

I wish I had notes on who is performing with Dylan on this. I keep hearing an organ, or organ like sounds. Might be that versatile dobro again. I'd be happy to hear from anyone who knows.

'Stuck Inside of Mobile with the Memphis Blues Again' is another case in point. This long, rambling song has its roots in talking songs like Bob Dylan's 115th Dream and Talking World War 11 Blues. It's a surrealistic trip through modern America, a kind of Fear and Loathing in a Mobile. It's a world of political corruption and madness. I've commented before that it's odd how lines from Dylan songs can resonate with our contemporary reality. While listening to his song, I was reading about Donald Trump's attack on the U.S postal service, apparently trying to run it into the ground. These lines floated into my head:

> And I would send a message
> To find out if she's talked
> But the post office has been stolen
> And the mailbox is locked

When I first heard the song, I loved it for its groundhog day ending. It reminds me of a much later line: 'I'm all boxed in, no room to escape' (Mississippi 2001)

> Now the bricks lay on Grand Street
> Where the neon madmen climb
> They all fall there so perfectly
> It all seems so well timed
> An' here I sit so patiently
> Waiting to find out what price
> You have to pay to get out of
> Going through all these things twice

Classic Dylan lyrics, but again, not an easy song to maintain onstage, given its length and repetitiveness. I don't know that Dylan ever nailed this one onstage, but here he gives it a fair go. Perhaps it's the sinister feel of the album version that's lost here.

[Stuck Inside of Mobile]

More successful, for my ear at least, is this 'Ballad of a Thin Man' from *Highway 61 Revisited* (1965). I have described this song as an encounter with strangeness, and with alternative sexualities. A Freudian would have a field day with the imagery in this song. Mockery runs deep here. Dylan is mocking not only the uncomprehending Mr Jones, but the weirdos and freaks that assail him. The hard, cutting edge of Dylan's 1992 vocal style suits the song just as well as the spooky-voiced album version. I wonder if anyone has noticed that the underlying riff or base line is the same as used by Ray Charles in his 'I believe it to my Soul'(1960).

[Ballad of a Thin Man (A)]

That performance was from early in the year, Sydney April 15. By the time we get to November the song has regained some of its old spookiness and accusatory power.

[Ballad of a Thin Man (B)]

We'll finish this post, and our study of 1992 with a rousing performance of 'Highway 61 Revisited.' This is fitting as Dylan often used the song as concert closer. I've said before that this song is not quite what it's rough and rowdy surface would suggest. It's not just a fun, throwaway song, an absurdist exercise or pounding rocker, but a savage attack on the godless materialism of modern America.

> Now, the roving gambler he was very bored
> Trying to create a next world war
> He found a promoter who nearly fell off the floor
> He said, "I never engaged in this kind of thing before
> But yes, I think it can be very easily done
> We'll just put some bleachers out in the sun
> And have it on Highway 61"

The idea that someone would try to 'create a next world war' seemed totally ridiculous. I mean, everyone was trying to stop a next world war, right? But what about today? Don't we have promoters who just fell off the floor already on the job?

[Highway 61 Revisited]

So what are we to make of 1992? I think we can say that the signs are hopeful. The band is starting to come together, and there are some exquisite acoustic performances (See NET 1992, part 3), but taken as a whole, there is a sense of strain, of things not quite falling into place. Dylan's voice has hardly improved from 1991, and he often rushes or elides the lyrics.

Standing back a bit, we can see 1991 and 1992 as pretty much a whole. We get the sense that Dylan is still feeling his way forward, not entirely confident of his direction.

I have a personal angle on this, as I saw Dylan in that year perform in Auckland, and things were not too good, folks. Dylan looked out of sorts and distracted (hungover?) and did not click with his band who seemed to keep clear of him onstage. He was visibly struggling. Most of the audience left disgruntled. And yet, when I hear his Sydney performance a few days later, he's right on form! Seems like I was in the wrong town.

In 1993, however, there is a dramatic change as Mr Guitar Man steps to the fore!

See you all soon. Stay alive and stay well.

Kia Ora

1993

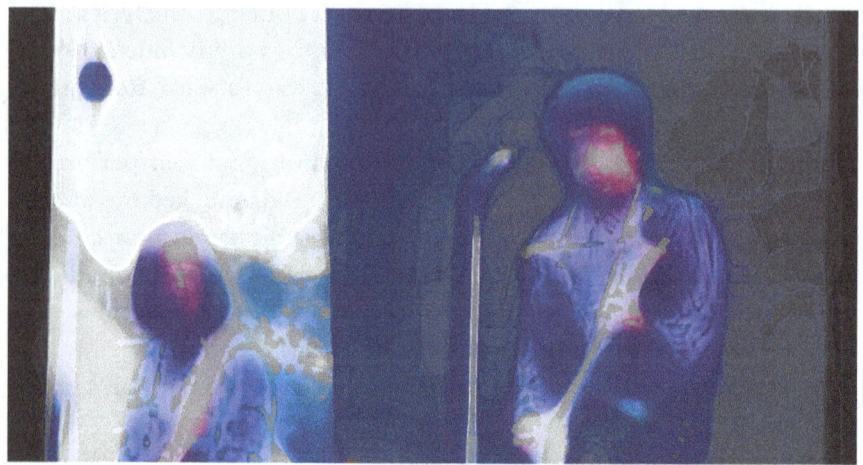

NET 1993: Mr Guitar Man Steps into the Light, Part 1 - Tangled up in Guitars

By Mike Johnson (Kiwipoet)

1993 is a stand out year for the Never Ending Tour. I'm tempted to rank it as one of the very best. All the hard work the band has been putting in for the last two years suddenly pays off. This is not just Dylan with band, this is a band, a unity and a formidable force. A five piece powerhouse with Dylan and John Jackson on main guitars, Tony Garnier on bass, Wilson Watson on drums, and, important for the sounds the band was developing, the brilliant Bucky Baxter on slide guitar and dobro.

The year is famous for the acoustic season Dylan did at the Supper Club, and we will drop in on that, but most outstanding is the emergence of Dylan as Mr Guitar Man. We've noticed him here and there in 1991 and 1992, with his odd, dissonant sounds, but mostly he's been content to play second guitar. However, in 1993 Mr Guitar Man steps out of the shadows and makes his presence felt in no uncertain terms.

Bob Dylan is not listed in the world's top 100 guitar players. This is somewhat surprising as the young acoustic Dylan inspired generations of young buskers and folk singers. Dylan plays adroitly on *Blood on the Tracks*, and his two solo traditional albums in 1992 and 1993, *Good as I been to You* and *World Gone Wrong* show that Dylan has not lost his touch when it comes to acoustic guitar. The 1992 acoustic performances show Dylan in fine form (see NET, 1992 part 3).

It is not Dylan's acoustic skills that cause disquiet, but his electric guitar playing, and we have to ask why it sounds so strange and 'off'. My jazz playing friends are only too happy to tell me that Dylan is playing 'off key' and that his breaks are full of 'bum notes'.

This is puzzling as Dylan rarely if ever sings off key. The accusation that Dylan 'can't sing' is baseless, as he has the most expressive voice in the business. Similarly his harmonica playing, while it often deliberately flirts with dissonance, is unique, Dylan is master of the little instrument (See Bob Dylan Master Harpist series).

The same can't be said with any confidence about Dylan's electric guitar playing. Obsessive and manic, and always unsettling, Dylan appears to be playing 'under the note' or just below the note. He plays percussively, often hammering away at one or two notes, and he seems more concerned with subverting the melody with his guttural tones than supporting it.

Dark and trenchant, it lacks the airiness of his harmonica playing. And yet, when he pulls it off, there is nothing quite like it, and I'm dedicating this and the next two posts to exploring Dylan's electric guitar sound as it emerged in 1993.It seems to me that the triumphant emergence of Mr Guitar Man in 1993 sees the best of his guitar performances, with a touch of Dylan-style genius. Maybe it is the joy of discovering his inner Eric Clapton, but to my mind Dylan's lead guitar work was never better than in this year.

Let's start with a raging performance of 'I and I' from September 12. Dylan must have decided that the album version was just too sweet

(*Infidels*, 1984). He worked it into a rocker with Tom Petty in the mid 1980s, and began re-exploring it in 1991 and 1992. Nothing, however can prepare us for this blast of sound, this tangle of guitars. And his voice! How he tears it out of his throat! A soundboard recording brings it right up close.

After the opening crash of the drums, the first guitar sounds you hear are from Dylan on his punky Stratocaster. From there on Dylan and guitarist Carlos Santana, who played with him from August 20 to October 9. get into a duet, a marvellous weaving of notes. The ending is all pathos. As the music draws to a dark close, with Baxter's long gloomy sounds heralding doom, Dylan continues, as if to keep the song alive, before the final shattering surrender. Crank up the volume and hold onto your seats!

[I and I (A)]

The 'I and I' story doesn't end there for this year, however. In August, Dylan did a memorable concert in Portland (20/8/93), also with Carlos Santana. While this Portland performance sees some gutsy guitar work by Dylan and Santana, with the ending more fully developed, it is Dylan's voice that is astonishing, emerging from those oddly forced, timbreless tones of the past two years, where the sounds seemed to be stuck in his throat, to soar clear and high. Dylan, at fifty, is rediscovering his voice, that high, wild mercury voice.

Those who have followed along this far can only rejoice, and I invite your to revel in Dylan's vocal on this 'I and I'. Back in the 1960s we tried to imagine what Dylan's voice might be like when he got older. I think we imagined something like this:

[I and I (B)]

We can't quite leave the song there. Since 1993 was the year this song reached a kind of perfection, I find it interesting to backtrack to a six show run Dylan did in London at the start of the year, 2/12/93. Here we find Dylan pushing his voice in all kinds of direction, testing the melodic limits of the song and his voice at the same time. The effect is a little more strained than the Portland performance, his voice hasn't quite loosened up, but no less epic. Then, quite unexpectedly and beautifully, the tangle of growling guitars recedes and a harp solo intervenes, with a few bars of sadness and reflection as a build up to a soaring conclusion, all of which brings a spontaneous roar of approval from the audience. It's not quite as ferocious as our first version, but it reaches further.

[I and I (C)]

What we have been listening to with these remarkable performances is Jackson (or Santana) and Dylan playing good cop bad cop. Jackson/Santana playing good cop, working the melody like a jazz man, keeping it clear and sharp, while Dylan plays bad cop, attacking the melody line, bitching at it, subverting it, throwing in jagged notes in the key of Dylan.

We now turn to our old favourite, 'Tangled Up In Blue'. We heard Dylan in 1992 turning this wonderfully adaptable song into an extended, pounding rocker. In 1993 Dylan stretches the song as far as he can, with twelve and thirteen minute performances, many of those minutes given over to Mr Guitar Man. In this (June 25) performance, we get an extraordinary introduction to Mr Guitar Man. While Dylan is playing hard and fast in the first guitar break, it's not until the second break, before the last verse, at 5.47 minutes, that we hear Mr Guitar Man in full flight.

It's a wacky, off the wall, positively demented guitar break. I used this performance in my Master Harpist series, and one of the correspondents suggested that Dylan was influenced by the jazz pianist, Thelonious Monk, who was always stabbing at the piano trying to find the notes between the notes. At 6.35 minutes Jackson takes over the lead, you can hear his clear melodic tones, while Dylan continues to stalk the melody with dark, punky sounds. The harp solo kicks in after the last verse at 7.36 minutes, after which, at 8.30 minutes, the two guitars take over again for a frantic two minutes of furious guitars, driven by Dylan's off the wall sounds.

[Tangled in Blue (A)]

This was no one-off performance. All through 1993 Dylan turned out these powerhouse performances of 'Tangled', throwing restraint to the wind and ripping into lengthy guitar duets with John Jackson or Carlos Santana. This kicked off a decade of ecstatic performances of this song, but none so wild or extensive as in 1993.

What's remarkable about the next performance, as well as the tangle of guitars, is the piercing harp break, taking us back to Dylan's 1989 form. At just over thirteen and a half minutes this must go on record as being among Dylan's most sustained guitar performances. The harp break finishes at 10.55 mins and the guitars take over for the next three minutes of wild duetting with Santana. Dylan tearing it apart. And we hear the best of many slow, ominous pounding endings, with Dylan slamming three or four notes over and over. Madness!

[Tangled Up In Blue (B)]

Madness is what we get too, in this hard driven performance of 'God Knows'. Originally recorded for '*Oh Mercy*' in 1989, it was re-recorded for 'Under the Red Sky' (1990). It's been a bit of a sleeper up to this point, when it steps forward in all its glory. It's all about the tenuousness and fragility of things. How stretched everything is:

> God knows it could snap apart right now
> Just like putting scissors to a string

That feels very contemporary, I have to say. Ah, but Dylan and Santana turn this song into an apocalyptic hurricane, with Dylan's hard, dark tones leading. I've heard some heavy metal that sounds pretty candified compared to this. Again that long ending as Dylan fights against the closing down of the song, the drawing in of night ... however you think of it.

[God Knows (A)]

At Portland in August, Dylan changes the whole build up of the song by starting with a low-key harmonica solo, keeping it quiet to begin with, only cranking it up after two and half minutes. Another wonderful vocal performance – note some lyrical variations. And of course the guitars:

[God Knows (B)]

So that's enough to get us started on this remarkable year. Next post I'll be back with more rocking, electric sounds from 1993.

Stay safe, keep dancing.

Kia Ora

The NET, 1993: Part 2 – The epic adventures of Mr Guitar Man

By Mike Johnson (Kiwi poet)

> 'You won't amount to much, the people all said
> Cause I didn't play guitar behind my head...'

Goodbye Jimmy Reed

In the previous post (1993, part 1, Tangled up in Guitars), we saw the emergence of Mr Guitar Man (Dylan on lead guitar), and something of a renaissance in Dylan's voice. And we saw some long, epic performances of 'I and I', 'God Knows' and 'Tangled Up In Blue'. I'll be following these development in this post.

Performing extended, epic versions of his songs is a feature of 1993. Often the last verse will come about half way through the performance, with the rest given over to harp and guitar breaks. In some ways this is backward looking, as the great age of rock guitar solos probably petered out in the 1970s. Endless blues solos became de rigueur for rock performances, and after a while they became boring as they really added nothing much to the songs, but rather became occasions for a lot of showing off.

By my reading of these songs, Dylan is not showing off, and his baroque extensions usually add to the song in some way. In my Master Harpist series, I showed how Dylan uses that little instrument to up the emotional ante of the songs, to give them an emotional colouring – sudden moments of whimsicality or a piercing sadness. Dylan's subversive guitar work may have a similar purpose, for it never allows a song to become just pretty or catchy. It often provides a disturbing undercurrent of dark sounds. We can never quite relax and just tap our feet with Mr Guitar Man keeping us on edge.

While we can still find some epic, extended versions fuelled by Mr Guitar Man right up until Dylan put the instrument down in 2002, after 1993 he was to rein in the songs. It is as if, in 1993, Dylan wanted to let his hair down and to allow himself and the band to rip loose. The evolution of the NET is towards more disciplined sounds, so I suggest we enjoy these free flowing epics while we can, even when things get a bit messy.

Take 'If Not for You'. It's a modest little love song, really. At least it started out that way. There's a lovely, plaintive version on the 'Alternative Self Portrait', official bootleg. In this 1993 performance it gets pushed out to 13 minutes. He keeps the tempo slow, slower than the released versions, which brings out the anthemic property of the song. It's not long before Mr Guitar Man begins to play around with the melody, but not in the fast, hard driving way we heard in part 1. He doesn't alter his punky sound, but shows how he can work it at a more gentle level.

[If Not for You]

You could say pretty much the same thing about 'Lay Lady Lay'. Part of what made that song a hit is its modesty and apparent simplicity. It's a lot more like a three-minute pop song than a lot of Dylan songs. And quite seductive when Dylan sings it in his Johnny Cash era voice on *Nashville Skyline* (1969). The song became pretty raucous during the Rolling Thunder years with the band joining in on the vocals.

None of this, however can prepare us for this impassioned nine and half minutes. Gone are the modulated vocals of the original, this is a raw appeal for love, ripped from his throat. Not quite so seductive. As he sings, his Stratocaster keeps up a constant dark under-thread, but stays in the background. He keeps it pretty minimal through some of the choruses as well, keeping the song dampened down. He finishes the verses in about four minutes, and the next five minutes is given over to Mr Guitar Man exploring some of the softer edges of his sound.

[Lay Lady Lay]

It's hard to know just quite how to take this. This style of playing does not hark back to the endless blues solos of the 1970s. It's not blues. It's a lot more like jazz, where the tradition of the lead instruments taking long breaks survives. And it's not necessarily pleasant listening; it's not supposed to be.

'She Belongs to Me' makes three of a kind here, although this song is not quite as modest as the other two. The original album version takes only 2.48 mins to make its statement. This 1993 performance runs to 8.30 mins. He slows the tempo right down, which adds to the time, but by 4.48 mins he's finished the last verse and we are treated to another four minutes of nicely lazy instrumental. Lead guitarist John Jackson sounds very sweet here, but Dylan doesn't. After all, it's not a sweet song. There is a bitter pill.

[She Belongs to Me]

At just under five minutes for the *Blonde on Blonde* album version, 'Just Like a Woman' can hardly be described as a modest little number. And it's neither simple nor a love song. I've said it's a song about vulnerability in love. I'll go further now and suggest that it is a song about wounding and being wounded; at least that's the way it comes over in this 8.30 min version.

It's a song better suited to epic treatment than the previous three, and Dylan is in fine vocal form. This would have to rank as one of Dylan's finest performances of the song. It sounds to my ear as if he's singing a full octave above the studio version, at least in parts, but it's in a different key as well, so I can't be sure.

Once again, the last verse is completed about half way through the performance, and we have another three and half minutes of Dylan and Santana working their way through several choruses. At about 6.15 mins Dylan quietens it all down for a while until his Stratocaster gets to work again, and we have another round hammering on the strings in the key of Dylan.

[Just Like a Woman]

Phew! It's a bit too easy to say that Dylan is ruining these performances with his kind of atonal guitar playing, but I'm sure tempted to stop listening after the last magnificent verse.

'I Believe in You' is another song that lends itself to epic treatment, since it's something of an epic expression of faith. I don't think there's any performance to match the Toronto 1980 show, but he does it full justice here, despite messing the words up a little at the end. This nearly nine minute version holds to the pattern we have seen in this post. In this case, the song finishes at about 5.30 mins, and in the guitar work that follows we get one of the clearest demonstrations of Dylan's method. John Jackson plays high and melodic, cruising on those sweet chord changes, while Mr Guitar Man pecks away those same sweet chord changes from below, threatening to overwhelm them.

[I Believe in You]

'One More Cup of Coffee' is another inherently epic song. None of us will be able to forget the soaring Rolling Thunder performances, when the song really had its day. Dylan's 1993 voice is up to the challenge, and he soon works his way into a passionate rendition, raspy as it might be, but the lucid beauty of those 1975/6 performances cannot be repeated, at least not with Mr Guitar Man eating away at the melody line with his guttural tones.

Once more the last verse is sung by 4.30 mins, and we get three more minutes of guitar work. Hard-edged and trenchant, the Dylan/Santana combo manages to pull this one off, fully exploiting the grandeur and pathos of the original.

[One More Cup of Coffee]

An odd thing happened to me while listening to this substantial performance of 'Just Like Tom Thumb Blues'. I had been listening to some 1940s big band swing to take my mind off Dylan for a while, and for a moment, listening to Tom Thumb's Blues, I got my signals crossed and I transposed the guitars to horns, saxes and trumpets, and I was suddenly back in the big band era. Dylan swings this junky's lament. Try it for yourself when the full band cuts in around three minutes and again at six minutes. I can see Stan Kenton smiling and tapping his feet. Dylan throws himself into the vocal while Mr Guitar Man and Santana do the swinging. Some great driving drum work too from Wilson Watson. This one just seems to fall together as they hit the groove.

[Just like Tom Thumb blues]
'Under the Red Sky' brings us back to quieter, more modest songs, in this

case rather sly and laconic as Dylan songs go. It has a dry, doleful edge to it, but in this 7.30 min version the sweetness of the melodic line is nicely set up by Bucky Baxter's gentle slide guitar. A vibrant vocal from Dylan. The last verse is over by 4.30 mins, and we get another couple of minutes of comparatively muted guitar work by Santana and Dylan, until the climax that is.

[Under the Red Sky]

So ends our survey of the epic, 1993 adventures of Mr Guitar Man. In later years he was to moderate his approach, and it is hard to know, when you boil it down, just what to make of it all. Is this genius or madness? Does Dylan really know what he is doing? Obviously that punky, key of Dylan sound is deliberate; there's a strategy behind it, the question is, does it come off? Your call.

Next post we'll discover what happens when Mr Guitar Man picks up the acoustic guitar.

Kia Ora for now

NET 1993: Part 3 – Mr Guitar Man Goes Acoustic

By Mike Johnson (Kiwipoet)

In the previous two posts we have sampled the sound and style of Bob Dylan's lead electric guitar work in 1993. When he picked up the acoustic guitar, however, Mr Guitar Man didn't always sound like the strumming Bob Dylan of old, but rather played his acoustic as if it were an electric guitar.

This enables him to tackle his longer songs in a new kind of spirit. Rather than just strum along, he can push the song forward with his distinctive lead guitar style. The problem he has with live performances of long songs like 'Desolation Row' is their repetitive structure. Such songs lack any bridge passages and their momentum is generated by their lyrics alone. So the challenge is, how to prevent a ten-minute song from becoming just the same thing over and over again.

Dylan solves this problem by using all the resources of his voice and his guitar to build the song to a climax. Typically these performances begin quietly, almost understated, then slowly build up energy. Sometimes reined in by a quiet harp break, as in the case of this 13.48 mins 1993 performance of 'Desolation Row'.

Dylan keeps this performance pretty subdued until after the last verse when the guitars have a fair go. All through the song Dylan patters away against the melodic sounds of Bucky Baxter, but the effect is much easier on the ears than the Stratocaster.

[Desolation Row]

It's not surprising that, when working out his acoustic setlists, Dylan should return to his early, acoustic period, songs written to be played acoustically in the early 1960s. Arguably 'Mr Tambourine Man' is Dylan's first great post protest song. As he sings, it's a song about 'escaping on the run,' and following the shaman wherever he may lead as long as it is 'far from the twisted reach of crazy sorrow'. In this song we hear Dylan the master rhymer at work.

> Though I know that evening's empire has returned into sand
> Vanished from my hand
> Left me blindly here to stand
> but still not sleeping
> My weariness amazes me, I'm branded on my feet
> I have no one to meet
> And the ancient empty street's too dead for dreaming

Reading lines like these, we have to conclude that Bob Dylan is the quintessential poet of alienation.

Dylan seldom messes up this song, and this powerful performance from his London show (02 – 07) is no exception. He plays it straight, no tricks, except the crowd teasing delay in getting his harp into action – and how they love it! Another gold star performance, with just the right amount of restraint and celebration.

After the harp break, around 5.15 mins, Mr Guitar Man steps in for some gentle notes before the last verse, which he builds vocally to a resounding ending. Wonderful. Then it's back to the harp to finish the last couple of minutes. Hard to find better performance than this.

[Mr Tambourine Man]

Another beautiful collaboration between Master Harpist and Mr Guitar Man. While on that subject, we can't skip the gorgeous 'Don't Think Twice' from the Portland concert. Dylan was in very good voice at this concert. It's a sensitive rendition, yet rousing too. The last line of the song, 'You just kind of wasted my precious time,' may seem cruel, but it reminds us that time is indeed our most precious commodity. The same concern drives these lines written almost sixty years later: (Cross the Rubicon)

> 'I cannot redeem the time
> The time so idly spent...'

Perhaps we all know people with nothing to do and who want you to do it with them. Time wasters. And, within the terms of the song, we can give our hearts but our souls belong to us, our soul's journey, whether we're on the 'dark side of the road' or not. Dylan wrote this one back in 1962, at the very start of his soul journey, if you like to see it that way. Again, at the other end of his life, he evokes the same imagery. (Cross the Rubicon)

> Take the high road, take the low
> Take any one you're on

It's curious that 'the low road' meant the road of death in the well-known Scottish ballad, just as the 'dark side of the road' puts the Dylan figure in the valley of the shadow of death (Psalm 23:4) in the earlier song. So here it is. Enjoy (Spoiler alert: exquisite harp work)

[Don't Think Twice (A)]

It's worth comparing that smooth performance with this one. Much rougher, and the harp solo more jagged. Same arrangement with the long slow ending, reminding us of how Mr Guitar Man slaughtered such endings in his electric sets (See NET, 1993, parts 1 and 2) with his Stratocaster.

[Don't Think Twice (B)]

And while we're in the 1962 zone, let's drop back into the Portland concert to pick up 'Boots of Spanish Leather'. A lot of Dylan songs contain conversations and snatches of dialogue, but this song is a sustained conversation over nine verses, and by the end has build up considerable pathos. Dylan never wrote anything else quite like this. The language is that of an old fashioned love ballad, almost an air of the 19th Century. Deep wells of sadness here, and right now I can't think of a better performance.

[Boots of Spanish Leather]

From the same era, we have yet another gentle yet passionate song 'Girl from the North Country'. As written it is a neat piece of nostalgia, but somehow Dylan's older, more cracked-voiced performance makes us really feel the distance of time. Like 'Bob Dylan's Dream', this song was remarkably mature, sensitively registering how the passing of time colours our memories and perhaps idealises our loves.

When Dylan was young, he liked to sing such songs in an 'old voice', with a put on crackle, as if he were much older than his tender twenty-two years. By 1993, he doesn't have to put on any old voice; he's got a crackle right at hand, forged in years of performance.

On the other hand, it is in performances like this that I think I detect a deliberate roughening of his voice. We can hear from his Portland and London performances of that year that Dylan can sing high and clear when he wants to, and that will become more evident in the next two years, but he can also sing rough when he wants to. When he wants to put a sandpaper edge on his voice. Go forward ten years to 2003 and that sandpaper edge has turned into a throaty roar, but I believe it all starts around 1992/3. Another gold star performance.

[Girl from the North Country]

We only have to skip forward a couple of years, to 1964, to find one of Dylan's most iconic songs, 'It's All Over Now, Baby Blue'. In previous posts I have described this song as love's last song, the final, painful ending of a love.

I want to draw attention to it here, as performances will build up to epic proportions by 1995, and while this performance doesn't scale those heights, it's fascinating to hear Dylan pushing the song with his voice, reaching for its emotional depths. Yes, it's hard and scratchy, but again I think some of that vocal texture is deliberate, pushing his voice for that emotional quality. The effect is a little spoiled by Dylan fumbling the lyrics at one point.

Towards the end of the song, after five minutes, you hear Mr Guitar Man playing his acoustic just as if it were his Stratocaster, driving the song along with his distinctive 'off' sounding guitar.

[It's All Over Now, Baby Blue]

Another song we have been following, and an acoustic favourite, is 'Ramona'. In previous posts I have commented on this song quite fully, cautioning against seeing it as a love song despite that lilting melody. I have a soft spot for this song as it is my daughter's favourite Dylan song, and she loves to quote to me these lines:

> 'You say many times
> that you're better than no one
> and no one is better than you
> If you really believe that you know
> you have nothing to win
> and nothing to lose'

Classic Dylan lines, showing his love of what I call 'parallelism' (echoing structures), part of what makes his songs distinctive.

[Ramona]

That's it for this little journey into Dylan's early, acoustic songs as he played them in 1993. We've heard Dylan not just strum along but play lead acoustic in his recognisable yet contentious style.

For the next post we'll drop in on Dylan's famous Supper Club sets and see what all the fuss is about.

Take care in the big bad world.

Kia Ora!

NET, 1993: Part 4 – The Supper Club and Beyond

By Mike Johnson (Kiwipoet)

On the 16th and 17th of November, 1993, Bob Dylan did a two-day season at New York's Supper Club, doing two concerts a day, morning and evening, ten songs per concert. The recordings made at these four concerts have become famous in collector circles as much for the well-balanced soundboard recordings as for the enhanced acoustic sound and a setlist that went beyond his usual suspects.

Some enthusiastic commentators suggest that these performances are better than those delivered the next year, 1994, in the commercially released Dylan Unplugged concert. They may well be right, but I have some reservations. The Supper Club performances are more adventurous, but Dylan's voice is still pretty patchy in 1993, and his Supper Club vocals are more ragged than the smoother, 1994 concert. His voice has been better in this year too – see NET, 1993, part 1.

One of the finest performances of the season would have to be this passionate rendition of 'Ring Them Bells'. Something of a sleeper, this one, from the 1989 *Oh Mercy* album, bursts into life here. It is an odd song, sounding a little like a leftover from the Christian era, but it's not quite that, remaining, as the best Dylan songs do, somewhat mysterious.

> 'Time is running backward
> and so is the bride.'

The last lines are the most telling.

> 'Oh the lines are long
> and the fighting is strong
> And they're breaking down the distance between
> right and wrong.'

It's the collapse of moral certainty that concerns the poet here. I can see a message in these lines that is very contemporary. Chaos results when a culture loses its moral compass. Dylan has approached this issue before, in 'Idiot Wind' (1974)

> 'What's good is bad, what's bad is good
> you'll find out when you reach the top'

and again in 'One Too Many Mornings'.

> 'You're right from your side
> and I'm right from mine'

and in 'Baby Stop Crying'(1978).

> 'Go get me my pistol, babe,
> Honey, I can't tell right from wrong.'

Despite this topsy-turvy world that has inverted good and evil or confused them, even from our fortresses we must ring them bells for the regenerative powers of spirit and nature.

> Ring them bells from the fortress
> for the lilies that bloom

[Ring Them Bells]

That one is from the late show on the 17th, surely Dylan's best live performance of the song, although I love the haunting piano demo version on Tell Tale Signs.

Another from that same late show is the more familiar 'One Too Many Mornings'(1964) just mentioned. I've commented on the effects of extending shorter songs to greater length in previous posts, in this year when Dylan favoured long, epic versions of even his shortest songs. 'One Too Many Mornings' only takes 2.43 minutes on the album (Times they are a Changing).

What made such songs feel miraculous was that they could

communicate so much in such a short time, especially a moment of acoustic bleakness that this song captures. Pushing it out to just over five minutes sacrifices that wonderful brevity. But there are gains as well. The more lavish and staged presentation allows for a more seductive unfolding of the sense of loss and hopelessness.

I prefer this version to the loud, high-pitched rock performances of 1966, epic and wonderful as they are. There's a delicacy of feeling here, and I'm certainly not averse to the minute or so of quiet harmonica solo at the end, reminiscent of Dylan's earliest harp playing.

[One Too Many Mornings]

Slipping back to the late show of the night before, we catch an epic version of 'Forever Young'. I've commented before on the paradox of the song and its yearning for the impossible, but what struck me about this performance was the pain, the anguish inherent in our doomed mortality. Dylan powers into the vocal, but what strikes us is how rich and full the sound is created here. It is all underpinned by Tony Garnier's solid double bass playing, but it is Bucky Baxter creating those 'orchestral' sounds with his slide guitar. I've called this enhanced acoustic because of the sound Baxter is creating. Dylan sings alone on the choruses, enhancing the pathos of the song, and keeps a tight rein on Mr Guitar Man.

[Forever Young]

'Tight Connection to My Heart (Has Anybody Seen My Love?)' from Empire Burlesque was something of a hit for Dylan in 1985, at least it was here in New Zealand. According to Wiki, Dylan performed 'Tight Connection to My Heart' 14 times in the early 1990s. He first performed it on January 12, 1990 in New Haven, Connecticut and then 11 more times in 1990. On November 16 and 17, 1993 he played the song twice in New York City.

I preferred the earlier formulation of the song, 'Someone's got a Hold of my Heart' from the *Infidels* recording sessions in 1983. The original is far less disdainful and more vulnerable. But this powerful live performance has almost persuaded me. It's far better than the album version, I have to say, and returns us to the full raw power of the song without the silly overdubs. Elsewhere on this site, Tony Attwood has registered his dislike for the song as it appeared on the album. I wonder if this live performance will change his mind. (This is another from the late show on the 17th)

[Tight Connection to My Heart]

'I Want You' is one of those songs that works well whether fast or slow. A bouncy little number off *Blonde on Blonde*, it hides its sophistication.

> 'The guilty undertaker sighs
> The lonesome organ grinder cries
> The silver saxophones say I should refuse you
> The cracked bells and washed-out horns
> Blow into my face with scorn, but it's
> Not that way, I wasn't born to lose you.'

This Supper Club performance is in the style of the original, just a somewhat more edgy expression of desire without that confident verbal leer of the *Blonde on Blonde* recordings. Note, however, the last verse which goes:

> 'But I did it, because he lied and
> Because he took you for a ride'

Dylan sings 'I did it because I lied...' A slip of the tongue? A deliberate change? We'll never know. This is from the early show on the 16th.

[I want you]

From the early show on the 17th, we find 'The Disease of Conceit', a song from '*Oh Mercy*'. This song was to drop from Dylan's set list in 1996. This Supper Club performance may well be the best ever.

[The Disease of Conceit]

Every now and again Dylan throws himself into an epic interpretation of 'Queen Jane Approximately' off Highway 61 (1965). This nine-minute performance is no exception. The song is as much about a yearning for companionship as it is an attack on living falsely.

> 'Now, when all of the flower ladies want back
> what they have lent you
> And the smell of their roses does not remain
> And all of your children start to resent you
> Won't you come see me, Queen Jane?'

[Queen Jane Approximately]

Earlier in this survey of 1993 we encountered an electric version of that wonderful love song with the hypnotic melody line, 'One More Cup of Coffee' (see NET, 1993, part two), and now the song turns up again at the Supper Club. As with the electric version, I don't think this acoustic performance lives up to the glory days of the Rolling Thunder Tour, but it's getting there.

[One More Cup of Coffee]

That completes our visit to Dylan's Supper Club season, yet as we saw in the previous post (part 3), excellent acoustic performances were not confined to that venue. Both the London and the Portland performances are at least as good if not better, even though there are no soundboard recordings of them. The same goes for the Toulouse concert (30th June). Take for example the performance of 'Gates of Eden' from that Toulouse concert. We have kept track of this song from the first, angry rock driven 1988 performance, always different yet somehow always the same, the same Celtic lilt. The same magic.

We've heard many wonderful performances of the song, but this one surely must stand out as one of the best, if not the very best. A ten minute epic in the year of epics, this is an extraordinary mood piece. The last verse is finished at about six and a half minutes, with most of the last four minutes sustained by a gentle, exploratory harp break before Mr Guitar Man steps in to land the song. How on earth did I miss this one in my Master Harpist series?

There's power too in Dylan's vocal performance, swinging between soft and sharp. My only issue is that there seems a little mix up in the lyrics. It was great however to hear the 'Motorcycle black madonna two-wheeled gypsy queen' verse which tends to get dropped.

We don't get anything quite like this at the Supper Club

[Gates of Eden]

I could say much the same about this eleven minute 'A Simple Twist of Fate' from the London concert (2/12). It's the same structure, right down to the harp break. This time, however, Dylan's main interest seems to be in giving Mr Guitar Man plenty of room to move, to explore that always oddly dissonant and unsettling guitar style.

[Simple Twist of Fate]

I think at this point we have to ask ourselves what function these guitar breaks really serve, to what extent they add to the song, and to what extent the emotion of the song is being explored in these extended versions. Perhaps the Supper Club performances are outstanding because they are more constrained, because the structure is tighter and Mr Guitar Man's playing is more closely integrated with the band.

Next post will be the fifth and last for this outstanding year. We'll hear live performances of some of the songs from Good As I Been To You and other bits and pieces that beg to be heard.

Kia Ora

NET 1993: Part 5 –
A Series of Dreams

By Mike Johnson (Kiwipoet)

> 'I'm not the songs. It's like somebody expecting Shakespeare to be
> Hamlet, or Goethe to be Faust...'

Bob Dylan

In November 1992 Dylan released an album of traditional songs and
covers. These were recorded in his own garage with only his producer and
sound engineer present. Apparently he undertook the album because of
a contract, not because he wanted to do it. Once he got started, however,
the project developed a life of its own as Dylan returned to his folk roots.

The resulting album, Good as I Been to You, was well received and
it was natural that Dylan would air these songs in the following year –
1993. On the album Dylan plays solo acoustic, and on stage he keeps the
acoustic feel while bringing in some subtle backing. One of my favourite
songs from the album is 'Blackjack Davy', a song of love and betrayal, right
up Dylan's alley. I loved the energy and rocking tempo of the song, and
there's no lack of that here (12/09/93).

[Blackjack Davy]

That sounds very close to the album version. Not so with Stephen Foster's
'Hard Times', a song from the depression era, reminding us that 'protest
songs' were not invented in the 1960s. By slowing the tempo down, Dylan
is able to wring every word for its effect, creating a powerful epic. Dylan
has done gentler performances of the song, but none as moving as this
one, at least for my ear.

NET, 1993, part 5, ins 2 Hard Times

135

He does something similar with 'Jim Jones', a song about the transporting of criminals from Britain to Australia in the late 19th Century, and the horror that awaited them when they got to Botany Bay. Again, by taking a bit more time, Dylan can build the song up in a way that didn't happen on the album.

[Jim Jones]

Let's slip back to the Supper Club for a moment (see previous post) and catch Dylan opening his second evening's concert with 'Ragged and Dirty'. With the band, he gives it a bounce, a kind of ragged 'Subterranean Homesick Blues' bounce.

[Ragged and Dirty]

Anyone in for a bit of weepy nostalgia? That background beat sounds just like the Inkspots, a 1950s black group. A lovely maudlin plodder with suitably agonised vocal delivery:

[Tomorrow Night]

Before finishing this rich and varied year, there are some performances that didn't quite fit anywhere else but were too good to leave behind. One is this rare performance of the percussion driven 'Series of Dreams.' According to rumour, Lanois, the producer of *Oh Mercy*, wanted to include the song while Dylan did not. In the end Dylan prevailed, but when the song finally surfaced in 1991 (the Bootleg Series 1-3) it was much admired. Driven by hammering drums, Dylan takes us through an underworld of dreams and visions. The lyrics for the song's bridge are as good as anything he's written. (This line arrangement is my own, attempting to mimic where Dylan breaks the lines)

> 'Dreams where
> the umbrella is folded
> Into the path you are hurled
> And the cards are

no good that you're holding
Unless they're
from another world'

Live, the song struggles a bit, deprived of Lanois' spooky arrangement and all the echoey stuff studios can do, but the performance builds up nicely, and Dylan is fully committed to his vocal.

[Series of Dreams]

Followers of lyrical variations in Dylan will be fascinated by the changes here. I can't pick up all the new lyrics but I do hear 'In one, doors were opening and closing…'. Someone with a better ear than mine would need to piece this together.

Another rarity in terms of live performances is 'Emotionally Yours' from the 1985 Empire Burlesque album. This has never been my favourite Dylan song. The lyrics don't go anywhere much. Dylan is a man of many masks, a protean artist capable of expressing a wide range of emotions, even sentimentalities such as this. But in performance terms, you won't find anything better:

[Emotionally Yours]

Another comparative rarity in performance is 'License to Kill', off *Infidels* (1984). The song was much praised, and taken as an indication that Dylan hadn't lost his anti-war heart. However, having it next to the much reviled 'Neighborhood Bully' on the album creates a paradoxical effect, as that song could be described as Dylan's one and only pro-war song. What remains is a powerful picture of a bereaved mother, and a killer who thinks he has a license to kill. The portrait of the killer seems very contemporary. It makes me think of the young Kyle Rittenhouse who shot two Black Lives Matter protestors in Kenosha recently. Dylan can do that sometimes – seem way ahead of his time.

'Now, he's hell-bent for destruction
he's afraid and confused
And his brain has been mismanaged with great skill

All he believes are his eyes
And his eyes, they just tell him lies'

Dylan was asked about this song in an interview he gave to USA Today in 1995. He was talking about the nature of creativity.

> Dylan: 'As you get older, you get smarter and that can hinder because you try to gain control over the creative impulse. Creativity is not like a freight train going down the tracks. It's something that has to be caressed and treated with great respect. If your mind is intellectually in the way, it can stop you. You've got to program your brain not to think too much.'

> Interviewer:' In 'License to Kill' you said, 'Man has invented his doom/first step was touching the moon.' Do you believe that?'

> Dylan: 'Yeah, I do. I have no idea why I wrote that line, but at some level it's just like a door into the unknown.'

[License to Kill]

'The Lonesome Death of Hattie Carroll' is the favourite Dylan song of poetry professor Christopher Ricks, famous for his study of Tennyson and Keats. One of the few Dylan books I do have on my shelf is Ricks' *Dylan's Visions of Sin* (Harper Collins, 2004). For Ricks, Dylan never did Hattie Carroll better than the album version (*The Times They Are A-Changing*, 1964). 'If he sings it more gently, he sentimentalises it. If he sings it more urgently, he allies himself with Zanzinger' (p16). Ricks has the same issue that I have with Visions of Johanna, and Tony Attwood has with Wicked Messenger – the originals are the best, so we think. This may be a very personal thing – the version we first bonded with. The New Yorker replied to Ricks, affirming the musician's 'license to expand his songs in performance'(Ricks, p 17).

Often in this account of the NET, I have questioned what purpose this 'license to expand' might serve in terms of what any particular song says or does. Some of Mr Guitar Man's long breaks are problematic in this regard, potentially turning a neat, crisp song into a quagmire. Dylan is a risk taker, he never plays safe, and risk takers are bound to fall at some point.

One of Dylan's best known protest songs, 'Hattie Carroll' covers the wanton murder of a black kitchen hand by a rich, self-entitled bar patron, Zanzinger. It is a song that carefully harbours and balances its rage. Ricks probably doesn't like this performance (the start is a bit ragged), but I find the semi-talking style, emphasising the reporting aspect of the song, effective. Arguably, Baxter's haunting steel guitar sounds sweeten the music a little too much for the message. Your call!

[Hattie Carroll]

Ricks makes a very interesting comment on the artfulness of the song's lyrics.

> 'Hattie Carroll was a maid in the kitchen
> She was fifty-one years old and gave birth to ten children
> Who carried the dishes and took out the garbage
> And never sat once at the head of the table
> And didn't even talk to the people at the table
> Who just cleaned up all the food from the table
> And emptied the ashtrays on a whole other level
> Got killed by a blow, lay slain by a cane
> That sailed through the air and came down through the room
> Doomed and determined to destroy all the gentle'

Of the discomforting repetition of the word 'table', Ricks observes, 'Hattie Carroll has her enslaved rhyming – or rather non-rhyming, since a rhyme would offer some change, some relief from monotony of 'the table...the table...the table as the grim ending of three consecutive lines.' (Ricks, p 225)

'It Takes a Lot to Laugh, It Takes a Train to Cry', a blues song from *Highway 61 Revisited* (1965), became a regular visitor to Dylan's setlists, and remained so right through to 2018. It works well as a late night, yearning for love, blues. When I first heard the album I was struck by the concision and beauty of the last verse.

'Now, the wintertime is comin', the windows are filled with frost
I went to tell everybody but I could not get across
Well, I want to be your lover, baby, I don't want to be your boss
Don't say I never warned you when your train gets lost'

Years later I learned about a Japanese four-line verse form, loosely called a tanka. The first line states the major idea or image; the second line extends that idea or image; the third line introduces a new idea or image, and the last line is the wild card line that somehow encapsulates all of it. The verse just quoted is a perfect tanka. I speculate that Dylan hit on the form naturally, its neat progression being aesthetically pleasing. This is far from his best performance of the song (wait until next year, 1994) but it's of interest as Baxter uses the chords off 'Rainy Day Woman' to background the vocals.

[It Takes A Lot To Laugh]

I'm up against my word limit here, but want to slip in three more performances. We are familiar with 'Cat's in the Well' from Under the Red Sky (1991). It often became a rather raucous concluding song. I like the stripped down minimalism of this performance.

[Cat's in the Well]

We can't leave the year without 'Ballad of a Thin Man', a song we have followed through the years of the NET. Dylan does a great vocal. The verses are sung by 5.30 mins and over the next four minutes Mr Guitar Man takes his Stratocaster for a walk, and we are treated to his punky, angular 'off key' style.

[Ballad of a Thin Man]

Last but not least, 'All Along the Watchtower', a suitably apocalyptic way to end a concert – and our brief survey of 1993.

[All Along the Watchtower]

We can see 1993 as a year of emergence. Dylan, still pretty ragged but starting to reclaim his vocal range, the band coming together and starting to work their sounds in interesting ways. There are some outstanding performances (see Part 1), but above all, the emergence of Dylan as a lead guitar player with a distinctive, unsettling style. Mr Guitar Man has arrived.

I'm very excited about 1994, as everything that is good about the 1993 performances just gets better.

Be Well

Kia Ora

1994

NET 1994: In Full Voice, Part 1 – Absolutely Vintage Dylan

By Mike Johnson (Kiwipoet)

> He can do it in Las Vegas
> And he can do it here...'

Just as, when we moved from 1992 to 1993 we noticed an all round improvement in the performances, from the overall sound of the band to Dylan's voice, so when we move from 1993 to 1994 we find a further improvement. More like a quantum leap.

For my money, 1994 and 1995 are the golden years of the NET, at least as far as the nineties go. In retrospect we can see that from 1991 to 1993 Dylan was struggling. 1993 was a year of great exploration, with Dylan extending himself in every direction, pushing his still emerging voice, his harmonica playing, and pushing his lead guitar playing to its limits, pushing his songs into extended epics.

In 1994 and 1995 Dylan brings it all back home. The arrangements bed down, the band sounds more cohesive than ever, Mr Guitar Man pulls his horns in a little and integrates his sound better, and, above all, Dylan's voice floats free from whatever it was that turned it strained and scratchy around 1991. His voice develops a softer edge to go with the acoustic orientation of his arrangements, what I have called his enhanced acoustic sound. With that high clear voice, which gets even better as we move into 1995, he sounds more like the Dylan of old, of the 1960s. Of course he can roughen his voice up when he wants to, just as he always could, even back in the sixties.

1994 was the year that saw Dylan re-emerge into prominence. On the 17th and 19th of November Dylan appeared on the MTV Unplugged television series, and the album of that concert was released in 1995 to some acclaim. We'll hear, however, a few outtakes from that session.

On August 14 1994 Dylan performed at Woodstock for a nostalgia concert, celebrating the original and famous 1969 Woodstock festival – which Dylan did not attend. That concert has been available on YouTube for some time, and was finally released, too belatedly I feel, in 2016. His performances at this concert were very well received and served to restore his legend somewhat.

Finally, most strangely of all, he took part in The Great Musical Experience in Japan (May 20/21) fronting a full orchestra, a concert also filmed for television. At first I thought that the superior sound that Dylan achieved in 1994 was owing to the commercial TV recordings, and to some extent that is so, but once we leave the professional recordings for the audience recorded shows we find the same thing.

In 1994 Dylan was right in the middle of his nineties dry period as far as song writing is concerned. His last album, Under the Red Sky, is three years behind him, and the great burst of creativity that produced *Time Out of Mind* is still three years ahead. But that does not result in any lack of passion or creativity as far as his performances are concerned. Quite the opposite. He pours all that power and passion into reconceiving his earlier songs, particularly that body of work from the 1960s that had made him famous in the first place. Those vintage years.

We can put aside all that brave talk of breaking free from the Bob Dylan mythos and creating a new Bob Dylan. Why bother when the old Bob Dylan is as close at hand as the check shirt he wore in 1965, and pulled out again for Unplugged in 1994. Wow! He sounds and looks just like the old Dylan.

I'm dedicating this and the next blog or two to those core sixties years, and invite you all along on a somewhat nostalgic ride through some of the greatest songs of the 20th Century, 1994 style.

Because it's such a rich, relaxed sound, I'll start with that gentle blues from 1965, 'It Takes a Lot to Laugh, It Takes a Train to Cry'. I commented on this song in my last post (See NET, 1993, part 5) and invite my readers to compare this performance with that 1993 performance. There's no sense of stress or strain here; the band relaxes into the rocking beat, everything fits and all runs smooth as oil.

[It Takes a Lot to Laugh]

That's from the Woodstock concert. This next is from Prague (July 16th), a brilliant, lucid performance of Dylan's great sixties epic Desolation Row. He's learned how to build the song, create tension and drive with his percussive, acoustic guitar sound.

It is highly unlikely that anybody reading this has never heard Desolation Row, but if that's the case, you are in for a treat. Desolation Row is a state of mind, a symbol, a place where everybody is in disguise as somebody famous, and strange and frightening events take place. It is a crazy-house reflection of a life that lies beyond the boundaries of what passes for our normal world. It's a circus world, and sane people might be advised to stay clear in case the doorknob breaks...

[Desolation Row (A)]

Note the echo in Dylan's voice, maybe an accident of the recording but it makes for interesting listening. It clips along at a fair pace too, avoiding any drag, always possible with a long song like this. Note also that thin, wiry harp break at the beginning to cue us into the song. Another masterly performance!

[Desolation Row (B)]

And while on the subject of famous compositions, you won't find much better than this 'Mr Tambourine Man'. I know of no other song that so powerfully expresses our desire to get away from the mad world, the world of 'crazy sorrow' and 'to dance beneath the diamond skies/with one hand waving free'. By slowing the song right down Dylan can make a meal out of those incomparable lines. Yet it doesn't turn into a ten-minute epic as it might have in 1993, but fits well into just over six minutes, a beautifully balanced performance.

[Mr Tambourine Man]

'Ballad of a Thin Man' is given the full epic treatment here. Like most of the songs in this post, 'Thin Man' is a regular. Listening to this full rock treatment, it strikes me that few live performances of the song evoke the spookiness of the album version, and tend to be more angry than eerie, like this one. Still, it hasn't lost any of its nightmarish quality. If you've ever found yourself in the wrong place and in the wrong company, you'll know what this is about. Best also if you're not too homophobic, or phobic about alternative sexualities, because there is something strange going on in this 'room' and you really don't know what it is.

[Ballad of a Thin Man]

Dylan's lineup remains the same as the previous two years: Dylan and John Jackson on main guitars, Tony Garnier on bass, Wilson Watson on drums and Bucky Baxter on slide guitar and dobro. For the Unplugged concerts, Dylan added the organist Brendan O'Brien. Together the organ and slide guitar create an 'orchestral' effect, a richness of sound we haven't heard on the NET so far.

You can hear that richness of sound on this wonderful performance of 'I Want You' (1966). A nice bouncy little number off *Blonde on Blonde*, it becomes here a sumptuous hymn to desire, and the way Dylan's voice lifts against the swell of the backing is sheer delight. Slowing the song way down brings out the hidden grandeur of the song's chord progression.

[I want you]

That's an MTV Unplugged outtake as is this next one, 'With God on Our Side', a protest song that leans towards a fatalistic view of history. The backing sounds much like the official Unplugged but I like the way Dylan builds the vocal on this one. A fraction slower than even the slow official performance, the song becomes even more dirgelike, a dreary, sorrow-filled encounter with American history.

[With God on Our Side]

We have watched 'One Too Many Mornings' develop over the last few years into a compelling nostalgic ballad. Keeping its acoustic roots, Dylan captures the agony and passion of the electric sets in 1966. With a wonderful climactic harp break, this has to come close to a 'best ever' performance (Boston, Oct 8).

[One Too Many Mornings]

'Masters of War' must surely be Dylan's least ambiguous protest song. Aimed at the heart of the war machine, the arms manufacturers, the song takes no prisoners. After all these years, the song is still pertinent. Somewhere along the way it has moved from strident to sinister, from outraged to threatening. These 1994 performances might be surpassed next year, in 1995, but they can still send a chill up the spine, especially with the echo Dylan gets on this one.

[Masters of War]

Over the last few years we have watched 'She Belongs to Me' grow quietly into this lazy tempo paean to the femme fatale, a woman too narcissistic and egotistical for comfort. The lazy beat, however, soon turns into a driving blues with a jazz-filled harp break and Mr Guitar Man adding a pounding edge to the song. Yet another candidate for best ever performance – at least until we get to 2013. (08/20/94)

[She Belongs to Me]

Previously, I have written that 'Tears of Rage' is one of Dylan's most mysterious songs. The key to understanding it may lie in discovering who the narrator is, who is singing? I don't know, but the song seems to lament the betrayal of the promise of America, and the consequent sense of alienation. That alienation is a response to the rank materialism of money-mad ethics.

> 'And now the heart is filled with gold
> As if it was a purse
> But oh, what kind of love is this
> Which goes from bad to worse?'

As always, love is sacrificed on the altar of materialism. I love the original, basement tapes version but probably only because I heard it first. It's a great song, and this is another vintage Dylan performance. The ease with which his voice can soar is a real pleasure. At first I thought this was another acoustic performance, but realized Dylan is playing his Stratocaster, only softly, in a sensitive muted fashion.

[Tears of Rage]

No song better evokes Dylan's glory years and his relationship with Joan Baez than 'Mama, You Been On My Mind'. I'm generally wary of biographical interpretations of Dylan songs, since Dylan loves to create personas or masks, but this song invites such interpretations, particularly as he and Baez would often sing duet. The frisson between the two of them onstage told its own story.

And yet it's a song that makes more sense sung with one voice, although the presence of the other, the one addressed, is very strong. If you've ever broken a relationship or let one slip away and later found it preying on your mind, this is the song for you, and this is a particularly poignant, lonely sounding performance. The piercing harp solo, reminiscent of Dylan's 1989 style, puts an edge of pain into it. Yet another incomparable performance (October 2 1994)

[Mama, You Been on My Mind]

That's it for openers. I think you'll agree with me that with performances of this quality, the NET is catching fire. I'll be back shortly with another round of absolutely vintage Dylan performances from 1994.

Kia Ora.

NET 1994: Part 2 - Absolutely Vintage Dylan Again

by Mike Johnson (Kiwipoet)

This and the previous post are dedicated to the songs of the 1960s, and how Dylan was bringing them back to life in 1994. Without any recent albums introducing new material into the shows, Dylan was thrown back on his old favourites and that core of songs that made him famous in the first place.

Prominent in this core group is 'A Hard Rain's A-Gonna Fall'(1963), one of Dylan's earliest and perhaps greatest protest songs. In musical form it is based on the 19th century ballad 'Lord Randal', but oh, what a makeover it gets when Dylan performs it in front of a full orchestra. If you haven't already found this on You Tube you're in for a treat. Dylan went to Japan for The Great Musical Experience, which is just what it was.

Dylan has learned with this song, and other long, repetitive songs like 'Desolation Row', to start quietly and build the vocal to a climax. Guitar and harmonica breaks are also staged to gather to a climax. These climaxes are not built into the musical form but created by Dylan to introduce an element of musical drama the originals lack. This 'Hard Rain' is a beautiful illustration of Dylan's developing vocal mastery. With the full orchestra, these climaxes are accompanied by the swirl of strings and the wail of horns. It shouldn't work but it does.

Readers of these posts know that I don't use YouTube links, partly because many of the songs I look at are not on YouTube, but also because those links may vanish as fast as they appear, and all too often we're confronted with a 'This video is not available' notice. But there is special fascination I think in seeing Dylan out of his usual habitat, with solemn Japanese playing their violins as if Dylan were Beethoven, and Dylan himself turning that ballad into a wonderful musical epic. It is lavish and extravagant. Enjoy.

[Hard Rain]

The rumourmongers have been hard at work explaining how come Dylan's voice improved so much. *Dylan got singing lessons before going to Japan. Dylan gave up drinking in 1994.* Take your pick or make up your own, but don't forget to enjoy the results. Not Caruso exactly but getting there...!

I have described 'Just Like Tom Thumb's Blues' as a junky's lament. It's a bleak song. Take this encounter with a prostitute:

> 'Sweet Melinda, the peasants call her the goddess of gloom
> She speaks good English and she invites you up into her room
> And you're so kind and careful not to go to her too soon
> And she takes your voice and leaves you howling at the moon'

The third line refers to the practice of allowing time before going to the woman's room in order not to alert the police to her activities. And we are in a place where 'the cops don't need you/and man they expect the same'. In performance, Dylan has found a tempo that kicks it along, and while it may not achieve the bone-grating desperation of the 1966 performances, it carries us along just fine.

[Tom Thumb Blues]

While we're hanging around *Highway 61 Revisited* (1965), what better than to go to the next track on the album, 'Highway 61 Revisited' itself. In previous posts I have suggested that this song is more serious than it sounds. On the album, it has a manic energy and a bouncy upbeat melody, as if this were some cheerful, throwaway exercise. It is, however, anything but cheerful and throwaway, being about God and Death and Mercy and World War III – and a girl whose complexion is much too white.

Not quite as energetic as the studio version, it also clips along at a fair, crowd-pleasing pace and Dylan's vocals are spot on. If it's energy and madness you want, wait until the guitars come in blazing...

[Highway 61 Revisited]

'Positively 4th Street', is from the *Highway 61 Revisited* era, but not included on the album, is one of Dylan's most famous attack songs. Most decidedly not a love song, and maybe best delivered in a jeering voice. Look at how

Dylan twists the popular saying that to have empathy for a person you need to able to 'stand in their shoes'.

> I wish that for just one time you could stand inside my shoes
> And just for that one moment I could be you
> Yes, I wish that for just one time you could stand inside my shoes
> You'd know what a drag it is to see you

[Positively 4th Street (A)]

The You Tube clip of this performance is replete with hyperbole: '*Fantastic!!! Exceptional...*' It's a wonderful performance but shouldn't be oversold. Because then we have no adjectives left, or run out of exclamation marks, when we come upon a truly moving performance like this understated one, so much more deadly for not being too accusative. Touches of gentleness and hurt are allowed to show, and the song's greatness is revealed. Not a single moment of the nine minutes feels wasted. It becomes more contemplative and dreamy, more in the vein of 'Queen Jane Approximately'.

[Positively 4th Street (B)]

My problem is that I can't confidently date this performance. It turned up in my lists, an orphan. I can't even be sure that it's from 1994, and would be happy if a knowledgeable reader could identify it. There was nowhere else to put it, and it's so good I couldn't leave it out.

'It's All Over Now, Baby Blue' comes at the cusp of Dylan's changeover from folk singer to rock singer and has often been seen as a farewell to his old life. Significantly, the last track on *Bringing It All Back Home* (1965). This may well be true, just as it may well be a farewell song to Joan Baez, but as I suggested in my Master Harpist series, it may be one of Dylan's greatest love songs – love's last song. The final gut wrenching moment of separation. Admirers of Dylan's 1995 Prague performance of the song will find earlier versions of that arrangement here, in 1994.

It's driven by an insistent, compelling beat we don't find in the original. Against that beat Dylan can pit his voice and his harp, using both to push and explore the emotional reaches of the song. Images of sadness and separation are all the more effective by being surreal and indirect:

> 'Yonder stands your orphan with his gun
> Crying like a fire in the sun'

The throes of love are expressed in an equally elusive and suggestive way:

> 'The empty handed painter from your street
> Is drawing crazy patterns on your sheet'

It's the wonder of poetry that in two lines you can express something it would take a couple of paragraphs of prose to explain, and you still wouldn't have it. The great thing about poetry is that it can't be reduced to prose explanations without loss of essence.

I've chosen two performances of this great song, partly just to enjoy a good thing, but also to show how hard Dylan was working on it. Each performance is just different enough for us to hear the search for the most perfect expression of the song. That would have to wait until next year. In the meantime this performance (Germany, don't have exact date) sees Dylan reaching for that balance between restraint and passion in a performance tremulous and heartbroken.

[It's All Over Now, Baby Blue (A)]

Dylan was trying out this new arrangement all through the year, giving rise to a number of brilliant performances, each one approaching the song with a slightly different emphasis and vocal intonation. This next one (date unknown) is slower and more empathic. A different kind of balance, Dylan's voice soaring in counterpoint to Garnier's long, low drawn out notes on the double bass.

[It's All Over Now, Baby Blue (B)]

This is a good place to pause. There is more but you can have too much of a good thing – Dylan's core songs given such rich and imaginative treatment. I'll be back soon with the final in this Absolutely Vintage Dylan season – Encore.

Stay safe and keep rockin.

NET 1994: Part 3 – Absolutely Vintage Dylan, Encore

by Mike Johnson (Kiwipoet)

Over the past two posts we have seen Dylan bringing his old sixties hits back to life for the nineties, in a series of stunning performances that mark a distinct improvement on previous years. If you take the last two posts and this one, we have twenty-five of Dylan's foundation songs given new arrangements and impassioned performances. With three years behind them, the band sound at home in the material, and Dylan's bizarre guitar style (Mr Guitar Man!) is still evident but often muted and, especially when he plays the acoustic guitar, well integrated into the overall sound.

A good place to start is that dirge to approaching death. 'Knockin' On Heaven's Door'. In these later versions, with the addition of the words, 'Just like so many times before', the song becomes a hymn of spiritual yearning and the desire for liberation. In this case the last verse finishes at 4.10 mins leaving another three and half minutes of guitar work in which Mr Guitar Man's complex weaving of dark notes does the work of expressing that yearning. This one's from the Boston concert.

[Knockin' On Heaven's Door]

The anthemic character of the song makes for a good encore, as does 'All Along the Watchtower'. I don't think this version quite matches the scintillating, jazzy 1992 performance, but it's getting there. The song lends itself to an apocalyptic clash of guitars. This one, from the Woodstock concert, is up on You Tube (at least for the moment) and I was amazed at the negative reactions to Dylan's vocal style, which some couldn't get their heads around. Here's a sample of the comments:

Lol I can't tell if he's being serious.

Why, oh why, is Bob singing it like that?

what the heck Bob?

This is disappointing to watch. Bob Dylan has the ability to sing a lot better than that,

it's like he's being awful on purpose.

Seriously he is taking the piss out of every one of you.

Dylan on helium amphetamine high speed dubbing.

It deadass sounds like Popeye is singing the lyrics.

He is too lazy to stop so he decided to say all the lyrics at once.

How did this auction end up then ? What was the highest bid ??

Did he drink helium?

I'm struggling, but I'm not able to enjoy that. I think if there's no Hendrix, that song stays in the drawer.

Good Lord! There is some serious disconnect here. I...er...like the performance. There is an urgency in those rushed vocals, and every word comes clear. Just because he doesn't try to sing it like Hendrix... But there is something else here, a tendency for Dylan to sing across the melody line. I see it (or rather hear it) as a deliberate ploy, not to wreck the song but to create a dissonance that draws attention to the lyrics. Heaven forbid that we become too comfortable with this song and its message. And Mr Guitar man may be no Hendrix, but he sure can be insistent. Over to you.

[Watchtower]

While we're on the subject of songs that work well as encores, let's try that sister song to 'It's All Over Now, Baby Blue', 'It Ain't Me, Babe'. This nearly nine minute performance joins the ranks of the great acoustic performances that Dylan has been springing on us for the last couple of years. Once more the vocals are passionate and inventive, and Dylan's spiky acoustic guitar sure pushes the song along. Brilliantly, he sings around the melody rather than right on it, pushing the words in unexpected directions. And then, the vulnerable, trembling harp that veers into squeaky climaxes. What more can I say? Vintage Dylan indeed.

[It Aint Me Babe]

Another powerhouse performance from the Woodstock concert – 'Just Like a Woman'. This is a contentio It Ain't Me, Babe'us song that I have characterised as expressing vulnerabili154 but many have seen it as a full on attack song dripping with contempt. The insinuating leer that marked the album version has gone from Dylan's voice in this rendition which is both open and passionate. There is more agony than spite in this 1994 version. And some great steel guitar work.

[Just Like a Woman]

Switching back to the gentler sounds of the Unplugged concert, we find 'My Back Pages', generally considered to be a seminal Dylan song, signalling his change of direction in 1964 from acoustic protest to surreal electric.

The lyrics are quite dense and the sound worked on. But the movement from moral certainty to moral uncertainty was to haunt Dylan for the rest of his life, and he would seek that moral certainty once more during his Christian period, 1979 – 81. In 'Ring Them Bells' he laments the 'breaking down the distance between right and wrong'.

> 'In a soldier's stance, I aimed my hand at the mongrel dogs who teach
> Fearing not that I'd become my enemy in the instant that I preach
> My existence led by confusion boats, mutiny from stern to bow
> Ah, but I was so much older then, I'm younger than that now
>
> Yes, my guard stood hard when abstract threats too noble to neglect
> Deceived me into thinking I had something to protect
> Good and bad, I define these terms quite clear, no doubt, somehow
> Ah, but I was so much older then I'm younger than that now'

[My Back Pages]

‹I Don't Believe You' was years later to be complemented by 'I Believe in You', which expresses the opposite sentiment. 'I Don't Believe You' is a strong reaction to a snub, to rejection. Remember the high-pitched yelling versions from 1966, when Dylan turned this acoustic song into an electric cry of pain.

This 1994 version, from the Krakow concert (7/17/1994), is most unusual for the sound the band creates. It may be the recording itself. It is very punky yet oddly muted. This one has slowly grown on me. The jazzy harmonica break certainly helps. I believe that's rain you can hear pattering in the background.

[I Don't Believe in You]

I don't think Dylan ever finished a concert with his *Blonde on Blonde* classic, 'Absolutely Sweet Marie' but I have no problem finishing this Absolutely Vintage Dylan series with it. It's a foot-tapper. I'm not quite sure what I think of it without the young Dylan's adolescent sounding whine, but I'm a sucker for the lyrics, how they hint at and rely on some unstated context, and how exactly they capture resentment, and resentment is what it's all about. The song contains one of Dylan's most famous aphoristic lines: 'To live outside the law you must be honest'. Paradoxical, but it makes perfect sense. I think, however that the line should be read in context:

> Well, six white horses that you did promise
> Were finally delivered down to the penitentiary
> But to live outside the law, you must be honest
> I know you always say that you agree
> Alright, so where are you tonight, Sweet Marie?

Those six white horses come straight out of the blues, perhaps from 'See That My Grave Is Kept Clean' but they pop up again in 'Yonder Comes Sin' (1981) as six wild horses.

> 'I say: See them six wild horses, honey
> You say: I don't even see one
> You say: Point them out to me, love
> I say: Honey I got to run'

However, back to the famous aphorism, the real kicker seems to me to lie in the following line. The two should be taken together:

> 'But to live outside the law, you must be honest
> I know you always say that you agree'

But is she honest? That's what the first line is building to. The world of

Blonde on Blonde is full of duplicity, and despite the aphorism, we just don't know whom to trust. This is another from the other Unplugged:

[Absolutely Sweet Marie]

So that brings to a close this three part survey of Dylan's 1994 performances of his sixties classics. I trust you have enjoyed yourselves. If you are having a Xmas break enjoy it. We look forward to a brighter 2021, we hope, and I'll be back to see how Dylan handled his post sixties work in this breakthrough year of 1994.

Kia Ora

NET 1994: Part 4 - I'd Give You the Sky High Above

by Mike Johnson (Kiwipoet)

In the previous three blogs for 1994, I considered Dylan's loving and adventurous treatment of his 1960 foundation songs. He brings that same inventiveness and passion to the 1970's material, which I'll look at in this blog.

As we have seen, 1994 was a strong year for the NET, perhaps the strongest yet, at least since 1990, and his treatment of his 1970s songs doesn't disappoint. We don't often hear much of the songs from *Planet Waves* (1974) as those songs were somewhat cast into the shade by grandeur of *Blood on the Tracks* (1974), but we can find love songs on *Planet Waves* that come very close to the songs on the later album, and may prefigure them.

'Hazel' is a good example. It lacks the cutting edge of the *Blood on the Track*s songs, but has a warmth and expresses desire without the ambivalences of the later songs. This is another outtake from Dylan Unplugged, and has a rich, sumptuous sound. If the Dylan Unplugged album had only included such wonderful performances as this, it would have been a real treat. Remember that Dylan added an organ to the lineup for these performances, which helps create that 'orchestral' effect.

[Hazel]

Of course *Blood on the Tracks* provides most of seventies songs performed that year, with the old favourites leading the charge. Tangled Up In Blue gets a brisk airing. I think the 1993 performances of this song might have the edge (see NET, 1993, part 1), but who's complaining? Dylan knows how to kick this song along, and gives a fine, spirited performance, using his guitar to drive the pace and his harmonica to add restraint and tension. A nine and half minute epic delivered with verve. The fast paced delivery makes the stories told in the song sound very exciting.

Special mention should be made to the long, slow ending, lasting almost as long as some pop songs. These slow endings have become a feature of the performances of many of the songs since 1992 and work to bring the songs to a crashing climax.

[Tangled Up In Blue]

We have three more favourites from *Blood on the Tracks*, including the ever popular 'Simple Twist of Fate.' This song evokes a brief but haunting love affair, a one night stand perhaps that lingers in the mind. Such an encounter can leave a particular kind of desolation.

> He woke up; the room was bare
> He didn't see her anywhere
> He told himself he didn't care
> Pushed the window open wide
> Felt an emptiness inside
> to which he just could not relate

In this nearly ten minute electric version, Dylan slows the pace and delivers a heart-ripping vocal to an appreciative audience that cheer at every nuance. This performance follows the pattern that has been evolving with these epic versions with the last verse being sung about half way through, the remainder devoted to Dylan's guttural guitar work and sensitive harmonica. Dylan's harp work is often at its best when it brings an element of poignancy and whimsicality to the emotion driving the song. In this case, regret, and the harmonica is good at regret. The harp solo on this performance is not to be missed.

[Simple Twist of Fate]

Lovers of Dylan's album performance of 'Shelter from the Storm', or those who might prefer the fast, hard edged 1976 performance, won't be disappointed by this 1994 version. All hyperbole aside, this could well be the best ever performance of this song. Readers will know that I'm pretty wary of these 'best ever' claims. Often performances may be the 'best ever' for that year, or that tour. Or two different interpretations of a song may both be 'best'. However it's hard to imagine a more powerful and convincing performance than this one. The vocals have a soundboard clarity to them, Mr Guitar Man drives the song along with this dark, subterranean sounds, and the harp brings that note of reflection.

[Shelter from the Storm]

This song may well be the best song on the album in terms of the lyrics. I find myself savouring every line. Maybe that's because it's Dylan's finest female worship song (We'll get another one with 'Golden Loom.') A song that celebrates women, or the divine female aspect, without any spite or ironical undercutting, and in which wry self-deprecation marks the song's humour.

> She came up to me so gracefully
> And took my crown of thorns

However, I'm sure there are *Blood on the Tracks* fans who might well favour, 'If You See Her Say Hello,' for its bitter sweetness. I find the sentiment a little too magnanimous to be entirely convincing.

> If you're makin' love to her
> Kiss her once for me
> I always have respected her
> For doin' what she did and gettin' free

That's very noble. I prefer the harder edged sentiment from the 'rogue' 1976 performance.

> If you're makin' love to her
> Watch it from the rear
> You'll never know when I'll be back
> Or liable to appear

Ah, yes, that make more sense to me. However this 1994 powerhouse of a performance, with its driving beat, lifts the song above any mawkishness and even convinces me. What helps is that some of the lyrics have been toughened up. In the original he sings:

And though our separation
It pierced me to the heart
She still lives inside of me
We've never been apart

In this performance he sings:

And though our separation
pierced me to the bone
she still lives inside of me
I've never been alone

There may not be a big shift in meaning, but there is a significant change in tone.
And if you want bitter-sweet, I'm sold on the change to the last line:

Tell her she can look me up
if I'm still on her mind.

Get ready for another 'best ever' performance.

[If You See Her Say Hello]

With its slow, sonorous beat and spooky atmosphere, 'Senor' is one of the most powerful songs on *Street Legal*. It captures that 'end of the line' feeling Dylan is so good at. The desire to escape meaninglessness and suffocation. When writing about this song in my Master Harpist series I said that the song reminded me of Thoreau's observation, 'the mass of men lead lives of quiet desperation, and what is taken for resignation is confirmed desperation.'It's a song that suits heavy treatment, and that's what it gets here. Dylan throws himself into the vocal and drives it forward with that insistent guitar.

[Senor]

I want to finish this post with a couple of rarities. In this series I haven't always allowed space for Dylan's treatment of other writers' songs.

There just seemed to be too many good Dylan songs to cover. However in September 1994 Dylan did a studio recording of some Elvis Presley songs, perhaps with the view to doing a tribute album. Only three songs were recorded, it seems, among which 'Any Way You Want Me' stands out. Dylan's broken voiced rendition gives the song a whole new and much rawer feeling. Quite a gem, this one.

[Any Way You Want Me]

As well as Presley, Dylan took part in a Jimmy Rogers tribute session. This performance of Blue-Eyed Jane reminds us of the strong influence Country and Western had on Dylan, and the role played by the great Jimmy Rogers in shaping that music and filling the radio airways with his sad ballads. Dylan sings it naturally and with obvious affection. Here he is accompanied by Emmylou Harris.

[Blue-Eyed Jane]

That's it for now. Soon I'll be back with the final installment of Dylan's 1994 performances that will include 'Jokerman,' 'Lenny Bruce,' and 'Born in Time'.
Until then, stay safe!

Kia Ora

NET 1994: Part 5 – Dancing to the Nightingale's Tune

By Mike Johnson (Kiwipoet)

We finish this survey of Dylan's monumental 1994 year with a brief look at his treatment of some of his 1980s songs. We start with 'Lenny Bruce' from *Shot of Love*, 1981, the third album in Dylan's Christian trilogy. It's not a particularly Christian song at all, rather a celebration of the life of the great comedian, Lenny Bruce, whose hard hitting comedy routines Dylan admired. The song is not that much admired, however, and some of the loose, proselike lyrics attracted adverse comment:

> 'Never robbed any churches nor cut off any babies' heads,
> He just took the folks in high places and he shined a light in their face.'

These may not be Dylan's finest lyrics, but they do provide us with an insight into those qualities Dylan admired that Christ and Lenny Bruce shared:

> 'He was an outlaw, that's for sure,
> More of an outlaw than you ever were.'

And

> 'They said that he was sick 'cause he didn't play by the rules
> He just showed the wise men of his day to be nothing more than fools
> They stamped him and they labeled him like they do with pants and shirts'

I have argued that what drew Dylan to Christ was Christ's outlaw status, and that's what draws him to Lenny Bruce. A man who, like Dylan himself, refused to be stamped and labeled. What makes this performance attractive is the easy pace it sets up. This is the case with many 1994 performances of Dylan's setlists. He often finds a rhythm, a forward, driving beat that carries the song along. (St Louis, April 10)

[Lenny Bruce]

Moving on from *Shot of Love* to *Infidels* (1984), we come to the opening track on that album, 'Jokerman'. Jokerman is clearly a major song, with some wonderful lyrics, but somehow I haven't been able to develop a tight connection to the song. I'm made curious by, and in some awe at the lyrics, but remain unmoved. I sense that the song registers Dylan's movement away from the Pentecostal Christianity with which he had engaged.

> 'Sheddin' off one more layer of skin
> Keepin' one step ahead of the persecutor within'

This sounds more like the Dylan of old, and in the repeated chorus there is the sensation of liberation and flight.

> 'Jokerman dance to the nightingale tune
> Birds fly high by the light of the moon
> Ohh, ohh, jokerman'

And it's still the same old bad-ass world out there:

> 'Nightsticks and water cannons, tear gas, padlocks
> Molotov cocktails and rocks behind every curtain
> False hearted judges
> Dying in the webs that they spin
> Only a matter of time
> 'Til night comes steppin' in'

Starting to sound like our world again. At the same time it's shot through with imagery from the Old Testament mixed with scenes from Hieronymus Bosch. Truly a magical mix. Don't really know why I can't get with it. There are two performances of the song in 1994 worth listening to. The first is from Krakow (Jully 7) and the second is from Portland (August 10)

[Jokerman A]

[Jokerman B]

Also from *Infidels* we have 'I and I', another song that seems to celebrate a liberation from Pentecostal restrictions:

'Been so long since a strange woman has slept in my bed
Look how sweet she sleeps, how free must be her dreams'

It is a complex, melancholy song, behind which lurks some Old Testament ferocity:

'I and I
in creation where one's nature neither honours nor forgives
I and I
one said to the other no man sees my face and lives'

The song also contains outstanding lines that belong with the very best of Dylan:

'Someone else is speaking with my mouth
but I'm listening only to my heart'

What better way of expressing a fundamental alienation of the self, a split between the I and I? To my ear, this song reached peak performance in 1993 (See NET, 1993, Part 1). This 1994 performance sounds post peak to me, but still magnificent. Like 'Man in the Long Black Coat', there's a sense of grandeur in the song.

[I and I]

Next we move to *Oh Mercy* (1989) and some of the songs from that album that Dylan cultivated in performance. Most notable of these is the aforementioned 'Man in the Long Black Coat'. This song is undergoing a change from a swampy ghost story into a cosmic drama. When we come to 1995, and the Prague performance, we'll have a useful comparison. In the meantime, this performance shapes up well enough, although I find Mr Guitar Man's work a little busy; too much being jammed in doesn't allow the song to breathe. This brings us back to the issue of Dylan's electric guitar playing and what it might contribute or fail to contribute to the song.

Dylan is working hard during these guitar breaks. He's packing the field with dark sounds, dark and always sounding a little off key, as if, as I have suggested before, he's playing under the note. The last half of this performance is a good example. This is not classic blues or rock guitar at all. It's more akin to jazz, but above all, it's Dylan's own distinctive sound.

[Man in the Long Black Coat]

Back in part 2 of this 1994 series, we heard Dylan singing 'Hard Rain' in Japan with full orchestra backing in a concert called The Great Musical Experience. That was a truly remarkable and memorable performance, but to my mind 'Ring Them Bells' is better suited to that full orchestral treatment given the grandeur of those chord changes. And of the words. On the surface it seems like a throwback to the Christian period (1979 -81), but for me it works emotionally on a deeper level that's difficult to explain. The command to 'ring them bells' is not as a call to prayer, or a celebration, but as a warning: (my own line arrangement, as I hear it sung)

> 'Ring them bells Saint Catherine from the top of the room
> Ring them bells from the fortress for the lilies that bloom
> Oh the lines are long
> and the fighting is strong
> And they're breaking down the distance between
> right and wrong'

[Ring them Bells]

From July 4th, Besançon, France, we get a brooding, powerful performance of 'What Good Am I?' While I like Dylan's piano versions of this song, I have to say that as soon as I heard this performance it immediately became my favourite. Arguably a peak performance of this wonderful piece of self-questioning. It's Dylan's vocal that won me over. You can hear Mr Guitar Man at his quiet and intricate best, but it's that cry-of-the-heart vocal that does the job.

The song has a political implication or dimension, questioning our indifference to the sufferings of others. When introducing the song in 1999, he dedicated to the 'rain forests', suggesting an environmental dimension, but for me the most telling verse is personal:

'What good am I while you softly weep
And I hear in my head what you say in your sleep
And I freeze in the moment like the rest who don't try
What good am I?'

What Good Am I

'Everything Is Broken' is a fast beaty number from *Oh Mercy*. It's a foot-tapper, but it shows Dylan re-evoking the spirit of protest. Everything is indeed broken. For me, however, the lyrics are a little unfocused. It's a kind of scatter-gun approach listing all those broken things.

'Broken hands on broken ploughs,
Broken treaties, broken vows,
Broken pipes, broken tools,
People bending broken rules
Hound dog howling, bull frog croaking,
Everything is broken'

The song doesn't have the coherence or the punch of 'Subterranean Homesick Blues'. This is another MTV Unplugged outtake. Just think, we could have had an amazing double album.

[Everything Is Broken]

On Under the Red Sky (1990), we find a modest little ballad called 'Born in Time'. Perhaps because the album was not well received, this little gem got overlooked. Like many of Dylan's great songs, it is steeped in fate. Love and destiny haunt the song, but something more too, a message: the more powerful love becomes, the more that love will test you. Here are the last three verses of the song:

> 'On the rising curve
> Where the ways of nature will test every nerve,
> You won't get anything you don't deserve
> Where we were born in time.
>
> You pressed me once, you pressed me twice,
> You hang the flame, you'll pay the price,
> Oh babe, that fire
> Is still smokin'
> You were snow, you were rain
> You were striped, you were plain,
> Oh babe, truer words
> Have not been spoken or broken.
>
> In the hills of mystery,
> In the foggy web of destiny,
> You can have what's left of me,
> Where we were born in time'

To be 'born in time' is to be born into love and suffering, a place where we 'hang the flame'. The song goes beyond complaint to surrender. The last two lines are devastating. 'You can have what's left of me' is hardly a come on line, but strips us back to the emotional core. I can't know why Dylan neglected this song and so rarely performed it. It's a little melancholy masterpiece. Dylan blurs a line or two, but these last verses are sung with such agony and passion!

[Born in Time]

So that brings to a close our trip through 1994, and what a trip it has been. Perhaps because he was not writing new material, he had to re-invent his back list. I can see that the NET tour itself has been on a rising curve since 1991 as Dylan found his voice and the band came together as a solid unit.

168

However, that curve is still on the rise and, I would argue, reaches its peak in 1995. I'm keen to try to prove that argument when I return to tune into that year.

Kia Ora.

1995

NET 1995: The Prague Revelation and Other Astonishments

By Mike Johnson (Kiwipoet)

> 'Well, it's sugar for sugar
> And salt for salt,
> If you go down in the flood,
> It's gonna be your own fault.'

'Dylan opens the year with one of the most remarkable performances of the "Never Ending Tour," despite still visibly suffering the after effects of the bug (at several points he sits on the drum rise, scrunched up in some discomfort)... the shock of the evening is not in his song selection. But the fact that he performs almost the entire show without a guitar, harmonica in hand, making strange shadow-boxing movements, cupping the harmonica to his mouth on nearly every song, blowing his sweetest harp breaks in years.'

Clinton Heylin (Bob Dylan: A Life in Stolen Moments Day by Day 1941-1995)

'Anyone who has watched a sunrise over the ancient city of Prague will feel they have visited a city of magic & wonder. Anyone who has heard Dylan's performance on the 11th will have felt a similar sense of awe.'

Andrew Muir (One More Night: Bob Dylan's Never Ending Tour)

On March 11, 1995, Dylan descended on Prague to kick off the year's tour with a sizzling three night stand. These concerts would astonish and tame a pretty unruly audience with a series of masterful performances that have gone down in NET history. It is possible to argue, as I will here, that the NET reached a peak in 1995, with these Prague concerts as the jewels in that crown. It would reach another peak around 2000.

At the end of the last post (see NET, 1994, part 5), I suggested that the NET had been on a rising curve since 1991 as Dylan struggled with his voice and the task of welding his band into a responsive vehicle for his wonderful songs. As we saw, 1994 was a lift off year, with an especially powerful set of acoustic performances, but in 1995 he soars into the stratosphere with some of his best performances ever, many of them from those three days in Prague.

The story of these concerts has now become part of the Dylan legend. Apparently he had the flu and was not up to playing the guitar. At least not until the 13th, the third and last concert, when he begins to get back into it. So mostly he fronted the audience with just his voice and his harp. This was new; Dylan had always put his guitar between himself and his audience – unless playing piano.

The flu might have knocked out his guitar, but his voice is capable of reaching a clarity and luminosity rarely heard since the 1960s. He can still give his voice a tearing edge when he wants to, but by softening the tones, giving them a quiet intensity, he achieves the vocal mastery we so much love in Dylan.

It's tempting to think that these performances are so good because Dylan is not playing the guitar. A heretical thought but a persistent one. Mr Guitar Man's insistent, complex, heavy electric guitar sound is not to everybody's taste. But there is more to it than that. These performances are the fruition of a long development.

Those of you reading this, and the next couple of posts, have a treat in store. I'm swerving from my usual practice of concert jumping to focus on Prague, 1995, working my way across the three concerts with some thirty performances lined up for you. I won't try to follow the setlists through as he plays them, but rather jump around to create my own extended setlist. I'm eager to get started.

So I'll start right from the beginning, the opening song of the first night, March 11, 'Crash on the Levee (Down in the Flood)'. The performance of this bluesy, irreverent song from *The Basement Tapes* (1967) is nothing too special, although the energy is all there. There are hints of Dylan's vocal power and the possibilities to come. After a bit of a shaky start, he soon finds his feet and away we go. A great song to get the energy pumping. A settling-in song.

[Crash on the Levee]

The recordings of this first night are somewhat sharper than the second and third nights. You can hear that clearly in the difference between the following two performances. This one is from the first night, the 11th:

[Ballad of a Thin man (A)]

And this is from the second night, the 12th :

[Ballad of a Thin Man (B)]

These performances show how effective the softly-softly approach can be, giving the song, with its bizarre characters and situations, a sinister touch. It also allows Dylan to stretch his voice on the high notes to dramatic effect. I prefer the second one, but that may just be the recording. And, as Dylan takes a rest at the end, the band find their feet without Mr Guitar Man.

There can be few performances of 'Mr Tambourine Man' as gentle and tender as the Prague versions, despite a couple of slip ups with the lyrics. By slowing the song right down, and taking advantage of the echo of the venue's sound system, this nostalgic rendition of Dylan's great hymn to escapism achieves a plaintive quality I haven't heard in previous performances. It's eerie, like an echo from the past. The invitation to go:

> 'down the foggy ruins of time
> far past the frozen leaves
> the haunted frightened trees'

has never sounded quite so ghostly. Listening to that 'spirit voice' reminds me of these lines from Percy Shelly:

> 'Oh! there are spirits of the air,
> And genii of the evening breeze,
> And gentle ghosts, with eyes as fair
> As star-beams among twilight trees:—
> Such lovely ministers to meet
> Oft hast thou turned from men thy lonely feet.'

Thinking of Shelly, a Dylan like character, at least in my mind, I'm reminded of Matthew Arnold's description of Shelly as 'a beautiful and ineffectual angel, beating in the void his luminous wings in vain.' I invite you to contemplate that quote as you listen to these two performances by our contemporary Shelly. The first one is from the 12th. A particularly plaintive, wistful harp.

[Mr Tambourine Man (A)]

This second is from the 13th. Except for a stuff up at the beginning with the lyrics, this is another superlative performance, equally ethereal.

[Mr Tambourine Man (B)]

And while on the subject of Dylan's sixties classics, while he didn't favour them as heavily as he did in 1994, we have two wonderful performances of Dylan's masterpiece 'Desolation Row.' In this song we meet some of the denizens of Dylan's circus, a host of crazy characters, all the outsiders and fucked-up ones, all in drag disguise ('I had to rearrange their faces/ and give them all another name'). This song, along with 'Visions of Johanna', stands at the apex of Dylan's post protest sixties song writing. This first performance on the 11th is wonderful by most standards, although it lacks the harp break, and Dylan's voice feels a bit under-recorded. In the light of the second performance, however, from the 12th, it sounds more like a rehearsal. The sharp-edged harmonica from the second performance caps it all off.

[Desolation Row (A)]

[Desolation Row (B)]

There are only a few videos from these Prague concerts and they tend to be patchy and too dark. The only one worth watching to my mind is 'Shelter from the Storm' and even then it is interspersed with stills. It does however give the flavour of the performance, Dylan's constant, restless movements on stage, that 'strange shadow boxing' referred to by Heylin.

This slow, soft version, from the 11th, stands in stark contrast to the harsh, fast 1976 performance. After a super-slow start, it kicks into an easy rhythm, and it soon begins to sound more like a love song than other performances. That easy pace allows Dylan to stretch his lungs. Listen to the magnificent vocal performance starting around 2.15 mins. (I have added the sound file in case the video should one day vanish)

[Shelter from the Storm]

'Lay Lady Lay' began life as a seductive, somewhat tongue-in-cheek number from *Nashville Skyline*, 1969, became a raucous cry of desire during the Rolling Thunder Tour (1975/76), to become here a tender, passionate love song. Again the hero of the story is Dylan's voice. He whispers, entreats and cries out for love. It is from the 13th, Dylan has picked up the guitar for this one, and Mr Guitar Man is in excellent form. You'll be hard put to find a better performance of the song.

[Lay Lady Lay]

While on the subject of tender love songs, let's consider 'Boots of Spanish Leather'. Not only is it one of Dylan's most affecting love songs, dealing with the feelings we have when about to be separated from someone we love, but perhaps his most successful conversation songs. Bits of conversation and dialogue are a hallmark of Dylan songs, but in 'Boots of Spanish Leather' we have a full two-sided conversation. The boots themselves become emblematic of all those strange exotic places his love will be visiting. His love, about to depart, presses him on the matter:

> 'Ah, but I just thought you might want something fine
> Made of silver or of golden
> Either from the mountains of Madrid
> Or from the coast of Barcelona'
>
> But all he wants, of course, is his love.
> 'Oh, how can, how can you ask me again?
> It only brings me sorrow
> The same thing I would want today
> I will want again tomorrow'

I don't know we can say that Dylan has ever written a tear jerker, but this comes pretty close. My problem here is I have two versions both dated 13th March. They can't both be right. I'm pretty sure that this softer performance is really from the 13th. Dylan fumbles the lyrics again near the beginning but soon finds his feet. My info has it that Dylan is playing acoustic guitar on this one.

[Boots of Spanish Leather (A)]

And I'm guessing from the sound quality that this next one is from the 12th. Either way, we have two stand-out performances of the song. And in both cases we get those 'sweetest harp breaks' that Heylin refers to, the first being more ethereal than the second.

[Boots of Spanish Leather (B)]

In the early sixties, Dylan would kick off his concerts with 'The Times They Are A-changing.' Sung in a strident, challenging voice, as he did then, it sounds like a call to arms. Sung in a more reflective tone, it becomes a meditation on time and eternal recurrence. Performed slowly it becomes,in Dylan's soft Prague voice, tinged with sadness.

[The Times They Are A-Changing]

For us, it's a good place to pause before the next instalment, The Prague Revelation Part 2, Salt for Salt.

Stay safe

Kia Ora

NET 1995: Part 2 - The Prague Revelation, Salt for salt, Peak Prague

By Mike Johnson (Kiwipoet)

In the first post in this 1995 series (See Part 1) I introduced Dylan's 1995 Prague concerts with some sample sounds. This post I've set aside for my favourite performances from Dylan's three night gig, 11th 12th, and 13th of March. For my ear, this is the cream of the cream, maybe the best Dylan you'll ever hear, although it's difficult to make such a claim because of the changes in Dylan's voice and style over the years.

There is magic in these Prague concerts. Perhaps the flu stretched him to the point where... I don't know, something else happened. A breakthrough of a kind in terms of the range of his vocal expression, and emotional expression in his harmonica playing. He wasn't just up there grinding it out; there is a fire in these performances, and a sense of restraint. We feel the banked up emotion behind the restraint, just as we do with the great blues singers like Lightning Hopkins and Otis Span.

The setlist over the three nights varied, with not many songs done on all three nights. 'Tangled Up In Blue', however, on its way to becoming one of the three most performed Dylan songs ever, did turn up on all three setlists. While Dylan achieves an extended emotional range by slowing down many of the songs performed in Prague, with 'Tangled' he speeds it up, or at least gives that impression from the urgency of the backing. All three performances crackle with energy. They are more disciplined than the ten, twelve minute versions we find in 1993/4, years in which epic versions ruled, but all the more punchy for it. (Those interested in the evolution of this song might enjoy the two postscripts to my Master Harpist series:

[Tangled up in Harmonicas: Part 1]

[Tangled up in Harmonicas: Part 2]

The first performance, from the 11th, scintillates with energy, with Dylan's voice swooping through the lyrics, with the sharp-edged harmonica to finish off. If you don't start moving your feet to this one, they may be glued to the floor.

[Tangled Up In Blue (A)]

The performance from the 12th kicks along at about the same speed but the sound is more full bodied. That might be the recording, it's hard to tell. With these faster versions we get the sense of a life flashing by, or hurtling by; it all goes by so fast. Before we can catch up with events, more events have piled on top. The slower version from the album and the even slower version from the 1974 New York recordings, the first takes of the song, make it a much more contemplative, reflective song than it is here, performed at this hectic pace. We fall headlong through life, from one scene to the next, with hardly time to remember, 'all the people we used to know.'

[Tangled Up In Blue (B)]

On the 13th Dylan introduces the song with the harp and launches into another faultless vocal performance. What is amazing is that if you listen to all three vocals you find he sings it differently each time, emphasising and elongating different words, creating different tonal effects.

[Tangled Up In Blue (C)]

'License to Kill' is a quiet, reflective protest song from *Infidels*. The chorus centres around a bereaved woman, lamenting the death of a loved one, maybe a soldier. The verses tend to focus on the training and brainwashing of a killer, and the subsequent plight of mankind. When I wrote about this song when it appeared in 1993, I quoted these lyrics:

> 'Now, he's hell-bent for destruction, he's afraid and confused,
> And his brain has been mismanaged with great skill
> All he believes are his eyes
> And his eyes, they just tell him lies'

I suggested that this reminded me of more current killers, those who think that a license to carry firearms is a license to kill. (See NET, 1993, Part 5) That was written before the January 6th attack on the Capitol in the US. Now the lyrics seem even more contemporary:

'Now he worships at an altar of a stagnant pool
And when he sees his reflection, he's fulfilled
Oh, man is opposed to fair play,
He wants it all and he wants it his way'

In this last verse the attack opens up to include all of humanity, the killers and the colluders. It's humankind's massive greed that gets in the way. This may not be Dylan's greatest protest song, but this performance from the 13th is certainly the greatest performance of the song. The power of performance is such that Dylan convinces us that it is a great song. The plaintive harp break at the end is the icing on the cake.

[License to Kill]

'Man in the Long Black Coat' is a spooky song based on the Devil at the Dance motif from *Oh Mercy* (1989). Dylan had been cultivating for three years. Those following these posts will have been alerted to the growing strength of this song in performance, with Dylan trying out slow tempos and varying musical arrangements. Its evolution has been from a swampy supernatural story to a cosmic drama of demonic seduction. As with the best Dylan songs, the drama pulls us into its orbit with its more universal application:

'Preacher was talking there's a sermon he gave
He said every man's conscience is vile and depraved
You cannot depend on it to be your guide
When it's you who must keep it satisfied'

The message is dark: we cannot alone find our way in the moral jungle, especially as, according to the old saying, the devil can quote scriptures.

'He looked into her eyes when she stopped him to ask

If he wanted to dance, he had a face like a mask
Somebody said from the Bible he'd quote
There was dust on the man in the long black coat'

This leaves us in a limbo where we are neither alive nor dead but 'float' in some kind of intermediary zone:

'But people don't live or die people just float
She went with the man in the long black coat'

These words remind me of 'the disrobed faceless forms of no position' we can find in 'Chimes of Freedom' way back in 1964. At Prague the song was another of those rare ones that was performed on all three nights, and what a magnificent sequence they make. At last we feel that the song has come into focus. Enjoy these three performances, as the song will never sound so good again. On the first night, the 11th, it's all in place except the harmonica. The long drawn out sounds on the steel guitar, the deep, thundery base. Magnificent.

[Man in the Long Black Coat (A)]

Magnificent as that was, it was just a warm up for what was to come on the 12th, with Dylan's triumphant harmonica to the fore. I wrote about the March 12th performance for the Master Harpist series. I can't say it better now than I said it then, so, with my editor's indulgence, I'm putting in this quote from that article:
'The pop and rock music of the 1980s veered towards creating sonic landscapes, orchestral sounds, and we don't normally associate Bob Dylan with this kind of music, but in this grand and grandiose version of 'Man in The Long Black Coat' you hear Dylan and his band aiming for a full orchestral effect, which is where the harmonica comes in, lifting the song into one huge wall of sound. It's a pity that the recording devices, or the original sound system for all I know, was not up to capturing the full range of this magnificent achievement – not to mention the limitations of MP3s! It's a sheer blast, with long sustained harmonica notes pushing the music ever higher, finally floating above the wall of sound, thin and insistent, and ultimately as haunting as the song itself. The first solo is just a warm up for

the climax to follow the last verse.' I can't add much to that except to say that every time I play this one, it exerts the same deep, magical pull. It is undoubtedly one of Dylan's finest moments onstage.

[Man in the Long Black Coat (B)]

The third performance of the song, on the 13th seems like an anticlimax when compared to the 12th, but of course it is another out of the box rendition. The vocal is just as magnificent and while the harp does not soar into the stratosphere, it has a sharp, cutting edge.

[Man in the Long Black Coat (C)]

Two songs always linked in my mind are 'It's All Over Now, Baby Blue' and 'It Ain't Me, Babe.' Both were written about the same time (1964) and both seem to be get lost songs. But things are not always what they seem when it comes to Dylan. These may be goodbye and good luck songs, but they are also love songs of the highest order, particularly 'Baby Blue'.

'It Ain't Me, Babe,' may sound brash and dismissive if it's sung that way, and it does work that way, but sung in a lonely, tender voice it becomes something else. Can we ever dismiss a lover without some tinge of regret, some strain of sorrow? And can love ever be banished by such brave assertions and protestations? Listen to this performance from the 12th and decide for yourself. And if you are in any doubt, try that most gentle and fragile harp break. Such exquisite restraint.

[It Ain't Me, Babe]

But for the final coup-de-grace as far as outstanding performances go, and a strong candidate for the best ever Dylan harp performance, we must turn to 'Baby Blue' on the first night, the 11th.

Once again, I wrote about this performance for the Master Harpist series, and again with my editor's indulgence I'll quote myself:

> 'Baby Blue', performed in a strident, declarative, in-your-face manner, might be classed as one of Dylan's put-down songs: get yourself together and piss off! But sung the way

he does at Prague, the song, all through the vocal, skirts the edges of heartbreak, and when the harmonica takes over, the mood is pushed into outright heartbreak. There's been a lot of tedious speculation as to whether this song is for Joan Baez (do we really care?), or was written as a farewell to the protest movement (ho-hum), but what these speculations might obscure is that 'Baby Blue' is a break-up song, which implies heart-break, finality, the end of love. It is love's last song.

Suddenly the lyrics don't sound so tough any more, and we wonder if he's exhorting himself to get a new life as much as the 'you' he's addressing. Listen to how Dylan lifts his voice in the last verse, how the harmonica takes over from where the voice leaves off, lays bare the real heartbreak and gives unrestrained voice to grief. Dylan can't cry onstage, but his harmonica can, and boy it sure does, and how painful it is at the end as he repeats the same notes over and over, like one of those protracted goodbyes everybody hates but sometimes you just can't escape. Just one more goodbye...one more... all the way to emotional exhaustion.

[It's All Over Now, Baby Blue]

What a note on which to end this post of the best of the best at Prague, 1995. I'll be back soon to finish off what Dylan started at Prague.

Kia Ora

NET 1995: Part 3 - The Prague Revelation – down in the Flood

By Mike Johnson (Kiwipoet)

In the first and second of these posts on his March, 1995 Prague concerts, I covered some of the finest performances of the 1990s phase of Dylan's Never Ending Tour. So what is left but the leftovers? you might ask. And it's true, but with Prague, even the leftovers make a wonderful feast.

Take 'Just Like a Woman', for example. Dylan performed this controversial song twice at Prague, on the 11th and 12th of March. It's controversial because of the sweet savagery of the lyrics and its outright attack on 'Queen Mary,' the subject of the song. Is this yet another example of Dylan putting down women? There is too much contempt in it for us to feel easy with it. And that 'breaks just like a little girl' at the end feels like a final kick in the guts. Or is it the line 'you fake just like a woman' that does it, as if being fake is particular to women? Interestingly, Nina Simone, a powerful woman if ever there was one, could take it to heart, identify with it, while avoiding the 'fake' line. Here's her version of the chorus:

> 'I take
> Just like a woman
> Yes I do
> And I make love
> Just like a woman
> And I ache
> Just like a woman
> But I break
> Just like a little girl'

But doesn't the singer indicate that he too might break like a little boy? Look at this last verse:

> 'It was raining from the first
> And I was dying there of thirst

So I came in here
And your long-time curse hurts
But what's worse is this pain in here
I can't stay in here
Ain't it clear that I just can't fit
Yes, I believe that it's time for us to quit
But when we meet again, introduced as friends
Please don't let on that you knew me when
I was hungry and it was your world'

Ashamed of his neediness? And vulnerable. Miserable in the rain, compelled to go to her. Also it strikes me that the real target here is not the woman so much as pretentiousness and falsity. The fakery of masks. The same target we find in a range of songs from 'Ramona' to 'She's Your Lover Now'.

Listening to these Prague performances, I hear the song as a love song, that desperate edge of a love that just can't fit. It's a confession, and we shouldn't be deceived by the opening line, 'nobody feels any pain', as the whole song is reeking with pain, and it might be that which saves it from its contempt. We often turn our vitriol on those who have exposed our weaknesses. Here's the first, from the 11th. Hard to find a more anguished performance. Or more wonderful harp work.

[Just Like a Woman (A)]

The performance on the 13th is somewhat more muted, perhaps a little more reflective. I like the strength of the first version, but the second is better structured, with the harp break taking us right to the end, rather than letting the band do the last chorus alone.

[Just Like a Woman (B)]

Time to kick back with something a bit more relaxed and watch the river flow. The easy beat of 'Watching the River Flow' (1971) might disguise the heavy dose of fatalism that runs through the song. A rather tongue in cheek expression of 'go with the flow' hippie philosophy. According to the session men, Dylan wrote the lyrics in a few minutes in the studio.

'Oh, this ol' river keeps on rollin', though
No matter what gets in the way and which way the wind does blow
And as long as it does I'll just sit here
And watch the river flow'

I love the down-home, gutsy sound of the band on this one.

[Watching the River Flow]

Speaking of the blues, and songs penned in 1971, this performance of 'If Not for You' is given a bluesy twist here, especially when Dylan pulls out the harp at the end. Those interested in the origins of the song could do no better than check out the version on Another Self Portrait (Bootleg Vol 10). This one, from the 11th, kicks along nicely:

[If Not for You]

I still think the song 'God Knows' reached its performance peak in 1993, with Mr Guitar Man playing a guttural, intricate weave of sound (See, NET, 1993, Part 1). I don't know if Dylan picked up the guitar for this one on the 11th of March, but it sure sounds like it. Dylan is in great vocal form. The song is a somewhat frantic mix of despair and hope:

'God knows it's fragile
God knows everything
God knows it could snap apart right now
Just like putting scissors to a string'

[God Knows]

Since 1992 Dylan had been developing slow, bluesy endings to his performances. Some of these endings last almost as long as a whole pop song. 'Don't Think Twice', especially when sung in a fast, peppy manner, lends itself to a slow, thumping end, which is what we get here. There is an unexpected emotional sophistication in what sounds like a bit of ditty, the title being a throw-away line.

'I'm a-thinkin' and a-wond'rin' walkin' way down the road
I once loved a woman, a child I am told
I give her my heart but she wanted my soul'

We might be hard put to explain the difference between heart and soul here, but we can feel the difference. Some people just want to consume you. They don't want you to be your own person, and Dylan is all about being his own person. In the last lines I detect a touch of tragedy. There's nothing worse for the artist than being trapped in a time wasting relationship. There's a deeper calling for the 'road', the dark side. The road would become perhaps the defining motif in Dylan's songs.

'I ain't sayin' you treated me unkind
You could have done better but I don't mind
You just kinda wasted my precious time
But don't think twice, it's all right'

This situation is repeated years later in 'Caribbean Wind', (1981).

'Would I have married her? I don't know, I suppose.
She had bells in her braids and they hung to her toes
But I kept hearing my name and I had to be movin' on.'

And again in 'I And I' in 1984.

'Noontime, and I'm still pushin' myself along the road, the darkest part
Into the narrow lanes, I can't stumble or stay put
Someone else is speakin' with my mouth, but I'm listenin' only to my heart'

In this performance Dylan keeps the bounciness of the original, and delivers another soft, intimate vocal.

[Don't Think Twice]

'I Don't Believe You' is another song from Dylan's early acoustic era that has gone through many changes. The original was a wildly sarcastic romp, which turned into a wailing screamer during the 1966 tour, which turned into... this upbeat 1995 version, with that easy, catchy, mid-tempo beat that Dylan had been working on for the last couple of years. It works as a foot-tapper. My complaint about these later versions is that they don't capture the wry self-irony of the original, the humour inherent in the situation that lifted it above being a mere complaint.

[I Don't Believe You]

Dylan performed 'All Along the Watchtower' twice, on the 12th and 13th. There is little to choose between the two performances. I once used the term ecstatic rock to describe this frantic, full on guitar fest. This one is from the 12th.

[All Along the Watchtower]

'Maggie's Farm' may be a rejection of stifling conformity, but it is also a good, beaty, hell for leather rock song. Who can forget the moment during the 1964 Newport Folk Festival when Dylan first belted out his new rock sound. This is the song Dylan chose to finish the shows on the 11th and 12th (with encores to follow). This one is from the 12th, and you can hear Dylan introduce the band which is: Bob Dylan (vocal & guitar),Bucky Baxter (pedal steel guitar & electric slide guitar), John Jackson (guitar), Tony Garnier (bass) and Winston Watson (drums & percussion).

[Maggie's Farm]

'Like A Rolling Stone' may be Dylan's most iconic hit. It was the way the song caught the public that did it. It is Dylan's sharpest 'attack' song, portraying a rich girl blinded to her own pretentions and having to face the truth about herself. Voted by Rolling Stone magazine as the greatest rock song ever, it was a wonderful way to finish the last evening of his Prague residency. A triumphant finish to three triumphant performances.

[Like A Rolling Stone]

Of course the year didn't end with Prague. Rather it started there. In the next post I'll be looking at 1995, post Prague to see what goodies we can discover. Until then, all the best and happy listening.

Kia Ora

Net 1995: Part 4 – Beyond Prague, London Calling

By Mike Johnson (Kiwipoet)

Of course, Dylan's revelatory three day residency on Prague was not the end of the 1995 story, just the beginning. He went on from there to performances equal to Prague, but not with the same consistency.

His three day residency in London, from the 29th to the 31st of March at the Brixton Academy, is a good example. It may well be that the recording of the London concerts was not as good. Despite their obvious audience source, there is something about the Prague recordings, how they capture the echo of the venue, and the clarity of the sound, that was not sustained in London. Yet there were some outstanding moments in London, such as this 'Masters of War', which equals the best of Prague:

[Masters of War]

For my ear, we have a 'best ever' performance of this song, at least in terms of acoustic versions. In my post for Master Harpist 2, I wrote regarding this performance: 'Dylan can let rip with this song, and turn it into a howling rocker, but this performance is all restraint, a sense of holding back that emotion, which just breaks through the voice here and there, until we get to the harp, where we get a sharper, more trenchant comment. Listen to the way the guitar and harmonica surge back and forward in a syncopated manner, while Dylan's vocal and harmonica phrasing drive the song forward. Hard to find a better Dylan performance than this.'

Another London performance we can't overlook is this 'Senor', a song that takes us right to the borderlands of spiritual despair. It's a wonderful moody song from *Street Legal* (1978) and never fails to create a spooky atmosphere on stage. There is a pretty good video of this performance, and you see Dylan, once more without guitar, putting on a very Prague-like performance. (I have added the audio link in case the You Tube clip disappears)

[Senor]

The London concerts are remarkable for a most rare performance of 'Joey' off *Desire* (1975). 'Joey' has never been my favourite Dylan song, as it appears to lionise a mafia figure. How different from 'The Lonesome Death of Hattie Carol' (1964) which presents us with a harrowing tale of how a poor black woman was randomly killed by a rich crook who might have been Joey, or at least a Joey type figure. As a story, this epic failed to move me, but if any performance of the song was going to move me it would be this one. Whatever you think of the song, the power of this performance turns it into a passionate narrative of betrayal. A remarkable vocal.

[Joey]

'Dignity' was written in 1989 for *Oh Mercy*, but Dylan was dissatisfied with the versions they tried out. He re-recorded it in 1994, and many of us first became aware of the song from the 1994 MTV Unplugged concert. A derisive humour lies behind this song. Dignity can no longer be found no matter where you search:

> 'I went down where the vultures feed
> I would've got deeper, but there wasn't any need
> Heard the tongues of angels and the tongues of men
> Wasn't any difference to me'

You can listen to it as if dignity was a person, and the effect is quite odd. I've just added the capital D to dignity.

> 'Somebody got murdered on New Year's Eve
> Somebody said Dignity was the first to leave

I went into the city, went into the town
Went into the land of the midnight sun'

This 1995 London performance recalls the MTV performance of the year before, but to my mind has the edge on the earlier performance, being a bit sharper and rougher.

[Dignity]

What I like about Dylan's 1995 vocals is the understated softness of his voice when he needs it. Yes, he can yell it out, and often the songs build from soft to loud, but in the case of the London performance of 'She Belongs to Me' he pretty much keeps it soft and intimate, as if it were a love song instead of a cautionary account of how one can be bewitched and end up 'peeking through a keyhole down upon your knees.' The woman in question is a charmer for sure – but what is the cost of getting involved? Serving another's ego?

[She Belongs to Me]

Feel like kicking back with a bit of rock blues? A song that belts along with a steady rock pace? Something to dance to? Try this London performance of 'Tombstone Blues'. On the album (*Highway 61 Revisited*, 1965) the song happens at quite a frantic pace, thirty years later it rollicks along. The lyrics come over nice and clearly too.

[Tombstone Blues]

Throughout Dylan's songs there is a resistance to over-educated intellectualism. Dylan loved baiting intellectuals, wanna-be intellectuals and pretenders. In 'Someone's Got a Hold of My Heart' he complains about 'too much educated rap.' There is an intellectual force behind his wild whirling words however, but it leans to the anarchic, the chaotic and the revelatory. In 'Tombstone Blues' we find this:

'I wish I could write you a melody so plain
That could hold you, dear lady, from going insane

That could ease you and cool you and cease the pain
Of your useless and pointless knowledge'

And this fucked up world is sure going to make you sick.

'Well, John the Baptist after torturing a thief
Looks up at his hero, the Commander-in-Chief
Saying, "Tell me great hero, but please, make it brief
Is there a hole for me to get sick in?"'

A regular on Dylan's set list, 'If You See Her Say Hello' wasn't played at Prague, so it's a pleasure to pick it up here, in London. These London performances make a nice complement to Prague.

The vocal is restrained, the harmonica sharp-edged and guitarist John Jackson gives the song a country twist. Again we get that easy, mid-tempo, catchy rhythm that makes these songs fun to listen to. It is less wrought than the album version (*Blood on the Tracks*, 1974), but no less nostalgic for that.

[If You See Her Say Hello]

Before leaving the London concerts behind, here's an unusual performance. On the last night, the 31st of March, Dylan is joined onstage by Elvis Costello for a rousing performance of 'I Shall Be Released.' Dylan's distinctive voice and vocal phrasing do not make him an easy partner in any duet. But here they take turns and sing together only on the chorus and it turns out pretty okay. The video of this one is pretty cool too.

[I Shall Be Released]

We now move from London to Edinburgh, 7th April, for another rarity, the last ever performance of 'What Was It You Wanted?' (*Oh Mercy* 1989)
I have always admired this song for its portrayal of devastating emotional disconnection. Imagine two people sitting at a table. They are apparently having a conversation but what we hear is what just one of them is saying, or perhaps thinking. Are you listening to me? Are you there at all? It's the ultimate disconnect.

'Whatever you wanted
Slipped out of my mind
Would you remind me again
If you'd be so kind
Has the record been breaking
Did the needle just skip
Is there somebody waitin'
Was there a slip of the lip?'

This verse is obsessively repetitive, the same notes repeated eight times before a chord change, making it sound as if the needle really is skipping on the track itself. Very clever. Structurally it's relentless, as is the alienation it portrays. Do we even know whom we're talking to or what about?

'What was it you wanted
I ain't keepin' score
Are you the same person
That was here before?
Is it something important
Maybe not
What was it you wanted?
Tell me again I forgot'

Of course people want something, even if they don't come out and say it. So what's their angle?

'Whatever you wanted
What can it be
Did somebody tell you
That you could get it from me
Is it something that comes natural
Is it easy to say
Why do you want it
Who are you anyway?'

This kind of hidden agenda makes us suspicious. 'Are you talking to me?' Do these two people even know each other? Self doubt intervenes.

'Is the scenery changing
Am I getting it wrong
Is the whole thing going backwards
Are they playing our song?
Where were you when it started
Do you want it for free
What was it you wanted
Are you talking to me?'

I don't know why he left it behind after 1995, for by the sound of this performance Dylan is fully engaged with the song. It's a great performance although Dylan's voice is a bit soft or under-recorded at the beginning.

[What Was It You Wanted]

While on the subject of songs from Oh Mercy, and still in Edinburgh, we find an equally committed performance of 'Disease of Conceit.' In 1996 this song too would be dropped from Dylan's repertoire. It's a very explicit song. There is nothing elusive in its imagery. It's almost embarrassingly direct, and so suits Dylan's understated, 1995 style.

[The Disease of Conceit]

That's it for now. Next time we'll be looking at some more compelling sounds from 1995. Until then, stay safe and happy listening.

Kia Ora

NET 1995: Part 5 - Acoustic Wonderland

By Mike Johnson (Kiwipoet)

Since Dylan no longer played alone on stage with just an acoustic guitar, amplified by a microphone, as he did in his early days, we have to ask what acoustic means in terms of the development of Dylan's sound in the 1990s.

I have made reference to a mingled, or modified acoustic sound, but for me the key indicator is whether or not Dylan is playing his electric Stratocaster or his Gibson acoustic. Dylan's Gibson guitar, and Jack Johnson's, are amplified rather than just played into a mic, so the sound can sometimes be as loud if not louder than some of the more muted electric sounds. Often, on the acoustic tracks Tony Garnier will play a double bass instead of an electric bass. Bucky Baxter's steel guitar, however, sounds pretty much the same, acoustic or electric.

The drums are another key indicator. In most of the acoustic tracks they are absent, giving the performance a more folky feel. This post is dedicated to the songs from 1995 which satisfy those criteria, and which we can unhesitatingly identify as acoustic.

'Hard Rain' of course began as an acoustic solo (*The Freewheelin' Bob Dylan*, 1963). During the Rolling Thunder tour (1975/6), it turned into a fast-paced crashing rocker, a hurricane of sound. This one (16th December), with its discreet backing, gives this performance the feel of Dylan's early 60's performances. The backing smoothes it out a bit too, reducing the dumpty-dum tendency of the ballad form. Given the apocalyptic content, this is a quiet, restrained performance. In Dylan's evolving style, however, it builds to climaxes, goes quiet again, then builds again. Powerful delivery of the last verse. An epic performance of an epic song.

[Hard Rain]

'One Too Many Mornings' (1964) has also been through its changes, but to my ear the loud Rolling Thunder version is just too raucous for the quiet melancholy of the song. It's a morning after song, full of bitter-sweetness and regret.

> 'From the crossroads of my doorstep
> My eyes start to fade
> And I turn my head back to the room
> Where my love and I have laid
> And I gaze back to the street
> The sidewalk and the sign
> And I'm one too many mornings
> And a thousand miles behind'

I love this performance (22nd July). It's a little slower than the album version, and the vocal is softly and lovingly delivered. This is a song that benefits from Dylan's maturing voice. On the album he artificially aged his voice by making it sound cracked and well lived in, even though he was only 23 years old. Now at 54, he doesn't have to try.

[One Too Many Mornings]

If I had a choice of attending any concert other than the Prague concerts I would choose the concert at Bethlehem on the 13th of December. The recordings are good and Dylan's performances are superlative.

What makes this Bethlehem performance of 'Desolation Row' so special is the inclusion of that which over the years has become the missing verse. Why Dylan chose to drop this verse will remain a mystery I guess, but I always thought it was one of the best verses of the song. In it, Dylan the post modernist reflects on the two great modernist poets of the early part of the 20th Century.

> 'Praise be to Nero's Neptune
> The Titanic sails at dawn
> And everybody's shouting
> "Which Side Are You On?"
> And Ezra Pound and T. S. Eliot
> Fighting in the captain's tower
> While calypso singers laugh at them

And fishermen hold flowers
Between the windows of the sea
Where lovely mermaids flow
And nobody has to think too much
About Desolation Row'

Interestingly, 'Which Side Are You On?' is a pro-union song by Pete Seeger. Dylan may have been taking a sideswipe at Seeger, but his real aim is at increasing polarisation of political attitudes, the sense of battle lines being drawn. In Desolation Row (the place) you can hear them all playing their penny whistles. You can hear a few members of the audience react when Dylan begins the verse.

[Desolation Row]

Listening to that, I can't help but reflect on Dylan's acoustic style. I don't think there is that big a difference between his acoustic and his electric playing, but the effect is sure different. I have suggested that Dylan's guitar playing is percussive rather than melodic or lyrical. It's there to drive the beat and build up the tension as the song progresses, not to sound pretty. This 'Desolation Row' is a particularly good example of how he pushes the song along with the guitar. With Dylan's singing it's all about phrasing; with his acoustic guitar it's all about timing.

Now for a rarity. Dylan and Patti Smith duetting on 'Dark Eyes', a rarely performed song from Empire Burlesque (1985). The magazine Far Out has a lovely article on this performance:

Apparently they performed the song seven times together in 1995. I think the best version is this one from that same Bethlehem concert

[Dark Eyes]

There is no video of that concert, but there is this one from Philadelphia on the 16th of Dec, three days after the Bethlehem concert. While on the subject of duets, 'Mama, You Been On My Mind,' described as one of Dylan's greatest love songs, was often performed with Joan Baez in the 1960s. It was often performed with a bit of a laugh or smile, but it's not really that funny, unless yearning itself is funny. There is however a wry,

196

almost throw away quality to the lyrics:

> 'Perhaps it's the color of the sun cut flat
> And covering the crossroads I'm standing at
> Or maybe it's the weather or something like that
> But mama, you been on my mind.'

In this performance Dylan plays it fast and straight, with an emphasis on the passionate rather than the humorous side of the song. Lovers of Dylan's harmonica have a joyous surprise in store with a peppy break at the end of the song, hitting the high, squealing notes Dylan first developed in 1989.

[Mama, You Been On My Mind

For those who have been following these posts, 'Gates of Eden' needs no introduction. I have always loved the mysteriousness and weirdness of the song.

> 'The motorcycle black Madonna
> Two-wheeled gypsy queen
> And her silver-studded phantom cause
> The gray flannel dwarf to scream
> As he weeps to wicked birds of prey
> Who pick up on his bread crumb sins
> And there are no sins inside the Gates of Eden'

The 'grey flannel dwarf' reminds me of something out of a David Lynch movie, and there are plenty who were there at the time who think the 'motorcycle black Madonna two-wheeled gypsy queen' to be Brigitte Bardot in this poster famous in hippy apartments far and wide in the 60s.

Caption: The motorcycle black Madonna two-wheeled gypsy queen?

It's a nice idea, but the term 'black Madonna' has other connotations. Representations of the Virgin Mary as black go back a long way in East European history.

Caption: The Black Madonna of Częstochowa, Poland

But I digress. This is another top performance of the song. All it lacks is a harp solo. There is some fancy guitar work by Mr Guitar Man to push the song along and bring out its underlying urgency.

[Gates of Eden]

Another song which should need no introduction to Dylanites is 'Visions of Johanna', probably Dylan's greatest song, at least in terms of the lyrics. I've never been entirely comfortable with the post 60s performances of the song. Nothing matches the bleak, subterranean intensity of the 1966 performances. And while it lacks the sinister edge of the album version, this 1995 performance is sensitive and moody enough to satisfy. (21st of June)

[Visions of Johanna]

I have two offerings of Dylan's great ode to escapism, Mr Tambourine Man. I'm a fan of these slow versions of the song. Arguably the faster versions belie the weariness of the opening verses:

> 'My weariness amazes me
> I'm branded on my feet
> I have no one to meet
> and the ancient empty street's
> too dead for dreaming.'

This sounds convincing sung in a slow weary voice rather than the upbeat sound of the original (1964) and early performances of the song. This is another song in which the ageing of Dylan's voice works in his favour.

[Mr Tambourine Man (A)]

This second offering is very similar, and comes from that wonderful Bethlehem concert on the 13th of December. The sound is a little sharper on this recording. And the weary, contemplative harp solo is incomparable. We'd have to go back to the sweeping 1966 performances to match it.

[Mr Tambourine Man (B)]

Normally, I'd be more excited over this strong acoustic performance of 'Tangled Up In Blue.' It sounds rough and raw, more like a well-known 1975 version albeit slower. Great as it is, it is disappointing that he misses out the verse beginning 'She lit a burner on the stove...' Everything else is in place for an outstanding performance. (21st June)

[Tangled Up In Blue]

While 1993 was the great year for extended epic performances, Dylan continued to deliver epic versions of his greatest anthems. This ten minute performance of 'The Times They Are A-changing' doesn't feel too long or over-extended. With the audience joining in on the punchlines, this has to be an exercise in nostalgia. The vocal is more world-weary than strident, which suits the song's underlying fatalism well. Remember, honey, when the times were a-changin' with such righteous force and it was all about youthful idealism? All the bad guys were going to get out of the way if they couldn't lend a hand. Well... times are still a-changing and there's nothing we can do about it, but it may not always be for the best, you know. The bad guys are still there. The more things change the more they stay the same, as the saying goes.

There's something of a broken-hearted feel to this performance (shouldn't things have changed by now, honey?)Whatever the torments of time, this is an oddly sad but rousing way to end a concert (Bethlehem again) and for me to top this collection of Dylan in acoustic mode, 1995.

See you soon with the last part of this tour through some of Dylan's key performances in this outstanding year.

[The Times They Are A-Changing]

Kia Ora

NET 1995: Part 6 - The Kingdoms of Experience

By Mike Johnson (kiwipoet)

So we come to the last of my posts on that most remarkable year in Dylan's Never Ending Tour – 1995. The performances I've included here did not fit neatly into any of the previous articles, but are no afterthoughts. Or if they are, they are necessary afterthoughts. We wouldn't want to be without them for a full understanding of Dylan's achievements in that year.

We'll kick off with something of a rarity, a live performance of the blues 'Pledging my Time' from *Blonde on Blonde* (1966). I remember around the time I first heard Dylan I was very much into the blues. I was not alone. The blues was sweeping into our musical world from the The Rolling Stones and rock music in general, from jazz and singers like Ray Charles, and the rural blues men like Lightning Hopkins. The blues was everywhere. I remember thinking when I heard Dylan's 'House of the rising Sun' and 'One Kind Favour' that Dylan could become a great blues singer, with his expressive inflections maybe the greatest.

Dylan loved the blues but also avoided it; he didn't want to be defined by it. He had other fish to fry. But when he decides to get into it, he can do it like no other. This is one of more successful adaptions of his *Blonde on Blonde* songs to live performance. Just leave the insinuating inflections of the album behind and you have, well... just the blues. (Don't know date of this one, I'm afraid)

[Pledging My Time]

Staying with *Blonde on Blonde* we have a committed performance of 'Stuck inside of Mobile with the Memphis Blues Again'. This is a long song and not an easy one to sustain in performance. Given the lyrics it's well worth perservering with, however. It takes into the same circus territory as 'Desolation Row' and 'Visions of Johanna'. Whereas 'Visions of Johanna' is a quezy evocation of a 3 a.m zonkout, 'Mobile' is a surreal trip through the maddness of the world, and all the freaked out people in it, and has its roots in Dylan's earlier more humourous madcap adventure songs like 'Talking World War 3 Blues' and 'Bob Dylan's 115th Dream'.

The sense of being trapped in a claustrophobic world is strong in Dylan, and has been right from the start. It comes through strongly on *Blonde on Blonde*. I always loved 'Mobile' for this devastating last verse. This performance may not have the gloomy instensity of the album version, coming over more like a raw cry for help. (No date for this one either, sorry)

> Now, the bricks lay on Grand Street
> Where the neon madmen climb
> They all fall there so perfectly
> It all seems so well timed
> An' here I sit so patiently
> Waiting to find out what price
> You have to pay to get out of
> Going through all these things twice

[Stuck inside of Mobile with the Memphis Blues Again]

Another of Dylan's mid-sixties classics is 'Highway 61 Revisited', another madcap song full of mysterious characters and events. Once more the meaninglessness of material accumulation comes under fire. A couple of circus characters have this conversation:

> Well, Mack the Finger said to Louie the King
> "I got forty red white and blue shoe strings
> And a thousand telephones that don't ring
> Do you know where I can get rid of these things?"
> And Louie the King said, "Let me think for a minute, son"
> And he said, "Yes, I think it can be easily done
> Just take everything down to Highway 61"

When the album came out, the buzz was that Highway 61 was a reference to the main artery in the arm, which junkies use to hit up. Maybe, but mabe not. The humour here is derisive. Highway 61 is the junkyard of the spirit. This song is deeper than it sounds on first listening.

For my ear, the virtues of the song have all too often been buried in a blizard of guitar sounds. Yes, it's supposed to rip along with the images flashing by, but this is one of my favourite performances with its dark, insistent, beat and minimal backing. There is no sense of strain with the vocals either which come across loud and clear. (2nd April, Birmingham)

[Highway 61 Revisited]

My favourite version of 'When I Paint my Masterpiece' (1967) has to be the piano demo found on the *Bootleg Series Volume 10 Another Self Portrait*. It has something of a lumbering beat and is not easy to pull off in performance as it can easily drag. In this performance, however, Dylan doesn't let it drag, using his wonderful voice to lift it at the end, working to build up the energy of the song. It seems to hit on the yearning of all artists to achieve something astonishing and superlative, but the message seems to be that lots of scenes go by and that masterpeice will probably never be painted.

> Sailing round the world in a dirty gondola
> Oh to be back in the land of, Coca-cola.
> Well I left Rome, and landed in Brussels
> On a plane ride so bumpy that I almost cried
> Clergymen in uniform, and young girls pulling muscles
> Everyone was there to greet me when I stepped inside
> Newspaper men eating candy
> Had to be held down by big police.
> Someday, everything's gonna be different
> When I paint my masterpiece.

The song reflects the crazy life of the rock star on tour, wishing he was back in America. It's also the first Dylan song to express Dylan's interest in the classics and the world of antiquity which would play such a big part in his compositions after 2000. (26th October, Bloomington)

[When I Paint My Masterpiece]

When 'Jokerman' appeard in 1994, I commented on the difficulties the song presented, not only in the complexity of its lyrics. I see the song in terms of Dylan distancing himself from the Christianity that had driven his gospel years (1979-81).

> Shedding off one more layer of skin
> Keeping one step ahead of the persecutor within

and moving closer to the Old Testament:

> Well, the Book of Leviticus and Deuteronomy
> The law of the jungle and the sea are your only teachers
> In the smoke of the twilight on a milk-white steed
> Michelangelo indeed could've carved out your features
> Resting in the fields, far from the turbulent space
> Half asleep near the stars with a small dog licking your face

I'm not sure where the small dog fits in, but I love the imagery of those last four lines. Again, it's not an easy song to carry, but the 1995 Dylan is up to the challenge. The song suits the softer treatment. (2nd April, Birmingham)

[Jokerman]

'The Man in Me' from *New Morning* (1971) is no masterpiece, and arguably the lyrics are a little weak, but it is a love song and Dylan's soaring vocals bring it too life. Mr Guitar man has a fair go at it too, with his strange repetitive guitar work, hammering away on the same few notes. (June 29th Oslo)

[The Man in Me]

Perhaps because it's such a crowd-pleaser, and a great song to end a concert. You can go out with an apocolyptic storm of guitars. I can't think of a song that better expresses that sense of impending doom – oh, he ain't no false prophet. Those riders arriving at the end are not bringing good news. In a few short verses Dylan is able to evoke a fantasy land under seige by external forces.

What I like about this performance is the way the band goes quiet while Dylan is singing. Between verses the guitars can let rip. Mr Guitar Man is in his element, his often discordant guitar sounds find their perfect home. (27the March Cardiff, Wales)

[All along the Watchtower]

To finish off this post, let's return to *Blonde on Blonde*, and that wonderful concert at Bethleham, Pennsylania on the 13th of December. Rainy Day Woman 12 & 35 is one of Dylan's funniest, most irreverent songs. 'Everybody must get stoned' became something of a rallying cry for all stoners, most of whom didn't get the more shadowy implication that to 'get stoned' also meant to be killed by stoning, an Old testament punishment. I like the story, true or not, that when the police busted The Rolling Stones in 1966 this song was playing full bore. A bit of an embarrasment, really.

This is a wonderful performance of the song, with the audience once more singing along on the punchline. This is pretty close to the in-your-face irreverence of the original, but after a minute and a half Dylan gives up singing and the song turns into an instrumental. Everybody's having a great time, and Mr Guitar Man excells himself for the next five minutes. It's a rough and rowdy goodbye.

[Rainy Day Woman]

So ends our account of the NET, 1995, a year in which Dylan's voice broke through the constrictions of previous years, building solidly on his 1994 performances. And the band feels happily at home in his material. Dylan's performances reach certain peak in 1995. There would be more peaks to come, but in 1996 new elements enter Dylan's great muscial adventure.

Until then, good luck and stay safe.

Kia Ora

1996

NET 1996: Part 1 - Busy being born, With Al Kooper in Liverpool

'It might look like I'm moving
but I'm standing still'

By Mike Johnson (Kiwipoet)

'It is not a year remembered with great fondness by
most long-term fans. In contrast to the innovation and

stellar performing levels of most of 1995, it was all too predictable; same band, same set structure, and not many song debuts. Overall the shows were solid enough, but, as in late '93 and periods of '94, just not particularly special. More alarmingly, some of the overlong, uninspired, unproductive guitar instrumentals were reappearing too.'

-Andrew Muir, One More Night: Bob Dylan's Never Ending Tour

Doesn't sound too hopeful, does it? From Muir's point of view, having reached a peak in 1995, Dylan had nowhere left to go but down. With dogged inspiration Dylan had led the band on its rising curve from 1991 to 1995, but without some new input or change, he could at best mark time. And of course he is talking about our Mr Guitar Man, Bob himself, when he identifies 'overlong, uninspired, unproductive guitar instrumentals' although he doesn't say so.

There tends to be more guitar work in 1996, as Dylan uses the harmonica less. For the next couple of years the harp would fall out of favour. CS, the anonymous compiler at A Thousand Highways, has a gentler perspective:

'1996 was not an especially noteworthy year of performances for Bob Dylan, though it would be the last full year of touring before Dylan shifted towards performing new and traditional material with his 1997 release of Time Out Of Mind. In the interim, he and his band stuck to the sound they had established over the past two years.'

In other words, Dylan was on the edge of another great leap forward. Tony Attwood, Editor of *Untold Dylan*, puts it this way:

'Bob Dylan toured consistently in 1996 from April through to August, before finally taking a break. And at this point, for the first time in over five years, he started writing and recording new songs again, and from this we have the first set of songs that became

Time out of Mind. The re-writing of the songs, plus the addition of new compositions, continued through to 1997, but 1996 clearly marks not just the end of Dylan's longest period without writing songs at all but the emergence of a new way of writing songs about moving on – and despair.'

Time Out of Mind, starting to incubate in Dylan's mind in 1996, would not be just another Dylan album, but arguably the darkest, most despairing album Dylan ever cut, although *Blonde on Blonde* (1966) and *Street Legal* (1978) are rivals for that distinction. I bear that in mind when watching some of Dylan's stony-faced performances of 1996 (The Hyde Park performances, for example, twenty minutes of which you can find on You Tube). We can only assume that Dylan was performing in the face of that despair during 1996.

However, as with other lesser years of the NET, we find a number of treasures and standout performances. There are also some concerts well worth tuning into. A standout in my mind are the Liverpool concerts of the 26th and 27th of June, when he was joined by his organist from the 1960s, Al Kooper, who came up with that famous organ opening to the album version of 'Like A Rolling Stone'.

These performances may not have the aura of magic of the Prague concerts of 1995, but if this is another day at the office for Dylan, these Liverpool performances are pretty damn good. New cracks are beginning to appear in his voice. The voice we hear on *Time Out of Mind* is far from the clear, high tones of 1995, but this is not the scratchiness of the early nineties, rather the beginning of a new stage or new maturity in his voice. There is no loss of power and conviction.

I see 1996 as a year of consolidation and preparation. There was, however, some innovation and experiment. Remember that bouncy 'Positively 4th Street' from the 1965/66 era. It is a song of complaint about the betrayal of a friendship. I liked the studio version as its message is at odds with the happy sounding music, creating a pleasing disjunction. Here, however, Dylan has slowed down the tempo and drawn it out, and it sounds less happily vicious. Great to hear Al Kooper doing the opening chords. (June 26th)

[Positively 4th Street]

Some of the songs get a bit of a country twist. That works brilliantly for 'Watching the River Flow', which up to this point has been given the full rock treatment. This may well be the most successful adaptation of this wonderful paean to indolence. Impossible not to enjoy this fast paced performance. Great work from the steel guitar. (Also from June 26th)

[Watching the River Flow]

A bit of country twang works well too for 'She Belongs to Me'. Almost sounds like a love song with that lazy beat and a vocal performance that reeks of regret.

[She belongs to Me]

Staying with the June 26th concert, and Al Kooper's backing, we come to that magnificent tale of temptation and loss, 'Man in the Long Black Coat'. This version doesn't have the soaring harmonica of the unforgettable 1995 Prague performances, but Dylan's vocal compares favourably to any previous performances. Beautifully atmospheric.

[Man in the Long Black Coat]

'Silvio', co-written with the Grateful Dead's Robert Hunter, makes for a great rock song. To my mind, these early performances of the song are the best. In later years it was to become a bit of beaty filler, but here (June 26th) we hear it fresh and full of life. I read that Hunter wrote the lyrics and Dylan wrote the music, but find that kind of hard to believe given how Dylan-like the lyrics are:

> 'I give what I got until I got no more
> I take what I get until I even the score
> You know I love you and further more
> When it is time to go you got an open door
>
> I can tell you fancy I can tell you plain

You give something up for everything you gain
Since every pleasure's got an edge of pain
Pay for your ticket and don't complain'

I'm not complaining, but can you see anything there that doesn't sound like Dylan? Hunter channeling Dylan? He was to do it again with Dylan in 2009 with the album Together Through Life.

[Silvio]

'Seven Days' was written back in 1976, and first performed in that year, but rarely played during the NET. This is one of Dylan's orphan songs, never recorded in a studio, and only known through the few performances of it. And yet it is a powerful expression of desire for an absent lover, and would have fitted the *Desire* album perfectly. It captures that impatience we feel anticipating the arrival of a lover. Joe Cocker did a great live performance of the song in 1982. This 1996 performance is as good as any with its descending guitar line. (June 27th)

[Seven Days]

'Drifter's Escape' was first played live in 1992, but rarely performed until 1996. It's another madcap tale from 1967. The website Songfacts makes this comment:

> 'The surreal absurdity of the song has been compared to the writing of Franz Kafka. Its ambiguous nature has provoked all manner of analyses. Some critics have noted that the song mirrored Dylan's own experience with the media and his fans and critics (which seemed to overlap more frequently than one might expect).'

From 1996, over the next few years, Dylan was to develop the song into a hard-hitting and powerful rocker. This particular arrangement was only to last for a couple years, and features some full-on rock harp. (26th July)

[Drifter's Escape]

'Ramona', a 1960s favourite, has been performed some 380 times. This 1996 performance is certainly no better than the 1995 version, but it's a solid performance. Again, don't be deceived into thinking that this is a love song. It may arise out of love, but is a song of admonition, and a warning not to be deceived by the appearances of life. (27th June)

[Ramona]

The arrangement of 'Masters of War' that Dylan came up with in 1995 for his stunning London performance of that year was pretty much the same as this 1996 version, minus the harp. Its surging, menacing beat is perfect for this song, one of Dylan's most explicit protest, anti war songs . As long as we have war, and companies manufacturing weapons for profit, this song will be playing in the background. As eternally true as warmongering itself. (26th June)

[Masters of War]

Andrew Muir, in the front quote to this article, says that there were not many debut songs in 1996. Well, one of those 'not many' is 'Alabama Getaway', another Grateful Dead, Robert Hunter song. It's a zany little number with Dylanlike, absurdist lyrics. It's a good spot to pause in this look at Dylan's Liverpool performances of 1996.

[Alabama Getaway]

I'll be back shortly to look further at the performances from that concert.

Kia Ora

NET 1996: Part 2 – More Liverpool

By Mike Johnson (Kiwipoet)

In the previous post we saw that although 1996 does not have a good reputation among Dylan commentators, the performances are solid and workmanlike. They are not as inspired as some of the 1995 performances, but you don't always need inspiration to bring these songs to life.

One way or another, acoustic or electric, Dylan has pounded the hell out of a core group of songs that have proved indestructible. Unless Dylan is in very bad form, which despite rumours to the contrary doesn't happen that often, the inspiration of the song itself will carry it in performance. Over the long term, it's the greatness of the songs themselves that shines through.

A perfect example of this is 'Girl from the North Country.' Written in 1963, this song has the feel of a timeless classic. Fond remembrance is the emotion it evokes, and every time I listen to it in various performances, it works the same magic. This is from June 26th.

[Girl from the North Country]

I have chosen the two Liverpool performances (26th, 27th of June) as they are perhaps the most typically representative of that year. Not breathtaking, but solid and satisfying. Dylan sounds fully committed to the vocal and his guitar picking is just as complex and dissonant as ever.

What I've said about 'Girl from the North Country', you could say about 'Don't Think Twice', a song from the same era. It suits the upbeat performance we find here, the audience is quite delighted with Dylan's spirited vocal and keen to join in. The darkness of the song is buoyed by the brisk pace. This wonderful performance reminds me, in spirit, of the 1964 upbeat performances. (June 26th)

[Don't Think Twice]

Let's make that three in a row by listening to 'It Ain't Me, Babe' (27th June). For me this song is about shrugging off all of those things people project onto you, about who you are and what kind of person you are. The singer's not buying into any hippie idealizations of love. Dylan's disenchantment with the more doozie aspects of the mid-sixties youth moment shows in this song.

At eleven and a half minutes, this is another epic performance. I might have wanted a little less guitar, but Mr Guitar Man was very much to the fore in 1996. Dylan works hard at these guitar breaks which Andrew Muir in his book on the Never Ending Tour describes as 'overlong, uninspired, unproductive', and while I'm not as set in my opinion as Muir, I do wonder what Dylan was intending or doing with these breaks, and his guitar work in general, both acoustic and electric. There is a driving quality to them that's hard to shake.

[It Ain't Me, Babe]

'My Back Pages' is credited with being the first song in which Dylan confronts his disillusion with the counterculture and his move away from the moral certainties of the protest movement. Its famous refrain 'I was so much older then/I'm younger than that now' suggests a return to a more open-ended view of the world.

This performance, from June 26th. Once more the audience joins in. It's not the most accessible of Dylan's songs, but here he makes it sound almost homely and familiar. Once of the reasons I like the Liverpool performances is the audience's response to the songs. This would have been a wonderful concert to attend as there is a special rapport between Dylan and his audience. This rapport gives these performances their singular feel.

[My Back Pages]

This 'When I Paint my Masterpiece' is one of my favourite versions of the song. It's carried along by a slow, easy beat and the lyrics come across sharp and clear. The perfections of the imagined masterpiece are contrasted to the messy imperfections and craziness of life. The nice paradox is that the song itself is a masterpiece in which the disparate elements of an itinerant life come into a momentary balance. (27th June)

[When I paint my Masterpiece]

In 1995 Dylan perfected a slow, thoughtful version of 'Mr Tambourine Man' that stands in contrast to the bright, assertive performance on the album (1965). The song is about surrender to the deeper, more magical forces of life, and must be counted as one of Dylan's top ten songs. It paves the way for much darker songs like 'Desolation Row' and 'Visions of Johanna'. These long, slow versions accentuate the yearning in the song, and the weariness explicit in the lyrics. Arguably, the original version was too bright and bouncy for the lyrics, although the 'skipping reels of rhyme' work with a faster pace.

I like these slower paced versions as they immerse me deeper into the song, and those lyrics are good enough to linger over and be savoured. (July 27th)

[Mr Tambourine Man]

Staying in the sixties, but moving away from acoustic performances, we once more encounter 'Ballad of a Thin Man,' Dylan's great ode to strangeness. The song lands us squarely in the circus world of geeks (circus performers who bite off the heads of chickens for the delight of audiences), freaks and other strangers. Anyone who's been pushed way out of their comfort zone will relate to this story, and, along with some other commentators, I can't help thinking that the Mr Jones of the song is not some convention bound reporter or squarehead but a freaked out kid from Hibbing.

Always good as a heavy, though slow rocker, this performance doesn't disappoint. I don't think any live performance has captured the sinister spooky atmosphere of the album version, but there's plenty of fright and anger in it, and Al Kooper is on home ground with his thumping organ. (27th July)

[Ballad of a Thin Man]

I've always had a soft spot for the song 'Under the Red Sky' from the album of that name (1991). There is a beautiful but world weary whimsicality to it, with its children's song, fairy-tale like structure and imagery. This performance brings out all the gentleness and the reflective quality of the song. It's a sad little number with a mysterious heart.

[Under the Red Sky]

Ah! Where would we be without a scintillating rendition of 'Tangled Up In Blue'? While my personal favourite for this kaleidoscope of a song, at least for the nineties, remains the 1993 performance, with Mr Guitar Man's whacky break and a brilliant harp break (See NET, 1993, part 1), this 1996 version can stand proudly with any previous versions, including the glittering Prague performances of 1995. You might have heard it a hundred times before, and Dylan might have played it a thousand times before, but from those opening chords tipping you headlong into the song, you're a goner until the final, grand chord sounds. Whew! What a trip.

[Tangled Up In Blue]

I was going to leave out this performance of 'John Brown' one of Dylan's great protest songs, as Dylan's voice feels under-recorded, and I didn't think it was quite up to scratch. Listening to it again now, however, I think it is worth inclusion, although I prefer the MTV Unplugged performance from 1994. The band sounds great, giving the song a relentless forward movement, with Tony Garnier providing a dark undertone by using the bow on the double bass. (27th July)

[John Brown]

Dylan finished off his two day gig at Liverpool with an abrasive 'Maggie's Farm.' This song was meant to be rough and rowdy and in your face. The phantasmagoric American family it portrays are a danger to your body and your soul. Better to get out quick while the going is good. This song is similar in spirit and imagery to 'On the Road Again,' (Subterranean Homesick Blues, 1965) which to my knowledge Dylan hasn't performed live. In it he sings, 'You ask why I don't live here/ Honey, how come you don't move?'

[Maggie's Farm]

That's it for Liverpool, 1996. Soon we'll be back to consider the Berlin concert from that year and other goodies. In the meantime, keep listening and stay clear of the plague.

Kia Ora

NET 1996: Part 3 – Berlin and Beyond

By Mike Johnson (Kiwipoet)

While I have taken the Liverpool concerts at the end of June as representative of Dylan's 1996 form (see NET, 1996, parts 1 and 2), those concerts may not have been the very best of that year. Many commentators point to the Berlin concert earlier in June, on the 17th, as being the high point of the year.

Certainly the recordings are better, so the performances come over more clearly and sharply. The song Dylan used to kick off the Berlin show, 'Drifter's Escape' is a good example. The Liverpool performance (See NET, 1996, part 1) sounds very similar to this one, even the harp break is the same, but this Berlin performance certainly has the edge.

[Drifter's Escape]

The same applies to 'Watching the River Flow.' The same countrified arrangement as in Liverpool, very similar vocals, with perhaps a bit more energy than the Liverpool concert. This is a real pleasure to listen to. I think this arrangement gives rise to Dylan's best performances of the song. While it suited to some extent the hard rock treatment he'd been giving it, there is a levity, a devil-may-care attitude in the song which suits this lighter treatment.

[Watching the River Flow]

One song that did not appear in Liverpool setlists is 'Seeing the Real You at Last' (from Empire Burlesque, 1985). Dylan is consistently concerned with false versus true appearances, being real in the world and true to oneself. This spirit animates many of Dylan's so called finger pointing songs like 'Like A Rolling Stone'.

Behind many Dylan songs, no matter how complex, there lies a recognizable, common emotion or experience. I'm sure many of us know what it's like to suddenly see somebody in a new, more real light. It's not a pleasant sensation, not if we've been seeing someone through rose-coloured glasses.

Dylan has often performed this song in a strident or triumphant tone. Ha ha! Now I've seen the real you! Here, however, we find a softer, more reflective performance. It's been a long time coming, honey, but now I see who you really are. The lyrics are studded with lines from tough-guy style, late 1940s movies.

[Seeing the Real You at Last]

'Friend of the Devil' is another Grateful Dead, Robert Hunter song, but Dylan makes a few changes to the lyrics. This verse from the Grateful Dead reads:

> 'I ran down to the levee
> But the Devil caught me there
> He took my twenty dollar bill
> And he vanished in the air'

Dylan changes that to:

> 'I went down to the crossroads
> and the devil met me there
> took my twenty dollar bill
> and vanished in the air'

'Crossroads' evokes that famous blues song of that name by Robert Johnson. He sang:

> 'Standin' at the crossroad, baby, risin' sun goin' down
> Standin' at the crossroad, baby, eee-eee, risin' sun goin' down
> I believe to my soul, now, poor Bob is sinkin' down'

[Friend of the Devil]

Another song not performed at Liverpool is that mysterious Sixties classic 'Love Minus Zero'. Since 1994 Dylan had been cultivating a slow version of the song, savouring each one of those puzzling lines. While 'She Belongs to Me' (also of the 1965 Subterranean Homesick Blues album) warns of the dangers of adoration, 'Love minus Zero' expresses and celebrates that adoration. When we love someone with sufficient intensity, they take on a mysterious quality which in turn suffuses and colours our vision of the world itself.

> 'The wind howls like a hammer
> the night blows cold and rainy
> my love she's like some raven
> at my window with a broken wing.'

I couldn't ask more of this lovingly delivered performance except perhaps a harp break at the end.

[Love Minus Zero]

1996 was a big year for 'Positively 4th Street,' one of Dylan's great sarcastic songs. Yet, as we saw with the Liverpool performance, these 1996 versions go beyond the whining sarcasm of the original 1965 recording. Performed more slowly and thoughtfully, the complaint goes deeper and we catch a glimpse of moral outrage at hypocritical, callous behaviour. I like the song better this way. It rubs off the nasty edge of the song, and takes us to that sinking feeling we get when we know we've been shafted.

[Positively 4th Street]

I must have introduced that kaleidoscope of life lived, that compelling foot-tapper of a song 'Tangled Up In Blue' at least a dozen times since starting this series, and every time I think 'this is a version that will blow everybody's socks off' and every time I am right. This is the performance of all performances that will blow you away, just like a last one. Another epic not to be skipped. Listen to how Mr Guitar Man drives the song forward with his relentless picking at a few notes, and how Dylan's harp achieves a beautiful balance between restraint and ecstasy.

[Tangled Up In Blue]

I'd like to leave the Berlin concert with this slow 'Queen Jane Approximately'. It's an invitation to share a world-weariness which sounds aged but has been a part of Dylan's emotional mix right from the start. I'm reminded of 'One Too Many Mornings'. However it goes deeper in suggesting that only when you have reached the depths of existential despair and alienation should you get in touch with me. Then we will have something to share. When you've had enough of the world and all its uses, come see me. As in 'It Ain't Me, Babe', Dylan takes a sideswipe at hippie idealism.

> 'Now, when all of the flower ladies want back what they have lent you
> And the smell of their roses does not remain...'

I don't think you'll find a more tenderhearted performance of the song than this ten and half minute, gorgeously sung version.

[Queen Jane]

I'm sorry I don't have the performance date for this wonderful acoustic version of 'To Ramona'. We know that Dylan no longer stands alone before an audience with just acoustic guitar and harmonica, but this performance comes the closest of any I've heard to capturing that quality. The common complaint that Dylan never sounds the way he used to, or sings the songs the way he used to, doesn't stand up in this case. Except for that crack of age in his voice, it's eerie how like a sixties performance this is.

The harp break is a rare treat, as this song usually lacks the harp. To me, despite the harshness of it, this performance is more loving and accepting than the original. The recording itself is a bit on the hard, metallic side. The song is unsettling in its accusations but not without compassion.

[To Ramona]

Again, I don't know the date of this powerful performance of that rarity 'Born in Time'. In performance Dylan's soft approach to the vocals can mean his voice gets overwhelmed by the band. This doesn't happen here.

In this case the sharpness of the recording works in our favour. Although the song is from Under the Red Sky (1991), it always sounds to me as if it were written later. It wouldn't go amiss on Time Out of Mind:

> 'In the hills of mystery,
> In the foggy web of destiny,
> You can have what's left of me,
> Where we were born in time.'

The seeds of the despair in Time Out of Mind, which Dylan started writing in 1996, can be found in the earlier album.

[Born in Time}

'The Ballad of Hollis Brown' is a masterpiece of storytelling. It tells of one desperate man's build up to murder and suicide, a crime born out of poverty. The plight of this small farmer has its roots in the 1930s depression, and the imagery of the song echoes the same era.

> 'The rats have got your flour
> Bad blood it got your mare
> The rats have got your flour
> Bad blood it got your mare
> If there's anyone that knows
> Is there anyone that cares?'

Coming from the same place, Harlan Howard wrote 'Busted' probably about a year before Dylan wrote 'Hollis Brown'. 'Busted' was sung by Johnny Cash and Ray Charles:

> 'My bills are all due and the baby needs shoes and I'm busted
> Cotton is down to a quarter a pound, but I'm busted
> I got a cow that went dry and a hen that won't lay
> A big stack of bills that gets bigger each day
> The county's gonna haul my belongings away cause I'm busted'

Unlike the Harlan Howard song, however, which is a long recitation of woes, Dylan's song builds narrative tension to a shattering climax.

> 'Way out in the wilderness
> A cold coyote calls
> Way out in the wilderness
> A cold coyote calls
> Your eyes fix on the shotgun
> That's hanging on the wall
>
> Your brain is a-bleedin'
> And your legs can't seem to stand
> Your brain is a-bleedin'
> And your legs can't seem to stand
> Your eyes fix on the shotgun
> That you're holding in your hand'

How wonderfully (in narrative terms) that shotgun moves from the wall into his hands as if by its own volition. I love the hard rock version Dylan did in 1974, because of its cracking pace, but this slower paced performance is just as relentless, and the band echoes the sound of those early blues records. Forget you are in 1996, you could be in 1936. Wonderfully rough and hard-edged. (2nd July)

[Ballad of Hollis Brown]

I would like to leave this post on an exciting note, what I believe to be the first ever live performance of 'This Wheel's On Fire' from *The Basement Tapes* (1967). The lyrics of this song are obscure, and point to events hidden from our sight by a veil of coded language:

> 'If your memory serves you well
> I was going to confiscate your lace
> And wrap it up in a sailor's knot
> And hide it in your case
> If I knew for sure that it was yours
> But it was oh so hard to tell
> But you knew that we would meet again

If your memory serves you well‘

It is uncertain if the anticipated next meeting will be a pleasant one. Maybe not. But what is certain is that this is a powerful song, serving as a reminder and a warning, a warning not to forget 'favours' done. Dark circumstances are hinted at.

I can't help feeling that it is no accident that Dylan returned to this song in the year he was to write most of Time out of Mind. The darkness of the lyrics suits the flavour of the new album that is brewing. This performance has a wonderfully gutsy sound, quite distinct from what has come before, and foreshadowing what is to come in later years.

[This Wheel's On Fire]

Catch you next post, when I will be wrapping up 1996.

Kia Ora

NET 1996: Part 4 - In the House of Blues Forever

By Mike Johnson (Kiwipoet)

Dylan's stint in Atlanta, at the House of the Blues (August 3rd and 4th), gave rise to some solid and even outstanding performances, and we are lucky enough to have some of these on video. My favourite is this impassioned performance of 'My Back Pages', Dylan's awakening in 1964 to moral complexity and the failure of a simple, black and white view of the world. We see here Dylan's restless style, and his one-handed harp playing – harp and microphone in one hand. The harp break is sharp and trenchant. As usual I've added the audio file in case the video vanishes.

[My Back Pages]

Another video worth watching is this 'To Be Alone With You,' a light-hearted love song from *Nashville Skyline* (1969) which takes on a harder edge in this poker-faced performance. Dylan doesn't expend energy needlessly on stage, which may be the secret of his longevity as a performer. It's a good song to kick off the concert as the 'you' in the song could be read as the audience. It's a good song to get people jiving and in the mood for some Dylan.

> 'To Be Alone With You
> At the close of the day
> With only you in view
> While evening slips away
> It only goes to show
> That while life's pleasures be few
> The only one I know
> Is when I'm alone with you'

[To Be Alone With You]

Time now to check out some of the usual suspects, songs that Dylan has been cultivating from the start of the NET and which regularly show up on his setlists. A core of songs, mainly from the sixties and seventies around which his concerts are built. If you have the patience, it's fascinating to follow these songs through the years, how they change over time.

One of the songs that doesn't change a lot, although we get both electric and acoustic versions, is 'Gates of Eden'. Dylan would continue to plumb the mystery and menace of this song right through to 2001. One of Dylan's great strengths is the ability to express a profound alienation from the world. 'Gates of Eden' hits both the unreal and horrific nature of the world and our separation from it.

> 'The foreign sun, it squints upon
> A bed that is never mine
> As friends and other strangers
> From their fates try to resign
> Leaving men wholly, totally free
> To do anything they wish to do but die
> And there are no trials inside the Gates of Eden'

Those two lines, 'Leaving men wholly, totally free/ to do anything they wish to do but die,' are a neat summing up of the kind of existentialism encountered in Jean Paul Sartre and Albert Camus, writers very much in the air in the mid sixties. At the same time, these lines foreshadow the biblically rooted sentiment we would later find in 'Precious Angel' (1979), 'Can they imagine the darkness that will fall from on high/When men will beg God to kill them and they won't be able to die.'

While I love the dark, plunging electric performance of 1988 (See NET, 1988, part 1), I think it's these minimal, acoustic versions that move me the most. No drums, a gentle sound, with Mr Guitar Man excelling himself picking thoughtfully around the melody. (date unknown)

[Gates of Eden]

Also in a quiet, reflective mood is this 'Shelter from the Storm.' This is a good example of the quiet electric sound. You think for a moment that it is acoustic. Again, while I like the fast, upbeat performances of the song, and the hammering performance form the Rolling Thunder Tour, I think the slower, thoughtful performances such as this one suit the song best. This song is surely a candidate for Dylan's best 1970's love song, maybe his best ever, particularly if we count the wry humour behind the lyrics.

> 'Suddenly I turned around and she was standin' there
> With silver bracelets on her wrists and flowers in her hair
> She walked up to me so gracefully and took my crown of thorns
> Come in, she said
> I'll give ya shelter from the storm'

While Dylan gave the hippie, flower-power philosophy short shrift in the 1960s, here the hippy chick is reborn as a goddess, goddess of protection and maybe even salvation, although that's a big ask. Be careful what you ask for, as they say:

> 'In a little hilltop village, they gambled for my clothes
> I bargained for salvation and she gave me a lethal dose'

[Shelter from the Storm]

Never too far away from 'Shelter from the Storm', you will find 'If You See Her Say Hello', another song about what once was. If you listen to the evolution of the song on the compilation More Blood More Tracks you can hear Dylan trying out the song with a number of different moods and tempos. Slow it down and you accentuate the nostalgia; speed it up and it sounds more like a happy hour recollection. Dylan keeps this one fast and upbeat, giving it a bit of a country touch. A lovely, generous, magnanimous song. I'm not quite sure than I believe the sentiment, it's a bit too nice for me, but I'm happy to try it on for size (July 3rd)

[If You See Her Say Hello]

There is something epic in the chord structure of 'Tears of Rage' so we don't mind getting a nine and half minute performance. The editor of *Untold Dylan*, Tony Attwood, has a fine discussion of the chord changes, but flounders a bit when it comes to the song's meaning, as indeed do I.

What I do get is the sense of betrayal, of selling out to greed, materialism and 'false instructions'.

I could take a stab at it, and suggest that if the song were sung by George Washington, or rather the ghost of George Washington, or one of the founding fathers of America, and if the 'daughter' were America, then the song would make some kind of sense. The betrayal would be the way America has betrayed the ideals of the founding fathers, and the upsurge of hope on Independence Day. As it stands, however, the song works on an emotional level and we can't say exactly why. (Date unknown)

[Tears of Rage]

'What Good Am I?' is an unusual song in Dylan's canon. He doesn't usually question himself, or his own veracity, in quite this way. We all know what it feels like to have to face the way in which we have ignored or sidelined important things. Facing that inner uselessness is not an easy thing to do. Sung in a hard, waspish voice, as we heard in 1989 and 1990, the song comes across as a bitter self accusation. Here, it is much more gentle, and our sins of omission sad rather than anything else. While I think the instrumental break goes on for too long at the end, Dylan's singing is soft and sensitive, a beautiful and therefore painful probing of our shortcomings. (date unknown)

[What Good Am I]

GE Smith tells a story of how, back in 1988, when he was auditioning for the role of Dylan's guitarist, Dylan played nothing but 'Pretty Peggy-O' over and over again. Smith comments that Dylan must have liked the song very much. And indeed it seems he does, for of all the folk songs he learned before starting to write songs himself, 'Pretty Peggy-O' survives and has been performed from time to time.

This song originated in Scotland several hundred years ago. Here's a summary of the story.

> 'The song is a fairly standard trooper-and-maid story: that is, soldier passes through town, soldier seduces girl, soldier is ordered to leave, girl says hey I'm pregnant, soldier says tough

luck and marches away. In some versions the girl follows him, though only for a little while, but in most versions she ends up abandoned.'

It's fun to look at the original Scottish lyrics. Here are the first couple of verses:

There once was a troop o' Irishdragoons
Cam marching doon through Fyvie-o
And the captain's fa'en in love wi' a very bonnie lass
And her name it was ca'd pretty Peggy-o

There's many a bonnie lass in the Howe o Auchterless
There's many a bonnie lass in the Garioch
There's many a bonnie Jean in the streets of Aiberdeen
But the floower o' them aw lies in Fyvie-o

Once the song migrated to America, various lyrical variations occurred, Dylan's cryptic version being one of them. Here are Dylan's opening verses:

I've been around this whole country
But I never yet found Fenneario.

Well, as we marched down, as we marched down
Well, as we marched down to Fennerio'
Well, our captain fell in love with a lady like a dove
Her name that she had was Pretty Peggy-O

Well, what will your mother say, what will your mother say
What will your mother say, Pretty Peggy-O
What will your mother say to know you're going away
You're never, never, never coming back-io ?

The story is not so much told as alluded to in Dylan's inimitable way. What is fascinating about this 1996 performance is that Dylan makes further lyrical variations which have not been written down. I don't have the ear to transcribe them all, but if you look at Dylan's known variation as you listen to this, you will be able to hear the differences. In Dylan's hands it becomes a Civil War ballad, and my suggestion here is that it underlays a group of songs with a historical aspect that he wrote while writing the *Time Out of Mind* songs. Songs such as 'Red River Shore', 'Girl on the Green Briar Shore' and 'Cross the Green Mountain' all seem to relate or look back to 'Pretty Peggy-O'. (date unknown)

[Pretty Peggy-O[

When looking at Dylan's 1995 performances, we highlighted two versions of 'The Times They Are A-Changing' (NET, 1995 parts 1 and 5) and noted how the song itself is a-changing in mood as the times change. By the mid nineties the song is no longer a rallying cry for action, but an occasion for nostalgia for those earlier, more radical times. The audience sings along on the chorus and a little sadness enters. It is both sad and uplifting at the same time.

In 1996 Dylan keeps the same, slow-paced arrangement, but for this performance he is joined onstage by two members of the Dave Matthews Band, a saxophonist and a violinist. You don't hear much of the sax, but the violin, after a tentative start, adds a melancholy strain to the song in perfect keeping with the mood. It's that violin that lifts this performance above others like it. He gets the words a bit mixed up, but that harp break cuts to the heart. The audience loves it and so do I. Enjoy. (July 3rd)

[The Times They Are A-Changing]

I've been holding back this one so that I can end this post, and our visit to the NET in 1996, with a real blast. It's 'Rainy Day Woman' like you've never heard it. It's got all of the insouciant lurch of the original, album version with the added dimension of the Dave Mathews band joining in, particularly the sax.

My usually reliable info sources tell me that Dylan is joined by a saxophone and a violin, but I can't hear the violin. The rollicking, instrumental break that begins at about 4.10 mins, seems to have two saxes, both wailing away in fine blues jazz style. It's over to your ear on that one. Whatever, it's a helluva way to go out, all that swagger and vigour, that

screaming sax.
Makes you wonder what's around the corner in 1997.

See you then.

[Rainy Day Woman]

Kia Ora

1997

NET 1997: Part 1 - The Lonely Graveyards of the Mind

By Mike Johnson (Kiwipoet)

> 'While I'm strolling through the lonely graveyard of my mind
> I left my life with you somewhere back there along the line
> I thought somehow that I would be spared this fate
> But I don't know how much longer I can wait'

1997 was a big and varied year for Bob Dylan. In September the album he'd been working on since August 1996, *Time Out of Mind* was released, his first since Under the Red Sky in 1991. This meant it was only later in the year that some of the songs from the new album made their way into the concerts. As well as a few of the new songs, Dylan introduced a couple of older songs he's never performed, most importantly 'Blind Willie McTell'. 'The Wicked Messenger', also, which hadn't been performed since 1987 I believe, was to become a staple over the next few years.

There were also some changes to the make up of his band, also the first since 1991. Larry Campbell joined in March, replacing John Jackson, and in October 1996 David Kemper took over the drums from Winston Watson. Watson has been criticised for being too heavy-handed on the drums. That heavy-handedness worked brilliantly for some performances – try 'I and I' in 1993 (see NET 1993, part 1) – but perhaps didn't always work so well. However you feel about that, Kemper did bring a new sensitivity to the drums, which subtly altered the sound of the band.

Larry Campbell, who would stay with Dylan through to 2004, is generally considered to be a better guitarist than John Jackson. I think Jackson did his best guitar work for Dylan in 1993, when Dylan was veering towards the jazzy side. Campbell is also credited with being a multi-instrumentalist. Wikipedia comments: 'Campbell expanded the role to multi-instrumentalist, playing instruments such as cittern, violin/fiddle, pedal steel guitar, lap steel guitar, mandolin, banjo, and slide guitar,' but I'm not sure of the accuracy of that. Bucky Baxter was retained as steel guitarist, and is also credited with playing dobro, pedal steel guitar and mandolin for Dylan.

In addition 1997 was the year the apparently unstoppable Dylan ended up in hospital with a chest infection. Official statements indicated that the ailment was histoplasmosis, a fungal infection of the lung that causes swelling of the pericardium, the sac surrounding the heart. After recovering, and going back on the road Dylan's only comment was: 'Thought I was going to see Elvis.'

Finally, in 1997, Dylan performed before Pope John Paul II, at the Piazza Maggiore in Bologna, with an audience of 400,000. (Sept 27th) The performances were not as outstanding as the occasion.

The anonymous CM, of the website A Thousand Highways, flatly declares that '1997 is one of the best years of Bob Dylan's NeverEnding

Tour.' I don't entirely agree, but I'm happy to put it to the test in the next few posts.

Let's start with those new songs from Time out of Mind. The first track of the album is 'Love Sick', a song which would undergo many changes in the next ten years. Dylan has indicated that he believes 'Love Sick' to be one of the few songs he's written that might be worthy of inclusion in what is loosely called the Great American Songbook. In the song we drift like ghosts through the nighttime world, observing the rites of humanity as if from afar.

> 'I see
> I see lovers in the meadow
> I see
> I see silhouettes in the window
> I watch them 'til they're gone
> And they leave me hangin' on
> To a shadow'

'Love Sick' is an astonishing and dramatic introduction to the despair and alienation of the album, setting the tone for the coming songs. Its slow, heavy, death-march beat, and sudden reversal at the very end, all make for one of Dylan's most memorable songs.

Dylan exploits a possible ambiguity in the term 'Love Sick' which he creates for the song. During most of the song he uses the term to mean being sick of love, which is not the conventional meaning of the term. Only at the very end does the sentiment return to the normal meaning of the term, to feel sick from being in love. The misery of that last line changes the whole meaning of the song. He's sick of love because he's love sick, if you can make sense of that.

This first performance is from San Jose, 14th of November. He sticks pretty much to the studio arrangement. The backing is good, Larry Campbell emphasising the heavy grandeur of the chords and the emotional anguish of the vocals.

[Love Sick (A)]

Dylan sounds a bit wan, but that's at least partly how he's singing the song.

He really does sound like a wandering ghost. That effect may be, at least in part, a result of the recording. Here's another version from December the 18th (El Rey Theatre, Los Angeles) that's stronger and more upfront:

[Love Sick (B)]

Overall, however, we'll find that Dylan's vocals are nothing too special in 1997. He doesn't soar the way he did in 1995, and despite the energy of some of the performances, I get the feeling that Dylan is once more struggling with his voice. New cracks and fissures are opening up in his voice which will eventually lead, after 2004 or so, to his fully cracked, circus barker voice. To my ear, this is not the scratchiness of the early nineties, which he eventually overcame, but a more genuine ageing.

This is his *Time Out of Mind* voice, full of bitter experience and marinated in awareness of mortality. Arguably, Dylan's songs have never strayed too far from an awareness of mortality; what is different in *Time Out of Mind* is Dylan's response to ageing. It crops up directly in songs like 'It's Not Dark Yet' and 'Highlands,' but permeates the whole album, and is cultivated in his voice.

It's hard to match 'Can't Wait' for desperate weariness, both as a song and in performance. Different studio versions of the song found on *Tell Tale Signs* (a compilation of outtakes released in 2008) show Dylan working hard to find the right sound and tempo for the song, and that experimentation would continue right up to 2019. Dylan may never have settled on a particular arrangement and sound for the song, but the journey itself is a fascinating one.

Even during 1997 Dylan was trying out different paced performances. This first, fast tempo performance is from the highly regarded December 19th show at the El Rey Theatre in Los Angeles (There were three shows at El Ray, the 19th is the second of them.) It's full of verve, yet sung by a man sounding at the very end of this tether. Can't wait for what? Love? Death? The end of time? The end of mind? Whatever, it's a real kicker.

[Can't Wait (A)]

In tailoring this song for the stage, Dylan eschewed the swampy sound Lanois achieved on the album. This is much more raw. But he didn't always play it at this pace. Sometimes he slowed it down. This one's from the 24th of October. The slower pace enables Dylan to relish the despair of the song.

[Can't Wait (B)]

'Cold Irons Bound' is one of the most acknowledged songs on Time Out of Mind, and won Dylan a Grammy award. In the song the love sick poet, whose love is 'taking such a long time to die,' is likened to a prisoner chained in cold irons.

> 'One look at you and I'm out of control
> Like the universe has swallowed me whole
> I'm twenty miles out of town in cold irons bound'

While this state of mind might have been sparked by a love he couldn't kill, the feeling is universalised into a general sense of alienation from the world. The 'too many heads' refers to the Greek myth of a Hydra who would grow two new heads for every one chopped off. We find the same desperation here as in 'Can't Wait'.

> 'Oh, the winds in Chicago have torn me to shreds
> Reality has always had too many heads
> Some things last longer than you think they will
> There are some kind of things you can never kill'

This hard-driving rocker suits Dylan's snarling delivery perfectly. This is from the 11th of November, and had only been played a couple of times. It's fresh and full of fire.

[Cold Irons Bound (A)]

No less compelling is this performance from the 19th of December, the Los Angeles show.

[Cold Iron Bound (B)]

Until I heard the following performance, I'd always thought of the bluesy 'Till I Fell in Love with You' as one of the lesser tracks on Time Out of Mind. One of those fillers you get from time to time on Dylan albums. But this rough and tearing performance, plus another look at the lyrics, has convinced me otherwise.

The album version can't match the sheer raw power of this 19 of December Los Angeles performance. The throat-ripping vocal takes me back to the early days of the NET, 1988/89, and the lyrics are some of the very best in terms of how Dylan can convey his inner state by the condition of his body. Remember 'Mr Tambourine Man':

> 'My weariness amazes me
> I'm branded on my feet
> I have no one to meet
> And the ancient empty streets too dead for dreaming'

Compare that to this from 'Till I Fell'

> 'Well, my nerves are exploding
> And my body's tense
> I feel like the whole world
> Got me pinned up against the fence'

Dylan songs are full of references to, and the feeling of, entrapment; as he'd later put it in 'Mississippi' – nowhere to escape. 'Till I Fell...' gives powerful expression to the physicality of that feeling:

> 'Well junk is piling up
> Taking up space
> My eyes feel
> Like they're falling off my face
> Sweat falling down
> I'm staring at the floor
> I'm thinking about that girl
> Who won't be back no more'

At the risk of getting sidetracked, I'm reminded of these lyrics from 'Don't

Fall Apart on Me Tonight' from *Infidels* (1983), a song Dylan has never performed as far as I know.

> 'But it's like I'm stuck inside a painting
> That's hanging in the Louvre
> My throat start to tickle and my nose itches
> But I know that I can't move'

Anyway, here it is. I can't help feeling that this is what Dylan really had in mind for the song, the way it should sound, the emotions right up front, not buried in an echo chamber.

[Till I Fell in Love With You]

I'm running out space, but I want to finish this post with two performances of 'Blind Willie McTell', performed for the first time in 1997 and which would, over the coming years, be developed alongside the *Time Out of Mind* songs. Although written for *Infidels*, but never included on the album, it fits well with the dark aesthetic of *Time Out of Mind*.

> 'Well god is in his heaven
> And we are what was his
> But power and greed and corruptible seed seem to be all that there is'

The first performance is from the 5th of October. It swings along and Dylan is in great cracked-voice form.

[Blind Willie McTell (A)]

This second performance, from the 23rd of October, slows the pace down a fraction, giving Dylan more time to savour those wonderful lyrics. Some great guitar work on both these performances.

[Blind Willie McTell (B)]

I'll be back shortly with more exciting sounds from 1997.

Kia Ora

NET 1997: Part 2 – Hanging on to a shadow

By Mike Johnson (Kiwipoet)

Time Out of Mind came out in September 1997, and as far as I can tell, Dylan performed only four songs from the album in the last months of that year, Love Sick, Till I Fell in Love with you, Can't Wait and Cold Irons Bound. However he also brought forward some older songs he had never performed or rarely performed, such as 'Blind Willie McTell' (See NET, 1997, part 1) and 'This Wheel's On Fire.' He also covered quite a few songs by other artists. We get the feeling that in 1997 Dylan was attempting to widen his field and push his boundaries.

Let's begin with some of the Dylan songs that were new to performance. 'Wheels On Fire' was first performed in 1996 (see NET, 1996, part 3) and I commented on that gutsy performance. The 1997 performance is somewhat more lush due to some wonderful steel guitar work. The song was associated with The Band, who recorded it on their first album and, up until 1996, it had remained that way, the only Dylan performances being on *The Basement Tapes*. At the beginning of this performance Dylan introduces Rick Danko, his old drummer from The Band. It sounds as though Danko takes the drums for this one (Sorry don't have the date).

[Wheel's on Fire]

This captures all the allusiveness of the song. I miss the harmonica Dylan used to kick the song off in 1996, but Dylan does a great vocal here. In 1997 generally, Dylan didn't bring out the harp much. There are whole concerts played without it. Seems like Dylan had almost forgotten his trust little instrument.

'Tough Mama' has always been my favourite song off *Planet Waves* (1974), and I regret that Dylan only rarely performed it. For me, the song belongs to a small group of 'goddess songs', a particular kind of love song which celebrates the divine female. Others I would put in that group include Golden Loom, Isis and Shelter from the Storm. It sounds a bit like a throw-away rocker, but the lyrics are a stand out:

> Ashes in the furnace, dust on the rise,
> You came through it all the way, flyin' through the skies
> Dark beauty
> With that long night's journey in your eyes
>
> Sweet goddess
> Born of a blinding light and a changing wind,
> Now, don't be modest, you know who you are and where you've been.
> Jack the cowboy went up north
> He's buried in your past.
> The lone wolf went out drinking
> That was over pretty fast.

This performance is very close in tempo and spirit to the album version, and sounds suitably rough and road-worn.

[Tough Mama}

Another rarity is 'The Wicked Messenger' from *John Wesely Harding* (1967). The song seems to come out of the same box as 'All along the Watchtower' but has been overshadowed by that more famous song. Perhaps it's not quite as focused as 'Watchtower' and one can't help but wonder if the 'wicked messenger' is not Dylan himself in disguise as some Old Testament prophet.

> Oh, the leaves began to fallin'
> And the seas began to part
> And the people that confronted him were many
> And he was told but these few words
> Which opened up his heart
> If you can't bring good news, then don't bring any

This song would become a staple over the next few years, with constant changes in the arrangement. The vocal is done well, but Dylan was to move away from the kind of thump-bash arrangement we find here. This arrangement flattens out the drama of the lyrics, but it's a good place to start for this long neglected song.

[Wicked Messenger]

Dylan began performing 'Born in Time' in 1996 (See NET, 1996, part 3). I suggested that the song fits very well with the weary of love theme in Time out of Mind. The line 'You can take what's left of me...' is not exactly a seductive invitation. To be born in time is to be born into the death of love. The 'rising curve/where the ways of nature will test every nerve' doesn't leave much but the rag ends. The 1996 performance may be a little gentler than this one, but once more the tone is suitably weary and road worn. The steel guitar gives it a little touch of country music which does it no harm.

[Born in Time]

'One of Us Must Know (Sooner Or Later)' was performed over fifty times in 1978, and not again until 1997, when it was performed twice. The song is an apology, and maybe one of the least interesting songs from *Blonde on Blonde* (1966). It's hard to know what might have drawn Dylan back to this song after nearly twenty years. The weary, laid back treatment suits it well, however. (13th August)

[One of Us Must Know (Sooner Or Later)]

Easier to see what drew Dylan back to another *Blonde on Blonde* performance rarity, 'Pledging my Time,' a wonderful urban blues which neatly encapsulates the suffocating feeling of being trapped somewhere, at the party maybe, where you'd rather not be.

> Well, early in the morning
> To late at night
> I got a poison headache

But I feel alright

I don't know how you feel alright with a poison headache, but I guess if you're stoned enough it doesn't really matter. As so often with Dylan, he's telling as story but only alluding to it:

Well, they sent for the ambulance
Then one was sent
Somebody got lucky
But it was an accident

What exactly was going on in this stuffy room we can't know, but we can guess. You don't get those kind of headaches from drinking mineral water and breathing fresh air. The murkiness in all this is a perfect way of leading up the next song on the album, Visions of Johanna. This is a great version with Dylan in fine voice. There's nothing better to listen to on a pale afternoon than Dylan singing the blues. The band nails it too. (22nd of April)

[Pledging my Time]

Dylan revived 'The Ballad of Hollis Brown' in 1996 (See NET, 1996, Part 3). This performance is not cleanly recorded as the Berlin concert version of 1996, and feels a bit unrecorded, but it is still a magical piece of storytelling. It's in this song that Dylan blues roots in the 1930s shows. We could be back there in the dust bowl of the south listening some blues singer telling us his story.

[The Ballad of Hollis Brown]

Now we turn to some of songs not written by Dylan he covered in 1997, and after 'Hollis Brown,' 'Stone Wall and Steel Bars' by Ray Pennington and Roy Marcum and released in 1963 seems to fit nicely. Dylan first performs this song in 1997, doing it twelve times. Tony Attwood has an interesting discussion and background to the song (see: bob-dylan.org.uk/archives/11475). As with Blind Willie McTell and Born in Time, I see this song as fitting in very well with the *Time Out of Mind* ethos, and the musical tradition that album evokes. It's not a big jump from 'stone walls and steel bars' to 'cold irons bound.'

[Stone Walls and Steel Bars]

Another take on love, murder and betrayal can be found in Lefty Frizzell's 'Long Black Veil' from 1959. The song has a very Dylanish opening verse:

> Ten years ago, on a cold dark night
> Someone was killed, 'neath the town hall light
> There were few at the scene, but they all agreed
> That the slayer who ran, looked a lot like me

It's a great ghost story of a woman who haunts her lover's grave, a lover who died to save her from dishonour. It has a melancholy beauty. Like Stone Walls it takes us back to the music of a bye-gone era, the 1930s and 40s.

[Long black Veil]

'Shake Sugaree' was written by Elizabeth Cotton, and is squarely in the Country tradition. It's a song about pawning everything and having nothing. The feel of country music starts to come through Dylan performances in 1996, and in 1997 that tendency continues. It's there on *Time Out of Mind* in 'Dirt Road Blues,' which has never been performed.

[Shake Sugaree]

'Viola Lee Blues' written by Noah Lewis pushes us even further back into musical history, into the 1920s, the era of the jug band and country blues, an era that could have produced a song like 'Dirt Road Blues.'

Exploring his musical past is nothing new to Dylan. He did it in the early sixties, when he began writing songs, and again in 1971 while working on *Self Portrait*, and again in 1993/4 with his two albums of traditional songs, and he would do it again in 2014/15 with his exploration of what's called 'The Great American Songbook.'

However no album of Dylan songs has quite the retro feel of Time out of Mind. It wasn't just producer Lanois with his swampy southern sound, but Dylan who wanted an album that sounded like the old Sun Records of the forties and fifties. These songs we're looking at here from that era. Here's 'Viola Lee Blues.' Incidentally, Lewis was known as a great harmonica player, and I'm a touch disappointed that Dylan didn't take him on.

[Viola Lee Blues]

Another song which provides a backdrop to *Time Out of Mind* is 'I'll Not Be a Stranger' by the Stanley Brothers who began performing their bluegrass back in the late 1940s. The song is both sentimental and yearning and Dylan does a fine job with the vocals.

[I'll Not Be a Stranger]

Buddy Holly needs no introduction. He was right at the cusp, as pop music was turning into rock and roll. His 'Not Fade Away' (1957) still sounds good, and hasn't faded away. Dylan tells of how, as a teenager, while attending one of Holly's concerts, a 'transmission' took place between him and Holly. A look in which the musical baton was passed on. It's a mysterious feeling, but I think I know what it's like. I felt something akin to that when I first heard Visions of Johanna. For Dylan, it must have been a bit spooky too, for Holly was to die shortly afterwards. Dylan's 'Not Fade Away' is a great tribute to Holly, and to that musical history, which, if Dylan can help it, will never fade away. (19th March)

[Not Fade Away]

I'll be back soon with more sounds from 1997.

Kia Ora

NET 1997: Part 3 – I Came in from the Wilderness

By Mike Johnson (Kiwipoet)

Releasing his first album in six years (Time Out of Mind) in 1997 did not mean that Dylan made radical changes to his set lists or song arrangements. His tendency with new albums is to slip a few new songs in here and there, providing a sense of continuity with past years. Some of the older standbys, like 'I and I', begin to fade, others are brought forward, and some, like 'Tangled Up In Blue', never go away.

While his 1997 performances confirmed the tendency to move away from lengthy epics, this does not apply to 'Tangled Up In Blue', so we kick off this post with yet another eleven minute version of the song. While Dylan tended to leave his harmonica at home in 1997, that also does not apply to 'Tangled', much to the delight of the audience.

While I have been pretty circumspect in my assessment of Dylan's lead guitar playing, I have to note here how effective it is in pushing the tempo of the song. He may only be playing two or three notes, but how wonderfully they act as a driver. I think this is Mr Guitar Man at his best, not trying anything too fancy, just hammering that song along.

[Tangled Up In Blue]

One of the enduring qualities of Dylan's performances is their roughness and rawness. Dylan never sounds smooth, slick and accomplished. There is always an edginess. This is made more so in these audience recordings, which many prefer to the studio versions for just that reason. These audience recordings are very much live, and even when Dylan sings a softer, more intimate song, like 'You're a Big Girl Now', his emotional rawness still comes across. While full of bitterness and regret, 'You're a Big Girl Now' never becomes a smaltzy tear jerker. Along the very edge of pain, there is a kind of resistance to pain. Whatever happens in life, well, that's a price you have to pay... (This one from Tokyo 10th Feb)

[You're a Big Girl Now]

From the same concert, we get a quietly paced 'Shelter From the Storm'. This is another from Dylan's regular stable of songs, and I'm glad of it. A sophisticated love song full of wry humour, it shows how love nourishes and protects even in a world where 'it's doom alone that counts'. As with "You're a Big Girl', it has that same rough tenderness.

[Shelter from the Storm]

By this time 'I and I', another song we've been following, is on the wane. It was only performed a couple of times in 1997, then once in 1998 and once in 1999. For my reckoning, the song reached its peak in 1993. The commitment is still there, but you get the sense that Dylan has nowhere new to take the song. For him, the magic was beginning to fade. For all that it remains a powerful, dramatic song in which he finds he's 'still pushing myself along the road/the darkest part.' He's the poet who listens only to his heart.

[I and I]

Now for a rather sumptuous performance of 'Shooting Star'. I've always thought that the 'shooting star' of the song refers to a lot more than just an old love affair. It's all our hopes for redemption, our fears. The shooting star is a portent, with a cosmic significance. Doom is never far off:

> 'Listen to the engine listen to the bell
> As the last fire truck from hell goes rolling by
> All good people are praying
> It's the last temptation the last account
> The last time you might hear the sermon on the mount
> The last radio is playing.'

[Shooting Star]

Digging back into the 1960s now, we discover some more regulars. Here's a rocking performance of 'It Takes a Lot to Laugh' from *Highway 61 Revisited*

(1965). Blues always sounds better rough-edged. While this was stadium rock in that it was performed to a large audience, it has a blues club feel to it, rough and ready and forever 12 bars. (18th Dec)

[It Takes a Lot to Laugh]

'One Too Many Mornings,' with its old before its time feel, also suits that rough-edged voice; Dylan doesn't have to pretend to sound old. We've slipped back to the Tokyo concert to pick this one up. At 7 minutes it's creeping up towards an epic. I loved the stark simplicity of the original album performance (*The Times They Are A-Changing*, 1964), but this slow, thoughtful version works just fine. Voice nicely upfront.

[One Too Many Mornings]

'Don't Think Twice' is another early song that has survived the test of time. It has a nice bouncy rhythm that is somewhat belied by the sadness of the lyrics. Some things were just never meant to be. Here Dylan gives it a bit of a country twist, especially in the instrumental. It wouldn't go astray at a country dance.

[Don't Think Twice]

Over the past couple of years we have been treated to some solid performances of 'Queen Jane Approximately'. This is one song that Dylan can't resist turning into an epic, and we have a ten minute version of it here. This is achieved mainly by Dylan slowing the song down to about as slow as it could go and still hold together. Again, I feel that the world weariness evident in the song is well suited to Dylan's *Time Out of Mind* voice. If anything, the song is a plea for friendship, comradeship in the face of the relentless demands of the world.

The live performances of this song have been particularly good, and this is no exception.

[Queen Jane Approximately]

Because of the depth and seriousness of most Dylan songs, it's easy enough for us to overlook the comic element in his art. His humour can be overt or sly. We find it perhaps most clearly in the early Dylan, those talking songs like 'Talking World War 3 Blues' and 'Bob Dylan's 115th Dream', where the intention is satirical and the lyrics lean towards the absurd.

Absurdism is not always funny, although always surprising. A song like 'You Ain't Goin' Nowhere', is absurd, and leans towards that particular kind of humour called nonsense rhymes.

Nonsense rhymes are an ancient if neglected tradition in poetry. The idea is that such rhymes should just be sheer fun, and a play with the sounds of words. They tend to be found in nursery rhymes and children's writers such as Edward Lear and AA Milne. The Britannica describes them as a 'humorous or whimsical verse that differs from other comic verse in its resistance to any rational or allegorical interpretation.'

Here's a part of a poem by Edward Lear (1812 – 1888) that reminds me a little of Dylan's 'You Ain't Goin' Nowhere'

> 'On the Coast of Coromandel,
> Where the early pumpkins blow,
> In the middle of the woods
> Lived the Yonghy-Bonghy-Bò.
> Two old chairs, and half a candle
> One old jug without a handle
> These were all his worldly goods:
> In the middle of the woods,'

Arguably, you can make more sense of that if you're trying hard (poverty?) than this from Dylan:

> 'Buy me some rings and a gun that sings
> A flute that toots and a bee that stings
> A sky that cries and a bird that flies
> A fish that walks and a dog that talks'

Having said all that, the song is clearly celebratory. 'Tomorrow's the day my bride's a-gonna come...' suggests a crazy and buoyant anticipation. Nothing makes sense because it doesn't have to. It's an expression of sheer exuberance.

For more on the song, see Tony Attwood's excellent discussion here, particularly on lyrical variations. Dylan just can't sing it the same twice: https://bob-dylan.org.uk/archives/228

In the meantime, let's listen to a fun and energetic performance of the song by Dylan. This nicely captures the countrified happy-go-lucky spirit of the original Basement Tapes version.

[You Ain't Goin' Nowhere]

'Tombstone Blues' is also absurdist, but the lyrics are sharper and the edge satirical. The effect is of strangeness, but it is not funny.

> 'The king of the Philistines his soldiers to save
> Puts jawbones on their tombstones and flatters their graves
> Puts the pied pipers in prison and fattens the slaves
> Then sends them out to the jungle'

The actions of the 'king of Philistines' don't make that much sense, but there is a vague atmosphere of threat and the abuse of power. Certainly something is going on beyond our everyday expectations. Narratives themselves can be absurd, or flirt with absurdity:

> 'The hysterical bride in the penny arcade
> Screaming she moans, "I've just been made"
> Then sends out for the doctor, who pulls down the shade
> And says, "My advice is to not let the boys in"
>
> Now, the medicine man comes and he shuffles inside
> He walks with a swagger and he says to the bride
> "Stop all this weeping, swallow your pride
> You will not die, it's not poison"'

What has happened to the hysterical bride? We're not told, but it doesn't sound too nice. Compare those lyrics with these from Highway 61:

> 'Now, the fifth daughter on the twelfth night
> Told the first father that things weren't right

"My complexion", she says, "Is much too white"
He said, "Come here and step into the light"
He says, "Hmm, you're right"
"Let me tell the second mother, this has been done"'

The elusiveness of this kind of absurdity is the point, I think. We have to imagine what might have happened to the hysterical bride and the fifth daughter. This is a great performance of the song which rattles along in fine 1997 style. Fans of Dylan's harp, like me, will be glad to hear a few brief blasts from that little instrument here, but the last few choruses of instrumentals don't seem to go anywhere (18th of April):

[Tombstone Blues]

'Maggie's Farm' is another song that uses absurdist humour to make its point. One method in comedy is to exaggerate to comic effect. Here Dylan is able to make fun of an intolerable situation in a family from hell by comic exaggeration:

'I ain't gonna work for Maggie's pa no more
No, I ain't gonna work for Maggie's pa no more
Well, he puts his cigar out in your face, just for kicks
His bedroom window, it is made out of bricks
The National Guard stands around his door'

[Maggie's Farm]

I love the minimal trenchant arrangement of this performance, one of the best of many in my opinion. For me, the backing has been too rowdy on many of the performances in previous years. This one just seems to hit the spot. (the 3rd of August). We'll leave Bob there, slaving away on Maggie's farm until next time when we'll finish off 1997. See you then.

Kia Ora

NET 1997: Part 4 - Like So Many Times Before

By Mike Johnson (Kiwipoet)

When I get to the fourth post of a particular year, I am sometimes left with a random collection performances that don't quite fit in anywhere else. That has led to some interesting results. It's the same this year, although I find most of my 'leftovers' are familiar songs from the 1960s, a bunch of the usual suspects.

There are, however, a couple of rarities. 'Roving Gambler' is new to us in terms of the NET, but is a song Dylan has been singing, with variations, since the early 1960s. I urge interested reader to see the full account of this song by Tony Attwood here – bob-dylan.org.uk/archives/15673

'So we have one answer to why Bob Dylan likes it – it is a long-lived song that has turned up in many places. And it is unusual with the drawn out final line and the harmony opportunities that offers the performers. The change of tempo is not unique to this song, but it is unusual, and seems to date back to some of the early performances.'

It's a good rollicking performance piece, and fun to listen to, but I'd add that Dylan may like the song because it fits in perfectly with the ethos of his persona: the lonesome hobo, the travelling man, the blues journeyman who goes from town to town gambling his genius on stage and maybe breaking a pretty girl's heart before leaving town at dawn, just like so many times before. A joyful performance. (9th August):

[Roving Gambler]

'Joey,' from *Desire* (1975), is another rarity, although we have had a couple of strong performances in previous years. 'Joey' is an ambitious song, telling the story of the life and death of Joey Gallo, a mobster murdered on his birthday in 1972. Joey Gallo is not as sympathetic a figure at Hurricane Carter, and other than his rebel, outlaw status it is hard to see what attracted Dylan to the story. It seems that Dylan saw him as an underdog hero:

'I was on the outside
of whatever side there was.'

In 2016 Dylan described the story as 'Homeric' (Gundersen, Edna (2016-10-28). "World exclusive: Bob Dylan - I'll be at the Nobel Prize ceremony... if I can" (The Telegraph), but also claimed that his collaborator on the *Desire* songs, Jacques Levy, wrote all the lyrics.

It is my least favourite song on the album, and was described by music critic Lester Bang as 'repellent romanticist bullshit,' a judgment I tend to share. I would have preferred to see 'Golden Loom' or 'Abandoned Love,' on the album instead and would have rather tiptoed past the song in silence here. However, it is the only *Desire* song that Dylan performed during the NET, and according to a Mojo poll, "Joey" was rated the 74th most popular Bob Dylan song of all time.

One thing I can say is that the live performances of the song are certainly heroic. Dylan throws everything he's got at this performance. (Sorry, no date for this one)

[Joey]

'To Ramona' (1964) is described by Wikipedia as a 'folk waltz' and 'inspired by traditional Mexican Corrido folk music.' The song has been linked to Dylan's relationship with Joan Baez, and is not as gentle as it sounds, or as the melody would have us believe. The song seems to attack the more apocalyptic wing of the protest movement:

> 'You've been fooled into thinking
> that the finishing end is at hand'

but is a more general exposé of the destructive effects of living inauthentically and personal fakery.

> But it grieves my heart, love
> To see you tryin' to be a part of
> A world that just don't exist
> It's all just a dream, babe
> A vacuum, a scheme, babe

That sucks you into feelin' like this

It is no fun being deceived by the appearances of the world. In this 1997 performance Dylan plays the vocals pretty tenderly, but it won't be long before he begins to give the song a rather nasty twist. There is an underlying element of jeering or mockery which balances the love in the song, and this can only be brought out in performance, the way it is sung. At this stage there are only hints of it. This is an intimate, acoustic performance, with some nicely restrained guitar work by Dylan.(13th August)

[To Ramona]

Another song linked to Joan Baez is the famous 'It Ain't Me, Babe.' This song can be seen as an extension of the sentiment in 'To Ramona,' and the further rejection of the role of supporter of a lover's illusions and delusions. No hippy bullshit for Bob. This performance relies heavily on Mr Guitar Man's acoustic work, and while I would have preferred a harp solo, which always gives the song a certain piquancy, the vocal is as rough and true as you could wish. (18th December)

[It Ain't Me, Babe]

Yet another song linked to Joan Baez is 'Positively 4th Street.' Here the gloves have come off, and it is one of Dylan's deliberately most nasty songs. As with 'Just Like a Woman,' however, it is too easy to miss the vulnerability and hurt revealed by the song. We always want to hit back when we have been betrayed and slighted by those who profess to love us. Dylan doesn't filter or censor his feelings. It tumbles out raw and tough and real. Things have turned very sour, as these things do when love turns to hate. You can see a progression from 'To Ramona,' through 'It Aint Me Babe' to this:

Yes, I wish that for just one time you could stand inside my shoes
You'd know what a drag it is to see you

The original had a deceptively bouncy tempo. This created a disjunction between the lyrics and the upbeat sound. It only sounded like a happy song.

In this 1997 performance, however, Dylan slows the tempo right down to create a nine minute epic. Oddly the effect is more tender and yearning than we would expect, and the passionate delivery is devoid of jeering edges. It is odd. It sounds almost like a love song. At least it sounds shot through with regret rather than anger. It has that world weariness more fitting to a *Time Out of Mind* state of mind. (sorry, no date for this one)

[Positively 4th Street]

A song closely associated with Dylan's move away from topical protest songs is 'My Back Pages' (1964). When introducing this song previously, I suggested that the loss of moral certainty, the subject of the song, would cost Dylan dearly later on. The loss of moral compass is an important thread in Time out of Mind, and what I find fascinating about this performance in the year Dylan released that album is the way he hurls it out so defiantly. It becomes a forceful declaration, not of faith but of lack of faith. A declaration of uncertainty.

[My Back Pages]

With 'God Knows' (1991) uncertainty turns into jeopardy. It might be important for considering *Under the Red Sky* to remember that 1991 was also the year of the first Gulf War, the year of the first US and coalition attack on Iraq. Suddenly the world was on a knife edge once more:

> God knows it's fragile
> God knows everything
> God knows it snap apart right now
> Just like putting scissors to a string

That's just what it felt like to live through that war, with the possibility always lurking that it could turn into a more general Middle Eastern war:

> God knows it's terrifying
> God sees it all unfold
> There's a million reasons for you to be crying

You been so bold and so cold

It's hard not to feel that that the repeated phrase God knows is meant sarcastically – God knows everything! And yet it is ambiguous. This same God 'knows the secrets of your heart' and might offer some hope, some prospect of a purpose, or even the ever elusive prospect of salvation.God knows there's a purpose God knows there's a chance God knows you can rise above the darkest hour Of any circumstance

Here Dylan sticks pretty much to the tempo and spirit of the original album version, although the last two minutes are given over to the hectic, apocalyptic musings of Mr Guitar Man on his punky Stratocaster. God knows, you could have knocked a minute and half off this performance with no loss, but maybe that ominous swirl of sound is the point. Remember the head-bashing 1993 performance? (see NET, 1993, Part 1) Note he changes the word 'purpose' in the last verse to 'reason.' (2nd October).

[God Knows]

As has been the pattern in the 90s, Dylan has sung 'Knockin' On Heaven's Door' without a chorus. During the Rolling Thunder Tour the song sounded magnificent with ragged chorus of voices all knocking on heavens door. In the 90s Dylan performs the song unaided, which creates an impression of heroic fragility, especially with this cracked voice. This is a wonderful vocal performance, with the voice upfront and well recorded. This is an encore, which might help explain the rough, end of the night voice. The song starts 1.40 mins into the recording. (13th August)

Knockin' On Heaven's Door

In this spirited performance of 'Ballad of a Thin Man' we hear Dylan 'upsinging' at least in one verse. Upsinging is when the voice is raised at the end of each line. Later this would become an annoying mannerism but at this stage he's only trying it out. Since this performance is faster than the album version (*Highway 61 Revisited*, 1965) it sounds a bit rushed, but Dylan's high-pitched singing gives it a suitably desperate edge. (18th April)

[Ballad of a Thin Man]

During the 90s Dylan was perfecting a slow, sumptuous arrangement of the mysterious 'Love Minus Zero/No Limit' (1965). This 1997 version is pretty much the same arrangement (minus harp) as the MTV Unplugged performance of 1994. But to my ear the vocal is stronger, Dylan's voice more expressive. The emotional range of the *Time Out of Mind* songs, and the voice he finds to sing them, takes us further than Dylan has gone before, and he now brings that extended range to his earlier songs with, in this case at least, gorgeous effect. (Date not known).

[Love Minus Zero]

The same applies to Mr Tambourine Man, another from 1965. With the youthful idealism leached from the song by Dylan's more aged voice, the desire to escape down 'the foggy ruins of time' away from this world 'of crazy sorrow' sounds world weary and disillusioned, just like the *Time Out of Mind* songs. (18th December).

[Mr Tambourine Man]

It is hard to overestimate the effect that recording *Time Out of Mind* had on Dylan's performances in 1997. A new maturity and emotional range is evident, and he delivers his familiar setlist with a renewed vigour and power. His voice is changing. There are new cracks. He takes advantage of this change, adding a feeling of being broken by age and experience – but still on the road, still the singing the old songs, just like so many times before.

We'll be back soon to have a look at 1998.

Kia Ora

1998

NET 1998: Part 1 – One who sings with his tongue on fire

By Mike Johnson (Kiwipoet)

With the success of Time Out of Mind, released in September 1997, which won three Grammy awards and Album of the Year, Dylan came powering into 1998 enjoying the comeback of his career. He ripped into his concerts like there was no tomorrow. There was a new energy and focus. Pretty much gone were the long epics and the wandering guitar breaks of the earlier nineties. His electric performances were pared down, hard-edged and tight, while his acoustic performances were as committed as ever. Dylan was on a roll. My only complaint is that he only rarely pulled out the harmonica.

He did 110 concerts in 1998, but I'm going to concentrate on a few ace shows rather than attempt to play the field. Most commentators agree that the San Jose show on May 19th was outstanding, and I'll be drawing heavily from that show, but his five day residency at Madison Square Gardens, New York (from 16th to 21st January) where he shared a billing with Van Morrison, is perhaps better known. My own favourite, after the San Jose show, is the Newcastle show (20th June), so I'll be dipping into that as well.

Dylan continued to drip-feed new songs from the album, with, as far as I can tell, only two new songs introduced in 1998, 'To Make You Feel My Love' and 'Million Miles'. 'Love Sick' and 'Cold Irons Bound', however, became regulars on his setlist with 'Till I Fell in Love with You' and 'Can't Wait' making occasional appearances.

Let's start with 'To Make You Feel My Love'. This of course became a huge hit for Adele, with some fans of the song not realising it was a Dylan composition. Adele's version is so marvellous, it becomes hard to listen to how Dylan does it. It may be the saddest song on the album, a hopeless kind of love song full of forlorn avowals.

> 'When the evening shadows and the stars appear
> And there is no one there to dry your tears
> I could hold you for a million years
> To make you feel my love'

I don't think he ever did it better than this one, from the San Jose concert. The cracked voice and weariness are perfect for the song.

[To Make You Feel My Love]

For 'Million Miles' we turn to the New York concerts (20th). This may well be Dylan's jazziest composition, and wouldn't have sounded out of place much earlier in the century, the late 1940s perhaps. Its skipping beat puts it in that era. It's another song of hopeless love, when that gap between two people just can't be bridged. You can be standing right next to somebody and still feel a million miles apart.

> 'I'm drifting in and out of dreamless sleep
> Throwing all my memories in a ditch so deep
> Did so many things I never did intend to do
> Well I'm trying to get closer, but I'm still
>   a million miles from you'

But there is something more going on here than just a yearning for a distant love. There's a metaphysical anxiety and spiritual loss, an existential disorientation that characterises the whole album:

> 'Well I don't dare close my eyes and I don't dare wink
> Maybe in the next life I'll be able to hear myself think
> Feel like talking to somebody but I just don't know who'

And again:

> 'Well, there's voices in the night trying to be heard
> I'm sitting here listening to every mind polluting word
> I know plenty of people who would put me up for a day or two'

[Million Miles]

The same existential disorientation drives the Grammy award winning 'Cold Irons Bound,' only with a more desperate edge. 'Cold irons' refers to the metal manacles worn by prisoners and slaves. In our lost and disoriented condition we are little better than prisoners. We cannot escape the human condition:

> 'Well, I'm waist deep, waist deep in the mist
> It's almost like, almost like, I don't (even) exist
> I'm twenty miles out of town, Cold Irons bound.'
> Note the use of repetition here to drive it home.

And again:

'Well the winds in Chicago have torn me to shreds
Reality has always had too many heads'

As I listened to this one from the San Jose show, I found myself admiring Dylan's electric guitar work. Mr Guitar Man has been reined in, his playing minimal and concise. He's not muddying the melodic waters with over complicated picking, as he too often does, but kicks the song along with some wonderfully spare, driving sounds. Everything here clicks, and the band has never sounded better; tight, integrated and compelling. This is rock music at its best, folks; a bit rough and punky (that hint of garage band sound) and hard-edged. Take a moment to appreciate the drumming. New drummer David Kemper proves his worth, as does guitarist Larry Campbell.

For my ear, this is much better than the murky, too cluttered, album version. I can't help but think that this comes closest to the sound Dylan was after for this song.

[Cold Irons Bound]

Staying with the San Jose concert, and the theme of existential displacement, we turn to 'Love Sick', the song that kicks off the album. I was immediately hooked by that opening song, which was doubtless the idea, but, listening to these live performances, I'm beginning to understand why Dylan expressed reservations about Lanois' production. The Lanois sound tends to smooth over the raw edges of the songs. Take the backslap out of Dylan's voice and sharpen the sound and you have this:

[Love Sick]

It sounds spooky enough, as it should, without the backslap on his voice. It's all about distance, feeling a million miles from everything. To the wandering ghost, everything is perceived at a distance: 'in a meadow,' 'silhouettes in the window,' and 'a distant cry.' There's no rest from grief for the loveless:

'My feet are so tired

My brain is so wired
And the clouds are weepin"

"Till I Fell in Love with You,' drives home the message of the album, that without love, either the human or spiritual kind, we are lost. Lost and insomniac. I was surprised to note how often sleeplessness comes up in these songs. Another song which finds the poet tired and wired.

'I've been hit too hard
I've seen too much
Nothing can heal me now
But your touch'

There are good performances of the song from New York and Minneapolis (23rd October), but I've chosen this one from Springfield (2nd Feb).

[Till I fell In Love with You]

Dylan worked hard on 'Can't Wait' to get the sound he wanted, and would go on experimenting with the song in future years. In 1997/98 he was playing it pretty much straight from the album, minus Lanois' embellishments. Waiting for love (or death perhaps) can be a soul destroying business. It's a pity Dylan didn't sing it more often in 1998. I had to go beyond my cluster of favourite concerts to find this one from the New London (CT) show, 14th January. Here we find both mind and heart at the end of its tether.

[Can't Wait]

One of the features of 1998 is the pretty much unvarying setlist. The same six or seven core songs keep recurring, with a few strays and wild cards thrown into the mix. Dylan would often kick the shows off with either 'Gotta Serve Somebody' or 'Absolutely Sweet Marie.' The latter song, particularly, was a good hard-driving crowd warmer. If you can leave behind the adolescent whine of the album version (*Blonde on Blonde* 1966), you have a rocker that doesn't sound too out of place among the *Time Out of Mind* songs. Failed love and capricious fate rule.

'Well, I don't know how it happened
But the river-boat captain, he knows my fate
But everybody else, even yourself
They're just gonna have to wait'

Here it is from the San Jose show:

[Absolutely Sweet Marie]

And while we're in the fast paced rock mood, let's stay in the sixties with 'Highway 61 Revisited'. In previous posts I've characterised this as a serious song pretending to be a throw-away rocker. To hell with this mad world; down Highway 61 anything is possible. Another San Jose kicker.

[Highway 61 Revisited]

Another regular on the 1998 setlist is 'Silvio', the Robert Hunter/Dylan song. It appeared on *Down in the Groove* (1988), perhaps Dylan's least regarded album. This is certainly the best performance of the song I have heard. It's great to hear Dylan doing this song before he became tired of it, and the performances became rote. As with 'Highway 61', the speed of the song can obscure the cunning of the lyrics:

'I can snap my fingers and require the rain
From a clear blue sky and turn it off again
I can stroke your body and relieve your pain
And charm the whistle off an evening train'

Wonderful. Or this:

'Honest as the next jade rolling that stone
When I come knocking don't throw me no bone
I'm an old boll weevil looking for a home
If you don't like it you can leave me alone'

On *Time Out of Mind*, in the song 'Not Dark Yet', Dylan sings:

'Well, my sense of humanity has gone down the drain
Behind every beautiful thing there's been some kind of pain'

This is not a new insight. In 'Silvio' back in 1988 we find:

'I can tell your fancy I can tell your plain
You give something up for everything you gain
Since every pleasure's got an edge of pain
Pay for your ticket and don't complain'

[Silvio]

Staying with the electric mood, let's finish this post with the last song from the San Jose concert, that glorious piece of irreverence 'Rainy Day Woman' from *Blonde on Blonde*. I don't think any performance can quite match the screaming saxophone version from 1996 (See NET, 1996, part 4), but Dylan's voice is better on this one. Everybody must have fun. Happy foot-tapping, and I'll see you soon with more sounds from 1998.

[Rainy Day Woman]

Kia Ora

NET 1998: Part 2 - Friends and Other Strangers

By Mike Johnson (Kiwipoet)

In Part 1 of 1998 (see previous post) I tried to cover the songs from *Time Out of Mind* new to live performance, and I found 'Million Miles' and 'To Make you Feel my Love.' However, I missed a song: 'It's Not Dark Yet'. I might have passed over it because I don't think this is the best performance of the song that Dylan did, or even a memorable one, but I am being influenced by how it was to develop over the coming years, and how good it was to become.

This is a song, I contend, that Dylan would grow into as the years passed and the shadows lengthened. After all, he was still on the sunny side of sixty when he recorded *Time Out of Mind*, and such a stark encounter with mortality would need the following twenty years to fully develop. It was almost as if he was too young in 1997 to fully feel the bite of the lyrics. No other song on the album quite confronts death the way this one does. For a man who's wrestled with his faith, the last verse is devastating, and signals a loss of faith.

> 'I was born here and I'll die here against my will
> I know it looks like I'm movin' but I'm standin' still
> Every nerve in my body is so naked and numb
> I can't even remember what it was I came here to get away from
> Don't even hear the murmur of a prayer
> It's not dark yet but it's gettin' there'

In the face of the gathering dark, our faith can fail us. To me, this performance from New London (CT) on the 14th of January sounds surprisingly tentative. He's stepped away from Lanois' swampy sound but doesn't seem to have found a new sound that will bring the song to life, although I don't want to judge this unfairly in the light of later performances that I prefer.

[It's Not Dark Yet]

In the previous post I pointed out that Dylan's set list was pretty unvarying for this year, with the same songs cropping up again and again. One of these is 'Serve Somebody', the first track of the 1979 album *Slow Train Coming*. Because of its context, Dylan's sudden conversion to Christianity, the song has been seen as a Christian song, but by 1998, nineteen years later, and set in the context of *Time Out of Mind*, I'm beginning to wonder. The song, in all its lyrical variants, merely states that no matter who we are, we are serving somebody, some force or other. We can serve the powers of good or the powers of evil, it's up to us.That's a much more universal message than a strictly Christian one. Are we really the good guys or not?

It's hard to get past the powerful 1979 – 1981 performances of this song, but this is much rougher than those earlier gospel versions, rougher but no less powerful, I think. And some of those lyrical variations bring us closer to a *Time Out of Mind* state of mind:

> Might think that you're living
> Might even think that you're dead
> Sleeping on nails
> Sleeping on a feather bed

Dylan would kick off his shows with either this song or 'Absolutely Sweet Marie' (see part 1). Here he is blasting his way into the 5th of November, Wollongong (Australia) concert, and he's in great voice.

[Gotta Serve Somebody]

The odd one out among these regulars, to my mind, is 'The Man in Me', a fairly minor song from *New Morning* (1970). I say this because there is a freshness of feeling in the song that is far from the spirit of *Time Out of Mind*.

> 'But, oh, what a wonderful feeling
> Just to know that you are near
> Sets my a heart a-reeling
> From my toes up to my ears'

Maybe that's why Dylan brought it to the fore, for the contrast of feeling. He'd typically bring it in around number three on the setlist. Here it is from that wonderful San Jose concert (19th May).

[Man in Me]

In 1997/98 Dylan brought two songs to the fore that he'd never played live. One was 'Blind Willie McTell' and the other was 'This Wheel's On Fire', a song Dylan wrote with Rick Danko. I've written before about how provocatively elusive the lyrics are to 'This Wheel's On Fire' (See NET, 1997, part 2), and the impression that the language is coded. Even the refrain is ambivalent in terms of its mood or intention; is it a threat or a promise?

> 'No man alive will come to you
> With another tale to tell
> But you know that we shall meet again
> If your mem'ry serves you well'

And dead men tell no tales…or do they? And is it a pleasant memory? Probably not, as it's a reminder of an obligation incurred, and somebody will be back to collect the debt.

This version from New London (CT) certainly brings out the element of threat or darkness in the song, more so than the nostalgia of the Band's recorded version (Music from Big Pink, 1968). That may be due to the ominous sound of the opening guitar riffs here, and the urgency of the drumming.

[Wheel's On Fire]

We find the same sense of threat in the guitar work on 'Blind Willie McTell' which I think we need to think of as a protest song. 'This land is condemned' and 'power and greed and corruptible seed' rule that land, America. This is justly considered one of Dylan's greatest songs, written in 1983, yet he seems to have become aware of that in only 1997/98. It contains unforgettable pictures of a fallen America with imagery that takes us back to the Civil War (1860s).

'Seen them big plantations burning
Hear the cracking of the whips
Smell that sweet magnolia blooming
See the ghost of slavery ship
I can hear them tribes moaning
Hear the undertaker's bell
Nobody can sing the blues like blind Wille McTell'

This is what he mostly sings. But there are variations and ellipses in performance, as well as in written versions. Consider this verse:

'There's a woman by the river
With some fine young handsome man
He's dressed up like some squire
Bootlegged whiskey in his hand
There's chain gang on the highway
I can hear them rebels yell
And I know no one can sing the blues
Like blind Wille McTell'

However, the official lyrics have this:

'There's a woman by the river
With some fine young handsome man
He's dressed up like a squire
Bootlegged whiskey in his hand
Some of them died in the battle
Some of them survived as well...'

... which I've never heard him sing. In most of the live performances the rebels disappear to be replaced by the undertaker's bell. Sadly, his tendency is to drop the wonderful 'big plantations burning' verse altogether. Whatever the lyrical variations, however, it remains a powerful song, powerfully delivered, and it sits very comfortably with the *Time Out of Mind* songs. (Sorry, no date for this one).

[Blind Willie McTell]

Another regular on Dylan's setlist in 1998 is 'Across the Borderline', a song by John Hiatt, Ry Cooder and Jim Dickinson. When you look at the lyrics it's easy to see what attracted Dylan to this song at this time. Dylan could have written it himself for Time Out of Mind:

> 'When you reach the broken promised land
> And every dream slips through your hands
> Then you'll know that it's too late to change your mind
> 'Cause you've paid the price to come so far
> Just to wind up where you are
> And you're still just across the borderline'

This one's from November 3rd, a sweet, reflective rendition.

[Across the Borderline]

Another song that never strayed far from the setlists is our old friend 'Tangled Up In Blue.' No stranger, this song. Ten years on the road and the song hasn't lost its bite; the memories it canvasses still sound fresh. Dylan rarely produced the harmonica in 1998, but he does here at the San Jose concert for this song. A sharp and edgy performance.

[Tangled Up In Blue]

On the subject of brief harp breaks, the opening harp work on this 'Just Like a Woman' sets a gentle and fragile tone. Strip the *Blonde on Blonde* jeer from Dylan's voice, make it sound more care-worn, and we get quite a different impression of the song. Indeed the mood can shift from scorn to compassion. Suddenly the details feel different, maybe more sad:

> 'Everybody knows
> That baby's got new clothes
> But lately i see her ribbons and her bows
> Have fallen
> From her curls'

A very telling detail. Like 'Miss Lonely' in 'Like A Rolling Stone', the woman here has fallen, her pretty pretences stripped away. And then there's the matter of the singer's hunger, of which he is ashamed. I think we tend to be scornful to those who we have revealed too much of ourselves to. Revealing our need, makes us vulnerable, so we hit back. But in this performance, there's not so much hitting back as regretting. (23rd October) It was just one of those things:

[Just like a Woman]

'Masters of War' is another song that got plenty of stage time in 1998. I still think his 1995, London concert version is the best, but by 1998 Dylan has settled on a slow, heavy beat for the song. He has largely abandoned fast electric versions for these ominous acoustic sounds. It's interesting that even within the confines of the same basic arrangement, the mood and tone of the song can vary a lot. In this first one, from San Jose, the song sounds urgent and intimate, the anger very evident. There's a furious crackle in his voice.

[Masters of War (A)]

In this following performance, however, from Los Angeles, 21st May, the sound is more distant, softer and more spooky. The differences in recording might play a part here, but it sounds to me as if Dylan is using the echo of the Los Angeles venue to effect that more distant voice.

[Masters of War (B)]

In 1998, Dylan often returned to that wonderful dirge, 'Forever Young'. As with 'Masters of War' the mood and tone of the song vary a lot from concert to concert. It's another old friend that ages well. Apparently Dylan wrote the song for one of his children in 1974, but by 1998 it sounds more grandfatherly. We oldies might grow old but you young ones please stay young. It's a plea from age to youth. The older Dylan's voice sounds, the deeper the irony becomes.

The first is from San Jose, another intimate performance, yet with the first signs of upsinging (lifting the voice at the end of the line) which will come to plague later performances. Here it works all right, as he's not doing it at the end of every line. The ragged chorus works well too.

[Forever young (A)]

This next one is slower, gentler perhaps, with no upsinging. Another irresistible performance. (23rd October)

[Forever Young (B)]

So that's it for this time around, folks. Stay young (at least at heart), and we'll be back soon with another round of friends and other strangers.

Kia Ora

NET 1998: Part 3 - What's a Protest Song?

By Mike Johnson (Kiwipoet)

In 1995, at Frank Sinatra's 80th birthday bash, Dylan presented a song I don't think he'd ever performed live before, 'Restless Farewell'. Apparently Sinatra requested the song. This is the last track on *The Times They Are A-Changing* (1964), and despite being a self-justifying exercise, it has a weary beauty with Dylan in fine lyrical form. The melody is from an old Scottish ballad, 'The Parting Glass'.

> 'Oh, ev'ry thought that's strung a knot in my mind
> I might go insane if it couldn't be sprung
> But it's not to stand naked under unknowin' eyes
> It's for myself and my friends my stories are sung
> But the time ain't tall
> Yet on time you depend and no word is possessed
> By no special friend
> And though the line is cut
> It ain't quite the end
> I'll just bid farewell till we meet again'

It is therefore a surprise to find it appearing in 1998, quite out of the blue. I don't think this is a particularly wonderful performance, or recording, but its sheer rarity value compels its inclusion here. This is from the Los Angeles concert 21st May:

[Restless Farewell]

From the same album, and in a very similar vein, we find 'One Too Many Mornings'. It's a sad farewell song in which the temporary, contingent nature of things is keenly felt. It captures that bleak, lonely feeling that might come upon you after a one night stand, or on realising that a love is all over. The song has a disarming simplicity, and is quite disingenuous in pretending to come from an unsophisticated, 'unlearned' man.

> 'From the crossroads of my doorstep
> My eyes start to fade
> And I turn my head back to the room
> Where my love and I have laid
> And I gaze back to the street
> The sidewalk and the sign
> And I'm one too many mornings
> And a thousand miles behind'

Within that 'restless hungry feeling,' there is no room for the moral certainty or moral absolutism that rule the protest songs. In 'Masters of War' we find the certainty that 'even Jesus would never forgive what you do', but in 'One Too Many Mornings' we find 'You're right from your side/ and I'm right from mine'. This moral relativism, if you like, prepares the way for a more thorough relativism in 'My Back Pages'.

This song has been a regular on Dylan's setlist over the years, and this a particularly good acoustic performance that captures the weariness and ambience of the original (31st March). That moral relativism sits quite naturally with the voice of the *Time Out of Mind* Dylan, the voice of the soul possessed by alienation and despair.

[One Too many Mornings (A)]

Perhaps a little better recorded, with Dylan's voice more to the front, is this performance. I think, from those opening chords, that the audience thinks they're about to hear 'Knockin' On Heaven's Door'.

[One Too many Mornings (B)]

Of course the early sixties was the era of the protest song, which Dylan himself made famous. Through the nineties, Dylan didn't forget his protest songs, despite his dislike of the term. 'What's a protest song?' he once famously responded to someone in the audience requesting one. It's a good question, but his best known protest songs are not that hard to identify. They are mostly topical and protest against war and social injustice.

'The Ballad of Hollis Brown' is a perfect example with its dark, brooding blues melody and its tale of desperation and murder-suicide. Its lyrics evoke the rural dust bowl songs of the 1930s

> 'The rats have got your flour
> Bad blood it got your mare'

but it has a contemporary force that makes it still relevant. Critic David Horowitz makes the following comment:

> 'Technically speaking, "Hollis Brown" is a tour de force. For a ballad is normally a form which puts one at a distance from its tale. This ballad, however, is told in the second person, present tense, so that not only is a bond forged immediately between the listener and the figure of the tale, but there is the ironic fact that the only ones who know of Hollis Brown's plight, the only ones who care, are the hearers who are helpless to help, cut off from him, even as we in a mass society are cut off from each other [...] Indeed, the blues perspective itself, uncompromising, isolated and sardonic, is superbly suited to express the squalid reality of contemporary America [...] A striking example of the tough, ironic insight one associates with the blues.'

This is a particularly good performance, sparse and hard-driving acoustic. The electric performances of 1974 make great blues based rock music, but this arrangement again captures the desolate atmosphere of the original. (Sorry, no date for this one.)

[The Ballad of Hollis Brown]

Perhaps Dylan's most famous protest song is 'Blowin' in the Wind'. This is the song that made Dylan's name. I believe there have been over sixty cover versions. It is built around a series of rhetorical questions designed to prick our consciences on matters of race and war. The song can easily become an anthem as it did in 1974 and 1984, but to my mind those anthem-like arrangements, despite audience participation, lose the frail intensity of the acoustic original. In this 1998 performance Dylan once more seems to be reaching back to the original sound and inspiration of the song, although the band joins him for the chorus.

Curiously, Dylan often stumbles over the lyrics of this song, or gets them a little wrong, but he covers up well for the gaffes and delivers a powerful performance. (23rd October)

[Blowin in the Wind]

While 'Blowin' in the Wind' might be Dylan's best known protest song, 'A Hard Rain's A-Gonna Fall' may be his most wide reaching outside 'It's Alright, Ma (I'm Only Bleeding)'. Dylan's 'surrealist period' of the mid-sixties is prefigured here in a stunning series of apocalyptic images that show rather than tell. The effect of this is that these images have not aged. They are as contemporary now as when they were written.

> 'I saw ten-thousand talkers whose tongues were all broken
> I saw guns and sharp swords in the hands of young children

That sounds like the 21st Century to me.

In 1998 Dylan does not seek radical arrangements of these old songs, but rather to reach back and uncover the impulse that led to the writing of the songs. With 'Hard Rain', we have a subtle reworking of the mood and tone of the song. We have had the loud, driving electric version of 1975/6, the slow, lush orchestral version of 1994, but here we have a gently lilting, discreetly adorned performance, not as strident as the original, but sadder and more contemplative (20th January).

[Hard Rain]

Aside from 'Masters of War' (see NET, 1998, part 2), 'John Brown' is Dylan's most effective anti-war song. It precisely identifies the generational gap between the young, anti-war movement and the parents of those young people. The song sets out to demystify war. The physically broken young returning soldier confronts his patriotic mother on the railway station upon his return. It's quite astonishing that the song was written in 1962, several years before the Vietnam War became an issue, and soldiers did come back from 'the war' their bodies and souls broken. In that respect the song is remarkably prescient. (Sorry, date not available for this one).

[John Brown]

Is 'Tears of Rage' also a protest song? Not as obviously as 'John Brown' or 'Masters of War', but the song seems to be driven by a moral outrage that at least belongs to the spirit of protest.

> 'It was all very painless
> When you went out to receive
> All that false instruction
> Which we never could believe
> And now the heart is filled with gold
> As if it was a purse
> But oh, what kind of love is this
> Which goes from bad to worse ?'

Whatever that 'false instruction' might be, it leads to the kind of greedy materialism that always provokes Dylan to outrage. Fast forward to 2020 and 'False Prophet':

> 'Bury 'em naked with their silver and gold
> Put them six feet under and pray for their souls'

Or 'Silvio' (1988), a regular in the concerts of the late nineties:

> 'Silvio, silver and gold
> Won't buy back the beat of a heart grown cold'

What we think of as a protest song depends on our frame of reference. In 'Tears of Rage', rage and grief go hand in hand. It's hard to find a more passionate performance of the song than this one, from 13th January.

[Tears of Rage]

So maybe 'Desolation Row' too is a kind of protest song:

> 'And the riot squad they're restless
> They need somewhere to go...'

Look at 'False Prophet' again:

> 'I'm the enemy of treason
> I'm the enemy of strife
> I'm the enemy of the unlived meaningless life'

Something of the quality of that 'unlived meaningless life' comes through in 'Desolation Row':

> 'To her death is quite romantic
> She wears an iron vest
> Her profession's her religion
> Her sin is her lifelessness'

But we all suffer from some variation of the same oppression:

> 'Now at midnight all the agents
> And the superhuman crew
> Come out and round up everyone
> That knows more than they do
> Then they bring them to the factory
> Where the heart-attack machine
> Is strapped across their shoulders
> And then the kerosene
> Is brought down from the castles
> By insurance men who go
> Check to see that nobody is escaping
> To Desolation Row'

Isn't there a deeper sense of protest here than in even the recognised protest songs? In 1997/98 'Desolation Row' fell into the background. It was only performed once in 1997, and rarely in 1998. I don't think this is a best ever performance, but I find it hard to pass over any performance of what might be Dylan's greatest song ever.

[Desolation Row]

Finally, what about 'All along the Watchtower'? Aren't the first verses, the conversation between the joker and the thief, all about the insufferable oppressiveness of our modern culture, which in itself is on the edge of a more ancient doom, doom the 'two riders' will bring with them. 'There must be some way out of here...' but maybe there isn't, except for that approaching doom. I always felt that 'Watchtower' was a protest song without quite understanding why. Perhaps it's that ominous tone, or the guitar war that breaks out after the last verse. Again it depends on your terms of reference. I like the way he breaks up the verses, fragments the lines, in this performance (6th June).

[All along the Watchtower]

> 'So let us
> not talk falsely now
> the hour
> is getting late...'

Words as true now as when they were written. May the spirit of protest never die, in whatever guise it comes!

That's it for now, gentle reader. I'll be back with more from 1998 soon.

Kia Ora!

NET 1998: Part 4 - You won't regret it

By Mike Johnson (Kiwipoet)

During 1998, Dylan shared the stage with other performers, notably Van Morrison, Mick Jagger and Joni Mitchell. Dylan's performances with others can be quite fun to watch, but rarely does Dylan do his best work on those occasions.

This scrappy 'Like A Rolling Stone' with Mick Jagger is a good example. Jagger jumps around plausibly, trying to look like one of those 'British bad boys' Dylan mentions in 'I Contain Multitudes'. Dylan tries to hunker down into the song but Jagger doesn't know the words. He can however belt out the chorus in fine style. Like a Rolling Stone? You bet. As I said, fun to watch...

[Like A Rolling Stone]

Dylan also did some shows where he was the opening act for Van Morrison. Van the Man was riding pretty high in those days. Occasionally they would join each other for a duet. Here Dylan and Van have a fair go at 'Knockin' On Heaven's Door'. There's a nice impromptu moment when master harpist Dylan finds a harmonica for Van to have a blast.

[Knockin' On Heaven's Door]

The two of them seem to enjoy themselves singing Van's 'More and More'. The grin on Dylan's face in the last verse gives the game away.

[More and More]

Joni Mitchell joins Van and Bob for a rather moving performance of 'I Shall Be Released'. It's nicely impromptu, with each pointing to the other for taking the next verse. It's great to see these three poets of rock music onstage together.

[I Shall Be Released]

But, as I said, Dylan usually does his best work alone. Let's pick up on 'I and I', a song Dylan has been cultivating since the heavy, thunderous versions he did with Tom Petty in 1986. My peak performance of the song remains the 1993, guitar heavy version (See NET, 1993, Part 1), but this 1998 performance comes a very close second. The song is slowly disappearing from Dylan's setlists by this time, but the power of the song is undiminished, as is Dylan's commitment to it (1st July).

[I and I]

'I'll Be Your Baby Tonight' and 'To Be Alone With You' are both in a lighter vein than the *Time Out of Mind* songs, and 'Blind Willie McTell', 'Silvio' and 'This Wheel's On Fire', songs Dylan brought forward to sit alongside the album songs.

One of the most laid back Dylan songs of the sixties must be 'I'll Be Your Baby Tonight', the last track on *John Wesley Harding* (1967), which was stylistically a taste of what was to come in *Nashville Skyline* a couple of years later. The lyrics are deliberately goofy.

> 'Well, that mockingbird's gonna sail away
> We're gonna forget it
> That big, fat moon is gonna shine like a spoon
> But we're gonna let it
> You won't regret it'

'I'll Be Your Baby Tonight' is a warm song, and his jokes at love's expense are gentle rather than sharp. It is, after all, an invitation to love, a night of boozy love by the sound of it (14th January).

[I'll be your Baby Tonight]

Another from *Nashville Skyline* (1969) that Dylan picks up on from time to time is the bouncy 'To Be Alone With You'. He relishes these lines:

> 'It only goes to show

That while life's pleasures be few
The only one I know
Is when I'm alone with you'

and I can't help thinking that the 'you' in the verse is the audience, even if that was not his intention when writing the song.

[To Be Alone With You]

'Tonight I'll Be Staying Here With You' also from *Nashville Skyline*, is in the same vein, only a touch more melancholy. I like the 1975 lyric change, 'Throw my ticket in the wind', but in this 1998 performance we get the original lyrics with the implied tiredness of the song beautifully rendered in Dylan's cracked, aged voice. That voice reminds us that Dylan is now a rich old man, and not the poor kid who wrote 'Only a Hobo'. These lines take on a special resonance because of that.

'I can hear that whistle blowin'
I see that stationmaster, too
If there's a poor boy on the street
Then let him have my seat
'Cause tonight I'll be staying here with you'

That 'poor boy on the street' might have been Bob in the winter of 1961.

[Tonight I'll Be Staying Here With You]

That pretty much does it for lightening up the mood, the dark, sombre mood of Time out of Mind. 'Born in Time' (from *Under the Red Sky*, 1991) fits so perfectly into that mood it could have come from the later album. This song has always been a favourite of mine. Although the frailty and contingency of love might be Dylan's overriding theme, to my mind it was never done with such delicacy of feeling.

'In the lonely night
In the blinking stardust of a pale blue light
You're comin' through to me in black and white

When we were made of dreams.
You're blowing down the shaky street
You're hearing my heart beat
In the record breaking heat
Where we were born in time.'

In keeping with the high quality of these 1998 performances, this is a particularly lush version of the song.

[Born in Time]

Talk about the frailty and contingent nature of love! 'A Simple Twist of Fate', with its elusive sub-textual narrative, says it all. We noted before how Dylan plays around with the pronouns in the song. In this version, the main character is the woman. The fact that it still works as well as the original, male centred narrative, demonstrates the equality of the sexes when it comes to regret and desire. The fact that the song sounds just as natural featuring a woman may be Dylan's point in playing with the pronouns in this way. In this version he sings:

> 'They sat together in the park
> As the evening sky grew dark.
> She looked at him and she felt a spark
> Tingle to her bones.
> 'Twas then she felt alone
> And wished that she'd gone straight
> And watched out for a simple twist of fate.'

It works for me, especially in this slow, thoughtful version.

[Simple Twist of Fate]

'My Back Pages' (1964) was starting to fade from Dylan's setlists, and this performance doesn't add much in terms of innovation, or interesting arrangements. Still, it's nice to hear a rare harp intro, and the solid acoustic performance. (23rd October). If you don't know the lyrics of the song, it's a good idea to check them out, for there are some interesting complexities.

I note how Dylan's love life somehow becomes a part of the changes he describes:

> 'Girls' faces formed the forward path
> from phony jealousy
> To memorizing politics
> of ancient history'

'Phony jealousy' becomes entangled in morally rigid politics. To be free from the latter means being free from the former. Faithfulness to an ideology gets tangled with faithfulness in personal relationships. Again:

> '"Equality", I spoke the word as if a wedding vow
> Ah, but I was so much older then, I'm younger than that now'

[My Back Pages]

Seen through this lens, 'It Ain't Me, Babe' flows naturally from 'My Back Pages'.

> 'You say you're lookin' for someone
> Who will promise never to part
> Someone to close his eyes for you
> Someone to close his heart
> Someone who will die for you and more'

He could be addressing these words to the 'corpse evangelist' of 'My Back Pages'. Again, there's nothing too special about this performance, which has a rough, acoustic feel to it.

[It Ain't Me, Babe]

'Don't Think Twice' doesn't come from the same place, more like the 'restless hungry feeling/that don't do no one no good' from 'One Too Many Mornings'. I quoted some of the lyrics of 'Don't Think Twice' to my wife who commented that it sounds cruel. I think that is an aspect of the song; the indifference you need to cultivate to keep moving on has its cruel side. But here it's an indifference touched with tenderness and regret. It's no fun being 'on the dark side of the road'. The song is best performed in a jaunty manner, as is this one from 20th February. I like the performance but the rowdy audience is a bit intrusive.

[Don't Think Twice]

Still in the acoustic vein, we have another old friend, 'Girl from the North Country,' a song animated by a gentle and loving nostalgia. It doesn't have the bitter edge of 'If You See Her Say Hello'.

[Girl from the North Country]

There's not much loving nostalgia in 'You're a Big Girl Now', either. Just the pain of the thought of what the woman in question might be doing without him. It's a fine way to torture yourself, imagining your lover 'in somebody's room'. Sometimes the 'dark side of the road' can be very dark indeed. Dylan does a fine vocal here, but to my ear the performance is compromised by Dylan's determinedly 'off key' guitar playing. I've mentioned Mr Guitar Man's disconcerting style before, and it certainly comes to the fore in this version. Maybe he doesn't want the sound to become too sweet. Your call, dear reader.

[You're a Big Girl Now]

Mr Guitar Man is less of a bother in this 'Senor,' and except for some upsinging, it's a raw and powerful performance of the song. Whenever I hear this song I imagine a seedy canteen or bar near the Mexican border somewhere, some lonely end of the world place where you might forget what it is you're waiting for, and you have to surrender to your gypsy fate.

[Senor]

The words that keep coming to mind to describe Dylan's performances in 1998 are rough and raw. Dylan never allows the performances to become smooth, easy listening. Others can do that with his songs, often to the songs' detriment. For Dylan, the experiences conveyed in the songs are never smoothed over or homogenised. The emotional edges are ragged, as the sound can be, often more so than the album versions, and Mr Guitar Man's insistent dissonances never allow us to let our guard down.

So that's it for 1998, folks, a big year, 117 shows, and there is another big, to my mind, better year coming up – 1999, on the edge of the millennium. We'll catch you then.

Kia Ora

1999

NET 1999: Part 1 - Every Night in a Combustible Way

By Mike Johnson (Kiwipoet)

'Touring is something you either love or hate doing. I've experienced both. I try to keep an open mind about it. Right now, I'm enjoying it. The crowds make the show.

> Going onstage, seeing different people every night in a combustible way, that's a thrill. There's nothing in ordinary life that even comes close to that.'

– Bob Dylan (Edna Gundersen interview for USA Today – April 1999)

At this point in our headlong dash through the NET, it is time to pause and take stock. The NET has completed its first decade, we are entering its eleventh year, we are on the brink of a new millennium, and it is fair to say that Dylan and his band have never sounded better.

When I began this series I observed that some commentators are tempted to see the NET as a work of art in itself. That would imply, however, some intentionality or deliberate structuring, and I certainly don't see that. That doesn't mean that the NET doesn't have some kind of shape or movement, but having said that, no two commentators see the same thing. Everybody who looks at the NET creates their own narrative, and I'm no exception.

One commentator claims that the NET's finest hour was the performance of 'Ring Them Bells' at the Supper Club in 1993. Another claims that 1997 was the strongest year of the NET. The same claim is made for 1998, suggesting that the San Jose concert of that year was the best NET concert ever. Another claims that 1994 was the peak year for the NET, with a distinct falling off in 1995. Still others (me included) see the Prague concerts of 1995 as a high point of the NET. And so it goes on.

Rather than a work of art, it seems, the NET is more like a Rorschach test with everybody reading their own narrative into it, creating their own version of Bob Dylan as they go. With over a thousand concerts for the decade and about fourteen songs per concert we have an incredible 14,000 plus performances, enough raw material for all sorts of constructions.

I have spoken of a 'rising curve', (from the song 'Born in Time') which I see moving from 1991, a low point generally, to 1995 and the outstanding Prague concerts. 1996 saw something of a falling off (but a fine concert in Berlin that year), with a strong comeback in 1997, and a new rising curve that takes us through 1999 to 2000.

> 'One of the peaks of the Never-Ending Tour, 1999 may be one of Dylan's finest years on-stage. After years of building

credibility throughout the 1990s, the performances exploded at the turn of the century.' (CS at A Thousand Highways)

Egil, at AllDylan, comments: 'Every N.E.T. junkie seems to agree that 1999 was a wonderful Dylan year. Strong performances in all 5 legs.' I have to agree with these assessments. Dylan finishes the decade, and the century, with a bang. Other than the galvanising effect of the success of Time Out of Mind, we have other factors to consider. First, there was another shake up in the band's line up. Bucky Baxter, who joined Dylan is 1992 playing steel guitar and dobro, leaves the band. But rather than simply replacing him, Dylan brings in Charlie Sexton, a guitar all-rounder, who will often play dual lead with Larry Campbell. Sexton would leave Dylan's band in 2002 and rejoin it in 2009.

Both Sexton and Campbell are superior guitarists, weave a wonderful web of sound around Dylan's voice, and at the same time provide an expanded context for Dylan's own lead guitar playing. Mr Guitar Man's insistent hammering at one or two notes during a guitar break sounds a lot better with these two ace guitarists backing him. To my mind, and I have to say I'm no expert, Sexton is easily a match for Eric Clapton. Clapton has a commanding grasp of the blues, and a rapid, fluid style. But Sexton is more adventurous, sharper and more passionate.

But it's not only the backing, it's Dylan's voice, his major instrument, which puts the icing on the cake for 1999. Dylan makes his voice as rough as any roadhouse blues singer, but can also sing softly and smoothly when the song calls for it. And power. There's little that is thin and reedy here, unless he wants it to be. His voice is full of power and expression. I have to go back to 1995 to catch him singing like this. Now, however, his voice is richer and fuller than it was in the mid nineties. The origins of Dylan's later crooning voice might be found here, although we could push that right back to *Nashville Skyline*(1969) and the Johnny Cash sessions.

My problem as your tour guide is that there is just such a surfeit of high quality material. Looking at the past three years, I have been able to hone in on two or three 'best' concerts, but that's not so obvious for 1999. The concert at Tramps, New York, is highly regarded, but most of the 117 concerts he did that year are good. I can't organise a post around three or four concerts. Furthermore, I suspect that technology took a jump around the end of the century, as the quality of the audience recordings is very high, better than we've ever heard, I think. There is a cornucopia of material.

While in 1997 and 1998 the setlists were pretty consistent, with essentially the same concert being delivered night after night with variations and wild cards thrown in, in 1999, particularly in the latter part of the year, Dylan throws the setlists wide open, singing a wide variety of his songs and cover songs.

So where do I start and, more urgently, what do I leave out? For 1996 and 1997, I began with new songs being drip fed from Time out of Mind, and we will certainly cover those songs, but I'm sorely tempted to begin with a kick, that old familiar warhorse 'Maggie's Farm'. This song may be so familiar that we can easily slip over it. Dylan might not have helped by, on occasion, ripping through it as if he just wanted to get to the end. It can too easily become a messy guitar fest. Not here. Listening to this, I'm taken back to 1964, the Newport Folk Festival, when Dylan rounded up some musicians from the Paul Butterfield Blues Band and blew everybody's ears out with 'Maggie's Farm', a hard-edged attack on those folkie sensibilities.

It's too easy to miss the bitter irony of his lampooning of the American family, and the claustrophobia inherent in that desperate desire to escape. Maggie's Farm just ain't no place to be, especially if you happen to be a restless young genius: 'They say sing while you slave and I just get bored.' This performance restores the song to its original power and vigour. Dylan is in wonderful voice and the band is working as sweetly as any freight train.

It's a good song to start with because it's all about busting loose, busting out of constrictions which is just what Dylan does in 1999, busting out of his setlists, busting into new vocal power, busting open the sound of the band (I don't have the date).

[Maggie's Farm]

If that doesn't get you up and rocking, I don't know what will. I think there's a bit of a fudge with the lyrics, well disguised, but it doesn't matter. And that nifty little riff Sexton puts in behind it gives it style. This has quickly become my favourite performance of the song, keeping well clear of the word definitive.

I could say the same about this masterful performance of 'Senor', in which there is also a glitch in the lyrics. If I was tortured into choosing just one superlative performance from 1999, it would be this one (I think...). 'Senor' is a wonderful song, easily my favourite from *Street Legal* (1978) and apparently Dylan's favourite too, as it's the only song from that album that has stayed the course in terms of live performance. The song has a sinister edge. To my mind it's about having your whole universe, your world view, shaken up, tipped upside-down. Unwelcome reality comes crashing in. You'd better watch out for that 'gypsy with a broken flag and a flashing ring'. He's (she's?) the harbinger of the most unbearable truth.

When writing about this song for the Master Harpist series, I commented that it reminded me of that famous quote from Thoreau, 'The mass of men lead lives of quiet desperation. What is called resignation is confirmed desperation. From the desperate city you go into the desperate country...' What are we waiting for, Senor? There's nothing left for us here. It's a song from the dark side.

I certainly get that sense from this performance. And, for fans of Dylan's harmonica playing (like me), the harp work here is a rare pleasure, for, as with 1997/98, Dylan mostly left his harp at home in 1999. The searing, cutting edge of Dylan's harp works well with the end of the line feeling that comes through the song. Unfortunately I have not been able to track down who is playing violin here, perhaps some helpful reader knows. But it's compelling, and transports us back to the Rolling Thunder Tour.

I wouldn't be tempted to equate the mysterious Senor of the song with Jesus or any particular figure. We may well all have our 'senors' who we hope will have the answers to our most desperate questions.

[Senor]

After completing the European summer tour Dylan returned to the United States to perform a thirty-eight date tour with Paul Simon. I believe that this 'Sounds of Silence' comes from Portland Oregon, 12th June. In my last post I commented that Dylan seldom does his best work when duetting with others, but I'm eating my words now. While avoiding hyperbole as much as possible, I now have to say this duet is exquisite. There's no other word for it. Maybe 'The Sounds of Silence' is a song Dylan wished he'd written. It's all about our moral silence, the creeping deadness of our outrage, the quiet apocalypse.

Paul Simon takes the lead with Dylan doing back up vocals. It's gentle and totally moving. And the harmonica. Talk about rare moments of harp magic in 1999, we certainly have one here, chilling and melodic. I can't imagine the song sounding any better. And doesn't the crowd love it!

[Sounds of Silence]

They look good together on stage too, a sense of close communion. They are both living the song. This video is not the same performance as the sound clip above, and is of poor visual quality, but gives us the idea of how these two work together. Another brilliant, but quite different, harp solo.

[Sounds of Silence B]

So I've run out of space, just when I was getting started. I'll be back soon to continue this exploration of this peak NET year.

Kia Ora

NET 1999: Part 2 - Is Everything as Hollow as It Seems?

By Mike Johnson (kiwipoet)

> 'Windows were shaking all night in my dreams
> Everything was exactly the way that it seems'

Time Out of Mind is all about the hollowness of life, how empty and meaningless it can all be. This theme or emotion is not new to Dylan. The struggles for faith and meaning are deeply intertwined and go way back to 'It's Alright, Ma' and even earlier. We could go even further and say that that struggle has driven Dylan's artistic development right from the start.

It's just that in *Time Out of Mind*, it reaches a certain pitch and intensity, and is linked specifically with ageing. No song deals more explicitly with the ageing process than 'Highlands', that long, ungainly song that finishes the album.

> 'I see people in the park, forgettin' their troubles and woes
> They're drinkin' and dancin', wearin' bright colored clothes
> All the young men with the young women lookin' so good
> Well, I'd trade places with any of 'em, in a minute if I could
> I'm crossin' the street to get away from a mangy dog
> Talkin' to myself in a monologue

,

Anyone with a few years under their belt knows what it's   like   to   see young people partying and having fun, oblivious of their youth and the passing years, oblivious of some old person slipping by in the shadows. It's a kind of jealousy or envy. Trade places with 'em? Sure thing. It's a feeling that alienates us, for we are forever separated from what we once were and would like to be again.

The whole song is one big monologue in which despair and meaninglessness are pitted against a paradisaical vision of 'the highlands'. This how it begins:

'Well my heart's in The Highlands, gentle and fair
Honeysuckle blooming in the wildwood air
Bluebells blazing where the Aberdeen waters flow'

By the end of the song the separation from the world is complete. A new, parallel world has come into existence, but it's 'over the hills and far away'. He remains 'a prisoner in a world of mystery'.

'The sun is beginnin' to shine on me
But it's not like the sun that used to be
The party's over and there's less and less to say
I got new eyes, everything looks far away
Well my heart's in The Highlands at the break of day
Over the hills and far away'

The central event of the song is a confrontation between the Dylan persona and a waitress. This encounter has been likened to the central encounter in 'Tangled Up In Blue', but that encounter is both sharper and more mysterious than the rather lumbering narrative in 'Highlands'. The waitress asks Dylan to draw her, he does a drawing which she rejects as it doesn't look like her:

'I said "Oh kind miss, it most certainly does"
She say "You must be joking", I said "I wish I was"
She says "You don't read women authors do ya?"
At least that's what I think I hear her say
Well I say "How would you know, and what would it matter anyway?"
Well she says "Ya just don't seem like ya do"
I said "You're way wrong"
She says "Which ones have you read then?", I say "Read Erica Jong"'

Dylan is probably referring to Jong's Fear of Flying, (1973) which was still popular. But despite some Dylanesque dry humour here, and his ability to weave conversations into his songs is evident, this prosy story fits rather uneasily into the overall structure of the song, and it's not quite clear what the story is intended to demonstrate.

Dylan rarely performed the song, which he débuted in 1999. I'm glad he sang all the verses and was not tempted to drop any out. It has a simple blues riff, but is not an easy song to carry in live performance (18th Nov).

[Highlands]

Dylan didn't overwhelm his setlists with songs from Time Out of Mind. He slips them in here and there, augmenting his setlists rather than dominating them with new material. Along with 'Highlands', another new song that appeared in 1999 was 'Trying to Get to Heaven'.

I have to put this latter song in my top ten (at least for the moment). It has a pleasing melodic line and musical structure, and is a further exploration of the hollowness of life. In his account of the song, Tony Attwood has suggested that it could be placed before 'It's Not Dark Yet' as a stepping stone to that final despair, and that's a helpful way to see it.

> 'When you think that you've lost everything
> You find out you can always lose a little more
> I'm just going down the road feeling bad
> Trying to get to Heaven before they close the door'

There is an elusive feeling here of a bygone era, both in the nostalgia of the lyrics and the overall musical effect, which takes us back to those 1930s and 40s which so haunt this album, and which Dylan consciously evokes.

> 'I'm going down the river
> Down to New Orleans
> They tell me everything is gonna be all right
> But I don't know what all right even means'

Note the archaism of: 'I was riding the buggy with miss Mary Jane...' Mary Jane is a street name for cannabis, but putting that aside, the scene could be from the civil war. The Dylan persona here has a 'lone cowboy' feel to it, also from a previous era:

> 'Some trains don't pull no gamblers
> No midnight ramblers like they did before
> I've been to Sugar Town, I shook the sugar down
> Now I'm trying to get to Heaven before they close the door'

Despite a contemporary drug reference to LSD in Sugar Town, shaking the sugar down has a somewhat archaic feel of having pulled off a successful scam or deal. It is perhaps a rather unflattering reference to Dylan's financial success.

I have two performances worth tuning into. This first is from 7th April, and is perhaps the sharpest and clearest recording. An example of how good an audience recording can be.

[Tryin to get to Heaven (A)]

This next recording is from 30th April, and is a little more lush in its sound. Another powerful vocal performance from Dylan.

[Tryin to get to Heaven (B)]

Besides these two new songs that Dylan débuted in 1999, he continued to develop *Time Out of Mind* songs he'd introduced in the two previous years. 'Love Sick' is never going to change too much over the years. It has a strict form that doesn't allow for too much improvisation. This one sticks pretty much to the album version, but notice how Dylan drops his voice at the end of the lines (the opposite of upsinging), creating a sinister effect.

[Love Sick]

We get the same effect from 'Cold Irons Bound.' Listen to how he drops his voice at the end of these lines.

> 'One look at you, and I'm out of controool
> Like the universe has swallowed me whooole'

Dylan would use this 'downsinging' to great effect in the next couple of years, giving familiar lyrics an ominous edge. We are prisoners of our love, the song seems to be saying. This is a very hard-edged performance. Maybe the recording is a little on the sharp side, but so is the song. There is no way to sugar-coat this pill: 'Up over my head nothing but clouds of blood'. Despair and anger do make a good couple, don't they?

[Cold Irons Bound]

Musically, 'Till I Fell in Love with You' has an archaic feel too. I keep hearing Jimmy Rushing or one of the old urban blues singers. It is driven by an unvarying bluesy riff, and with no bridge or other musical breaks, it relies totally on its lyrics and swing to keep it going. This is not so much rock music but pre-rock music, the more ancient blues and big-band era music. Replace the guitars with saxes and trumpets, and you'd almost be slap-bang in the dance-hall music of the late 1940s.

Dylan was consciously after that sound when he made the album. He apparently told producer Lanois that he was after the kind of sound of the early music studios, of what were known as 'race records' which brought forward many black performers. Lanois told him it could be done, but in the end the sound on the album was too sophisticated, too nuanced, to capture the raw sound Dylan was after.

On stage, however, he could do it, and does it brilliantly in this performance of 'Till I Fell in Love with You'. Again I avoid the word definitive, but this one ranks as my number one version of the song. Dylan's voice is up front, the lyrics crackle out, and the band swings along, a touch of bluesy swagger.

[Till I Fell in Love]

'To Make You Feel My Love' evokes the same era, but the sentimental ballad tradition, rather than blues. I can imagine Vera Lynn singing it (almost), it has that tearful 'We'll Meet Again', feel to it. These lyrics could have been written for Billie Holiday:

> 'I'd go hungry, I'd go black and blue
> I'd go crawling down the avenue

No, there's nothing that I wouldn't do
To make you feel my love'

Such lyrics are quite formalised, quite generic. Going 'black and blue' was not an uncommon phrase, and 'crawling down the avenue' has a similar well used feel to it. The lyrics are not intended to sound original, rather to signal the sentiment through familiar references.

'The storms are raging on the rolling sea
And on the highway of regret'

The effect of this is to evoke a sense of familiarity, as if we've heard the song before somewhere, maybe in a speakeasy in the small hours of the morning. Hasn't every singer who's ever pulled on your heart strings sung from 'the highway of regret'? There's a lot of traffic on that highway.

In this performance Dylan introduces it as 'a song to my ex-wife, who's a tennis player...' Make of that what you will. And again, a performance that tops those of the two previous years.

[To Make You Feel My Love]

The oddest aspect of these 1999 performances of 'Can't Wait', which Dylan regularly performed, is the disconcerting 'off key' playing of Mr Guitar Man. Again, I have to ask, what does Dylan intend here, what does he think he's doing? I ask the question because it's clearly deliberate. It throws the song off-centre with guttural sounds. It makes its own weird sense but its relationship to the melody is problematic to say the least.

[Can't Wait]

Perhaps, to return to Tony Attwood's comments on 'Trying to Get to Heaven', it was not just that song, but the others as well, 'Can't Wait', 'Till I fell in Love', 'Cold Irons Bound', that lead, somehow inevitably, to the total loss and despair of 'It's Not Dark Yet'. Seen that way, 'It's Not Dark Yet' could be seen as the quintessential song on the album, the song which pushes the darkness and alienation of the collection to the very extreme. An epic performance from a beautifully scarred voice.

[It's Not Dark Yet]

That's it for now. I'll be back soon with more goodies from 1999

Kia Ora

NET 1999: Part 3 - Touchdown at Tramps – Archaic Music

By Mike Johnson (Kiwipoet)

The story goes that in 1989, while recording *Oh Mercy*, Dylan exclaimed to producer Lanois, 'This is archaic music we're making.' In other words, Dylan realised he was no longer on the cutting edge of rock music, which had become increasingly sophisticated during the 80s, and arguably increasingly over-produced, or at least elaborately produced – a tendency that continued into the 90s. Along with that sophistication came a certain slickness, the kind of slickness you hear in the Spice Girls, whose music now seems to typify the commercial sounds of that decade.

In the face of these developments, Dylan's approach in the 90s seems determinedly retro. Not for the first time. At the end of the 1960s, when bands like the Beatles and the Rolling Stones were making albums that were increasingly baroque, complex and sophisticated, and the Cream were producing their creamy sounds, Dylan released, *John Wesley Harding* which had a thin, minimal sound, deliberately backward looking musically.

Listening to some of these recordings from 1999, I'm struck by how 1950s the sound is, or at least how obviously and deeply rooted in the origins of rock music Dylan's music is. Call it primitive, call it primal, call it dance music, call it roots music, call it whatever, Dylan determinedly evokes music from a previous age. Not just rock music but rock-and-roll, pre-rock. While the album *Time Out of Mind* shows the influence of that 'archaic music,' more consciously and deliberately than *Oh Mercy*, his live performances tap directly into the music of a previous age. He loves to sing those old songs.

Buddy Holly was right on the cusp, as rock-and-roll was turning into rock music. Holly wrote 'Not Fade Away' in 1957, but in the late 90s we find Dylan doing wonderful performances of the song, heavier than Holly would have conceived, but smack-bang in that tradition. The one thing we know when listening to Dylan performing the song at Tramps, New York, is that this is not the Spice Girls, that this is as far away from that kind of music as you can get. That this, most joyfully, taps into the roots. While I love the more minimal version of 1998, the sheer verve and energy of this performance carries me away. I think I'll just listen to it one more time.

[Not Fade Away]

Wow! that was as good as I thought it was. Even better. Buddy Holly would have loved it. Dylan does some nifty guitar work on this one. Stand up and dance!

'Not Fade Away' is not an isolated example. 'Alabama Getaway' is a Robert Hunter song, released by the Grateful Dead in 1980, but it taps right into Chuck Berry and the more 'primitive' tradition of 1950s countrified blues. I imagine Dylan likes the song because it's doing what he wants to do, to return to the golden age of Sun records when the music was still fresh and you could go to jail for playing it. This is another from Tramps.

[Alabama Getaway]

Dylan's music is haunted by these 50s, early 60s pre-rock singers like Buddy Holly, Jean Vincent, Dion – and of course Elvis Presley. Presley released 'Money Honey' (written by Jesse Stone) in 1956. Dylan clearly enjoys raking it over here, in 1999 (date unknown). It feels just like coming home.

[Money Honey]

It's not hard to see how firmly rooted Dylan's own rock songs are in this 'primitive' tradition, however sophisticated the lyrics might be. This performance of 'Tombstone Blues', for example, takes us right into the simple, jangling chords of old rock-and-roll, jump music. Dylan's twin guitarists, Charlie Sexton and Larry Campbell, make all this possible with their happily expert, retro playing. It's that disjunction between the 'primitive' music and the wild lyrics that makes Dylan's rock songs so distinctive. This is another one from Tramps.

[Tombstone Blues (A)]

Fascinating lyric change here. This is what I think he's singing:

> Mama's in the alley, she ain't got no shoes
> Daddy's in the graveyard, looking for the fuse

I have tended to argue throughout this series that Dylan didn't really stop writing protest songs, he just extended and deepened the range of protest. In 'Tombstone Blues' we find surrealist mockery as a form of social criticism.

> 'The ghost of Belle Starr, she hands down her wits
> To Jezebel the nun, she violently knits
> A bald wig for Jack the Ripper who sits
> At the head of the Chamber of Commerce'
> Where, I assume, he's still sitting.

'Tombstone Blues' (1965) is not really a blues in the strict sense of the word. It's not a three chord, twelve bar structure, with a repeated first line, and nor is 'Most Likely You Go Your Way'. This latter song is fast and hard-driving, and the more advanced technology permits sounds impossible to achieve in the 50s, but it wouldn't have sounded too out of place in a rock and roll dance hall of the late 50s. Some of these lyrics, though, might have sounded a bit strange. They still do:

> 'The judge, he holds a grudge
> And he's about to call on you
> But he's badly built and he walks on stilts
> Watch out he don't fall on you'

Gone are the long, wandering epics of the earlier 90s. This is short and sharp and takes no prisoners. And the way Dylan drops his voice at the end of the lines (down-singing) makes for an ominous, nastyish effect. I start to reach for that word definitive when I think of this performance. It captures all the turbulence and bile of the original (*Blonde on Blonde*, 1966), but ups the tempo to a frenetic pace. It's sharp and punky. Another Tramps performance.

[Most Likely You Go Your Way (A)]

That Tramps version is very hard-edged, but Dylan didn't always perform it like that. This performance (date unknown) changes the mood a bit with a more echoey sound and a less strident vocal. I sometimes wonder if these variations of sound and mood have to do with the acoustics of the venue, and even the nature of the recording, but this one certainly has a different feel to it. Both are great vocal performances.

[Most Likely You Go Your Way (B)]

The rise of rock-and-roll, and later rock music, is closely associated with the blues, and how blues spilled across racial boundaries to became popular with young white kids. (For those interested in that history, I recommend the acclaimed multi-part PBS series 'Martin Scorsese Presents the Blues'.) Also, listen to Dylan's early 1960s recording of 'One Kind Favour' and you'll get the feel for how important the blues were in shaping Dylan's music and vocal style.

A catchy little blues number, 'Down Along the Cove' comes as the second to last track on *John Wesley Harding* (1967), but we had to wait until 1999 to get the first live performance. Bringing it forward at this point, nested among the *Time Out of Mind* songs, and antique songs, is yet another indication of the influence of this retro music on Dylan's own songs. It's a Dylan song but could almost be someone else's. It's a straight no frills rock blues. A treat for the ears. (8th November)

[Down Along the Cove]

While on the subject of the blues, let's consider 'Leopard-Skin Pill-box Hat,' a derisive social commentary in blues style. But while he keeps the twelve bar, three chord structure, instead of repeating the first line, he makes up a new one for line two:

> 'Well if you, wanna see the sun rise
> Honey, I know where
> We'll go out and see it sometime
> We'll both just sit there and stare

Me with my belt wrapped around my head
And you just sittin' there
In your brand new leopard-skin pill-box hat'

Dripping with sarcasm, it's a comic put down. Taken out of *Blonde on Blonde* and transferred to 1999, with Campbell and Sexton on the job, it loses none of its jeering insouciance. (Date unknown)

[Leopard-skin Pill-box Hat]

Funny thing is, this song sounded pretty retro even in 1966 when it first appeared. It was a throwback to an earlier urban blues sound.

Mockery as social criticism is again to the fore in 'Highway 61 Revisited,' another retro sounding song, although less obviously derived from the blues. Again the complexity of the lyrics is set against a simple, 'primitive' jump music structure. It's a lot of irreverent fun. This Tramps performance really pushes it along, the wild lyrics flying by before we can get a hold of them. Taming Dylan's lyrics to the page hardly does justice to the madcap, whirling effect this song creates.

[Highway 61 Revisited]

A little less hard and fast, but no less rooted in the early history of rock is the 1985 'Seeing The Real You at Last'. Its dramatic portentous style might hark back to early Ray Charles, but it's that same jump rhythm that marks these Dylan songs. The lyrics too, some of them lifted from late 1940s movies (the Humphrey Bogart connection), reinforce the antique feel of the music. I keep thinking I've heard it before somewhere. There's an echo of Presley in it. This snarling Tramps performance does it full justice. The song is starting to fade from Dylan's setlists, so it's good to hear it get such lively treatment.

[Seeing the Real You]

Let's end this post where we started, with that pivotal figure Buddy Holly, that mid fifties rock and roll singer whose music pointed firmly towards the future. 'That'll Be The Day' (1957) is another Holly song that fits quite seamlessly into Dylan's setlists in 1999. In this case, Dylan creates a medley with Dion's 'The Wanderer'. Dion DiMucci is another transitional figure, the last of the great doo-woppers who didn't quite make it into rock music, and whose sound had already dated by the mid sixties. Yet there are echoes of Dion's high, clear voice in Dylan, and some of Dylan's 1999 performances of 'The Wanderer' sound uncannily like Dion himself.

By morphing without changing the beat from Holly to Dion, it says a lot about 50s pop music. These songs are sort of interchangeable. But it also says a lot about the influence of these singer/songwriters on Dylan. In some respects Dylan belongs more to that era of pop music which featured the vocalist (Dion, Elvis, Buddy Holly, Bobby Darin...) than to the rock music of the 60s which was oriented towards groups, bands (the Beatles, the Rolling Stones, the Hollies, the Animals...).

Even in his heyday in the 60s, there was something retro about Dylan – 'the last of the best...' I think he's singing here with Paul Simon, another lone singer/songwriter (20th July).

[That'll be the Day/The wanderer]

In the light of all this, I'm tempted to declare Dylan to be the last and the greatest of the old rock-and-roll merchants, yet he was able to do what those 50s singers didn't or couldn't do, namely bring rock-and-roll into the rock era.

Of course there was another side to Bob Dylan, that of the folk singer, another kind of retro, it is there we'll be turning in the next post.

Stay cool and safe.

Kia Ora

NET 1999 Part 4 – Minstrel Bob

By Mike Johnson (Kiwipoet)

For practical purposes, we can invent two Bob Dylans (there are a lot more; the man contains multitudes, after all). One is a rock singer with his feet firmly planted in the 1950s and the era of rock and roll. I explored the Rock Dylan in my last post. There we saw Dylan singing 'Not Fade Away', 'Money Honey', 'That'll Be the Day', and the rock and roll derived 'Alabama Getaway'. There are others we'll catch up with in the next post. We saw how the rhythms and chords of rock and roll influenced Dylan's great early songs like 'Tombstone Blues' and 'Most Likely You Go Your Way'.

Full credit is due to guitarists Sexton and Campbell for brilliantly echoing the sounds of that earlier era of music. But as well as the Rock Bob we have the Folk Bob. In the 1960s, Dylan acknowledged these two Bobs by breaking his concerts into acoustic and electric sections. That division carries through into the 1990s largely intact, although Dylan evolved a 'soft rock' sound which tended to blur the gap. He didn't necessarily divide his shows into two halves, as he did in the 60s, but the two sides of Bob Dylan were evident every time he switched guitars from acoustic to electric and back again.

In this post I want to explore the Folk Bob because, in 1999, Dylan covered some of the folk songs that influenced him, just as he did with the rock and roll songs. The two Bobs have distinct musical lineages, although when it comes to the blues, the line gets blurred.

Let's start with 'Roving Gambler' This is a traditional song, first recorded by Samantha Bumgarner in 1924, but which dates back to 19th Century England. The Folk Bob has an English/Celtic connection, sometimes direct but more often, as in this case, after the song has entered the American tradition.

Dylan has been singing it since 1960. It's peppy and a good performance piece. Like 'Pretty Peggy O' it's a root song for Folk Bob's own songwriting. As evidenced in this performance, the song has lost none of its charm for Dylan (9th November, Atlantic City.) Here he uses it as an opener.

303

[Roving Gambler]

'You're Gonna Quit me' is credited to Blind Blake, first recorded in 1926, and included in Dylan's folk collection Good as I Been to You, in 1993. The title of the album is a phrase from that song. Here Dylan plays it straight, just as he does on the album, and the ambience of it takes us right back to the folk clubs in New York in the early 60s (8th April).

[You're Gonna Quit Me]

It is well known that Dylan began his songwriting career by writing his own lyrics for pre-existing melodies. (I believe 'Mr Tambourine Man' was Dylan's first fully original melody.) One of the first songs Dylan wrote, 'Song to Woody', takes its melody from the Woody Guthrie song, '1913 Massacre'. The origin of the melodies of these songs is often obscure, which suggests they come from more ancient folk traditions.

In 'Song to Woody' the major features of a Folk Bob song are established – a simple ballad like structure with multiple verses, and no bridge. In revisiting the song, I was surprised at how good it is. Dylan didn't begin by writing bad songs; he was good right from the start. Like 'Bob Dylan's Dream', another early song, there's a sense of nostalgia, as if the singer is much older than he was, a sense of a life travelled and lived. There's a world weariness that belies his youth, but of course by 1999 his voice has grown old enough for the song. The song celebrates and is quite explicit about these folk and blues singers from the 1930s and 40s whose melodies and attitudes underpin Dylan's own.

> 'Here's to Cisco an' Sonny an' Leadbelly too
> An' to all the good people that traveled with you
> Here's to the hearts and the hands of the men
> That come with the dust and are gone with the wind'

The reference is to Cisco Houston, a comrade of Guthrie. Sonny is probably Sonny Boy Williamson, a bluesman from the 1930s and a great harmonica player, while Leadbelly and his prison songs were getting known in the early 1960s, mainly thanks to the efforts of collector Alan Lomax.

Once more, Dylan plays it straight, with no frills.

[Song to Woody]

The early 'Masters of War' shows how effective welding his own lyrics to pre-loved melodies could be. The melody comes from 'Nottamun Town,' an ancient traditional English song, a nonsense rhyme, which was collected and then arranged by Jean Ritchie.

In an article on Dylan.org.uk, Tony Attwood has a fascinating discussion of the 'Dorian Mode' in which the song is written, a mode that is in neither the major nor the minor keys, but a more ancient key which has largely fallen out of use. This Dorian Mode helps create that ominous, threatening effect we hear in the song, something that has come from a more ancient place. The genius of the song lies in this combination of hard hitting, contemporary anti-war lyrics with this antique Dorian Mode. Somehow, I am reminded of Samuel Taylor Coleridge's 'ancestral voices prophesying war' (Kublai Khan) and Matthew Arnold's 'Dover Beach':

> 'And we are here as on a darkling plain
> Swept with confused alarms of struggle and flight,
> Where ignorant armies clash by night.'

Dylan has done this song as a hard rocker, but in the 90's he developed a more quiet but no less threatening arrangement, not as rigidly dumpty-dum as the original (Freewheeling, 1962), but more a syncopated, surging sound better suited to the song. I'm still stuck on the 1995 London performance, but I have no quarrel with this powerful version (a harp break would have been nice, though). The audience is a little rowdy for my taste, but what interests me is the guitar work, with Sexton, Campbell and Dylan giving the song a Celtic drive both moving and spooky.

[Masters of War]

Dylan does the same thing with his anti-war drama, 'John Brown'. In this case he uses a traditional Irish melody from 'My Son John', an anti-war song in its own right. Again it is this mix of antique folk melodies and contemporary themes that drives the song along. There is a curious sense of antiquity to the lyrics of this song also, however. The term 'cannon ball' takes us back to wars of previous eras.

Probably the best live version of 'John Brown' remains the 1994 MTV Unplugged performance. It's very smooth. But by the late 90s Dylan had evolved a slower, starker arrangement, with banjo, that rivals the Unplugged performance. This 1999 performance (From Tramps, New York) is both simpler and more deadly. The antique nature of the melody is brought to the fore by the arrangement.

There is however a problem. By the late 90s Dylan has lost his grip a little on the lyrics (same with 'Blowin' in the Wind'), and he fluffs them a couple of times (while brilliantly covering up for it) and this mars the performance for me.

[John Brown]

'Tomorrow Is a Long Time' (1963) is built on three simple chords common to many songs, which is maybe why it sounds familiar, even if we haven't heard it. It's a wonderful love song, I put it alongside 'Girl from the North Country' – it has a similar innocence. In this performance Dylan doesn't try any clever tricks, or attempt to add chords, but plays it in all its original simplicity, giving it a gentle melody with the band joining in on the chorus. It is done without sacrificing the delicacy of feeling we find in the original.

[Tomorrow Is a Long Time]

It's not exactly clear where the melody for 'Girl from the North Country' comes from, and it doesn't really sound much like 'Scarborough Fair' to which it has been linked. It does, however, have an old worldly sense to it in some of the phrasing. Love songs are as old as folk music itself, and it's the sense of deep time, a long tradition, that gives these songs their gravitas. In singing these compositions, Dylan becomes the archetype of the travelling bard or minstrel. Once more the 1999 performances honour the feeling of the original. This is a softer version from 2nd April.

[Girl from the North Country (A)]

And here's a somewhat sharper version. (Date unknown)

[Girl from the North Country (B)]

'Blowin' in the Wind' is derived from 'No More Auction Blocks', a song about slavery dating back to the American Civil War. The wind may be elusive, but the questions are eternal. It was one of the first protest songs Dylan wrote that wasn't based on a topical event. The antique feel of it, and its anthemic quality, give a sort of timelessness. Again the use of 'cannon ball,' a deliberate archaism to give the message a more universal feel.

[Blowin' in the Wind]

Fast forward three or four years and we have 'Fourth Time Around', a narrative which evokes the English ballad tradition and was a poke at the Beatles song, 'Norwegian Wood', which Dylan felt was too much like one of his own songs. But the lyrics tell a sordid, unsavoury little tale quite at variance with the sweetness of the melody. It is a deadly little song about an un-romantic encounter. It is dripping with venom and bitterness.

> 'She threw me outside, I stood in the dirt where everyone walked
> And after finding out I'd forgotten my shirt, I went back and knocked
> I waited in the hallway, she went to get it, and I tried to make sense
> Out of that picture of you in your wheelchair that leaned up against
>
> Her Jamaica rum, and when she did come, I asked her for some
> She said, "No, dear," I said, "Your words aren't clear,
>   you'd better spit out your gum"
> She screamed 'til her face got so red, then she fell on the floor
> And I covered her up and then thought I'd go look through her drawer'

But what a beautiful, spooky performance Dylan gives here. The complaint that Dylan never sings his songs the way they sound on the album doesn't apply here. The thirty-three years between the writing of the song and this performance drop away. Yep. This is just the way it sounded.

[Fourth Time Around]

Well that's me this time around. Back soon with more sounds from 1999.

Kia Ora

NET 1999 part 5 Inside the Museum

By Mike Johnson (Kiwipoet)

My problem with reviewing Dylan's 1999 performances is that there is just too much good stuff. I have settled into doing about four posts per year, with about 10 audio files per post, and here I am at post five in 1999 with about thirty songs clamouring to get onto my setlist, and one more post to go of the covers Dylan did of other songs, some of which he'd never done before, at least on the NET.

So I've cut the thirty songs down to nineteen and will have to rip through them pretty fast. All these songs I have introduced before in previous posts, so those following these posts won't need any reminders. If you're a new reader, I suggest you look at some of the previous posts. (There is an index to the series here).

Without further ado, let's pick up from where we left the last post, looking at Dylan's folk roots, the acoustic Folk Bob, and we can't do better than start at Tramps, New York, with this vigorous, upbeat performance of 'The Times They Are A-changing'. The times might change but the song doesn't. The crowd loves this one. Wonderful vocal, and, glory be, a blaring harp solo, as jazzy and discordant as it ever was.

[Times They Are A-Changing]

'Boots of Spanish Leather' is one of Dylan's great conversation songs. The sadness of parting, the sadness of gifts. This is a quiet, reflective performance. No tricks, just the unadorned song. (18th November)

[Boots of Spanish Leather]

Staying in the same bandwidth, 'Don't Think Twice' also gets the simple, unadorned treatment. After the age of the epic versions of these short songs, it's a pleasure to be able to appreciate the brevity of the song once more. There is some guitar work but it is not excessive, and the instrumental break at the end gives it a country twist along with that pattering beat. It's so easy to listen to you can almost forget the sting in the lyrics.

[Don't Think Twice]

What's a protest song? 'It's Alright, Ma' is a comprehensive blast at all things false and phoney, and a declaration of resilience in the face of all that crap.

Originally, Dylan would rap it out fast, the words almost too quick to catch (try the 1990 performance, NET, 1990, part 1) but by 1999 he was searching for new ways to present the song. Here he slows it down a bit and puts that pattering beat I mentioned behind it. I think I prefer the earlier hard-driving approach, but I can hardly fault Dylan's vocal on this one. Instead of flattening his voice, as he did in the 60s, he raises and softens it.

[It's Alright, Ma]

Moving forward in Dylan's chronology a little, we come to his great blues composition 'It Takes a Lot to Laugh, It Takes a Train to Cry'. This performance has a country edge (courtesy of the steel guitar) rather than a hard urban edge. Nice lazy beat. A masterly performance. (date unknown)

[It Takes a Lot to Laugh]

One of the songs Dylan experimented with the most has been 'She Belongs to Me' and he would go on evolving new versions right through to 2013. All through the 90s Dylan developed a quiet, laid-back version of the song, quite different to the more upbeat, peppy album version. It would be some years before he developed the hard-driving, bluesy versions of the last years of the NET. But don't let that foot-tapping, laid back performance beguile you into thinking that it's a nice song.

[She Belongs to Me]

Time to hop back to Tramps for a gutsy performance of 'Ballad of a Thin Man'. The song is addressed to someone who is way out of their depth at some seriously bizarre party. Dylan's low, snarly voice is as effective as the high, keening voice of the original. More effective maybe, as there is no escaping the nastiness of the tone here, augmented by the equally nasty tones of Dylan's Stratocaster. If ever Dylan's off centre, 'off key' guitar playing is appropriate, it is here.

[Ballad of a Thin Man]

Before leaving the world of *Highway 61 Revisited*, we have to drop in and hear 'Desolation Row', one of Dylan's greatest masterpieces. I couldn't overlook this one even though there is nothing particularly notable or outstanding about the performance. There is a beauty in the melodic structure of the song that belies the dark visions that impel it, and Dylan's rough, late 90s voice suits the subject matter just fine.

[Desolation Row]

Coming to *Blonde on Blonde*, we find a gentle performance of 'I Want You'. Not as transcendent as the 1994 MTV Unplugged performance (not included in the official release, see my NET, 1994), or as desperate as some live performances, this one finds the softer, more romantic, less driven side of the song.

[I Want You]

The greatest song on *Blonde on Blonde* has to be 'Visions of Johanna', maybe Dylan's greatest ever song. A subterranean masterpiece, a moody, early hours of the morning kind of song. As I've said before, none of the subsequent performances have the spooky power of the album version, or the 1966 live versions, but this one holds the mood. At least it doesn't have the pattering beat Dylan often uses during this period. This performance carries the weirdness and darkness of the song, probably due to Dylan's dark-edged vocal.

[Visions of Johanna]

What Dylan show would be complete without 'Forever Young'? This brings us into the 70s, and the most popular song from *Planet Waves*, a sad anthem to the passing of time and the inevitability of old age. But it's not really about physical age, is it? It's about staying young in spirit. It was amazing to hear the 80 year old Dylan give the song a good airing on *Shadow Kingdom*. As long as you can draw breath, the song holds. There's a bit of a fumble with the lyrics, and a ragged chorus, but that's all right if you're young at heart.

[Forever Young]

'Shelter from the Storm' brings us into the 70s and *Blood on the Tracks*. Arguably, the song benefits from a slower, more thoughtful version than on the album. Both a wonderful love song and a tribute to the loved one, it reminds us that we are nothing, just a 'creature void of form,' if we are not loved. It is a song about the redeeming power of love. Again the steel guitar gives the song a country flavour, gentle and twangy, without sentimentalising the song at all, although there is more of a nostalgic flavour than the brisk album version.

[Shelter from the Storm]

We'll pause briefly at Dylan's gospel period for the provocative 'Gotta Serve Somebody', a song Dylan often used as an opener in 1999. It has a good strong rock beat. Here he delivers it to an ecstatic audience at Grand Rapids, 15th Feb. While you are up and dancing, listen for lyrical variations and verse mix ups. It really doesn't matter with this song.

[Gotta Serve Somebody]

We can't pass over *Shot of Love* without listening to 'Every Grain of Sand'. It's a song hanging in the balance between profundity and sentimentality, and works best with an unsentimental performance. If the album version is just a tad too smooth for your taste, this rougher more down-home late 90s style might be more fitting. Again there's the steel guitar to give it that country feel, but that doesn't push it towards sentimentality, not with that ragged, doubt-filled voice.

[Every Grain of Sand]

Lets move forward to 1989, *Oh Mercy* and the forever atmospheric 'Man in the Long Black Coat'. Best served soft and menacing. I still hark back to the 1995, Prague performance with its soaring harp, but this rougher, gutsier version does the job just fine. Ever taken your love to a dance or rave only to have her leave with another, and a dodgy character at that? If you want to indulge that feeling, now's your opportunity. Innocence falls into the thrall of evil. It's a cosmic drama.

[Man in Long Black Coat]

Oh Mercy and *Under the Red Sky* also saw something of a revival of the old, radical, protest Dylan. What's a protest song? Well, 'Everything Is Broken' can't be anything else. This performance bustles along, just as it should, a recitation of modern evils, but I'm afraid it can't match 'It's Alright, Ma' for the denunciation of everything. It lacks a melodic line, and is too mono-tonal for my taste. I guess it leans towards punk. It's not designed for aesthetic pleasure, and he rips through it with vigour and alarm.

[Everything Is Broken]

I could have dropped 'I and I' as this is not the best performance of the song, but we have been following it from the early 90s, watching it grow and develop, and this will be the final year Dylan will perform it. It's full of the lyrical force of someone listening to their heart, whatever they might be saying. It has sadness, nostalgia, defiance and threat. One of Dylan's great performance songs. Goodbye is too good a word.

[I and I]

Before finishing, *Shadow Kingdom* arrived just I was finishing the previous post. I was intrigued to see that the ambience, the scene portrayed, was of the 1930 or 40s clubs, dives and speakeasies, and he made his early songs sound like they came from that era. This movement towards the roots of modern music really gets serious with Time out of Mind, its consciously antique feel. There was no Folk Bob in *Shadow Kingdom*; all the music was brought home to that between the wars milieu. In 1999 you can feel Dylan positioning his songs in that way, a path that would lead to *Shadow*

Kingdom.

Pity he didn't play his great stadium rock epic, 'Tangled Up In Blue'. With the right arrangement, it would have fitted *Shadow Kingdom* just fine. But the song was very much alive in 1999, with two very solid performances I could not choose between – so here they both are. The first is a little shorter and faster (date unknown), while the second feels a bit more adventurous. Funny how that guitar backing can bring a Celtic or Irish flavour to the melody. 'Tangled' has deep roots in old music, that's why it sounds so compelling.

[Tangled Up In Blue (A)]

This next one is from New Orleans, 3rd Feb. We welcome back the epic, and Dylan's harp improvisations.

[Tangled Up In Blue (B)]

Next post will be the last for 1999. We'll hear Dylan covering the songs of others, his 'uncovers'. Until then, stay well and stay tuned.

Kia Ora

NET 1999: Part 6 - Honky Tonk Dylan: Despair and Sentimentality

By Mike Johnson (Kiwipoet)

This post, the last for 1999, is dedicated to the non-Dylan songs Dylan performed in that year. We have already seen some of these songs in previous posts; 'Sounds of Silence', (NET, 1999, part 1, don't miss it!), 'Not Fade Away', 'Alabama Getaway', 'Money Honey' (NET, 1999, part 3), 'Roving Gambler' and 'You Gonna Quit Me' (part 4). But that doesn't cover the range of songs Dylan does in 1999, which is particularly rich in cover songs, as Dylan keeps returning us to an earlier era of music, mostly country and cowboy songs, thus establishing a context and background for his own songs.

Some of these songs, like 'Friend of the Devil' have cropped up in Dylan's setlists for a couple of years. That song is from the Grateful Dead, with the lyrics written by Robert Hunter. Released in 1970, it has been widely covered by a number of artists, and has been described as progressive bluegrass. It has that classic feel to it. The themes of insomnia and relationship woes put the song firmly in *Time Out of Mind* territory (18th Nov).

[Friend of the Devil]

Remember when you first put Dylan's 1980 *Saved* on the turntable? The first song is 'Satisfied Mind', a slow, bluesy intro to the album. The song was written by Jo Hayes and Jack Rhodes and was number 1 on the billboard Hot Country Song list in 1955. It was the kind of song the child Dylan would have been listening to on his radio during those lonely Hibbing nights. Dylan's first known performance of the song was in 1967, during *The Basement Tapes* era. Those who know it from *Saved* are hardly going to recognise it performed in this antique fashion. It turns out to be a rollicking cowboy song with suitably melancholy lyrics about the illusory nature of money (9th Nov).

[Satisfied Mind]

As far as I know, 'Pass Me Not, Oh Gentle Saviour,' written by the blind Fanny Crosby in 1868, was not performed by Dylan prior to 1999, and would only be performed five times over 1999 and 2000. It's a country music hymn, an interesting fusion that produced many such songs. Fanny Crosby herself wrote dozens of them. Still a cowboy song, it's about salvation rather than whisky or love woes. Dylan's arrangement here is similar to The Stanley Brothers version released in 1960.

It's something of a curiosity in this context, a dark period for Dylan in which his faith is deeply called into question by the *Time Out of Mind* songs. 'Don't even hear the murmur of a prayer', he sings on 'It's Not Dark Yet'. Perhaps this expression of a simple, old fashioned faith appealed to Dylan during such a time, a crisis of faith if we can call it that. There's a strong flavour of nostalgia in all of this (23rd Feb).

[Pass Me Not, Oh Gentle Saviour]

Not quite so maudlin, and more upbeat, 'Honky Tonk Blues' by Hank Williams turns out to be a crowd pleaser. Not to be confused with 'Honky Tonk Woman' by The Rolling Stones, Williams' song was released in 1952, and was made famous by Charlie Pride in 1980. The song is about a farm boy who goes to the city and becomes disillusioned. There may be an echo here of Dylan's experience – a kid from the northern provinces goes to New York to suffer his own rude awakening. But of course, you can never go back again... (23rd Feb).

[Honky Tonk Blues]

'You're Too Late,' by Lefty Frizzell, recorded in 1954, was only performed once by Dylan at Daytona Beach, FL, Jan 29, 1999. (See Tony Attwood's post: bob-dylan.org.uk/archives/16040). Again, we're in country, cowboy music territory, sob songs I like to call them. They are sentimental in the way that 'To Make You Feel My Love' from *Time Out of Mind* is. Despair and sentimentality are a matched pair. This is a wonderful, robust performance of the song. Highly recommended. Perhaps this sentimentality is an antidote to despair, or maybe a traditionally safe way to channel it (29th

Jan).
[You're Too Late]

'Oh Babe It Aint No Lie', by the incomparable Elizabeth Cotton, was released in 1958 and has been covered by many artists including Gillian Welsh and Anita Carter. There is a wonderful YouTube video of Cotton performing the song (looks like the early 60s to me, but there is no date on the performance). In her lengthy intro she tells how the song came about. Captivating: youtube.com/watch?v=FhQLxGmU4QA

Dylan did the song on 27th July and gives it a brisk treatment, changing the lyrics around a bit, making it more of a love/regret song. Still it's a lot of fun. This is from the Tramps concert in New York.

[Oh Babe It Aint No Lie]

Dylan's admiration for Johnny Cash is well known, and around 1969/70 Dylan sought to emulate the iconic country singer, wearing white suits and adopting a 'country singer' voice. Dylan mimicked Cash as he did Guthrie years before. That admiration never faded, perhaps because they both went to the same musical well to draw their inspiration. Apart from 'Walk the Line', 'Folsom Prison Blues' is Cash's most famous song, not without controversy, as Cash was never a prisoner there, nor anywhere else. Dylan doesn't have Cash's deep, majestic voice, but he gives the song a vigorous airing with his own nasal twist. You'd almost think Dylan had been a prisoner there too, you know – cold irons bound (10th Nov).

[Folsom Prison Blues]

Dylan also sang 'Big River', another Johnny Cash song released by Sun Records in 1958. Perhaps it was from Cash that Dylan learned the power of place names, and how to use them in a song. Here's a verse from 'Big River.'

> 'I met her accidentally in St. Paul, Minnesota,
> And it tore me up every time I heard her drawl, Southern drawl,
> Then I heard my dream was back Downstream cavortin' in Davenport,

And I followed you, Big River, when you called.'
Listening to the opening bars, you might think you are about to hear a Dylan song, 'Tombstone Blues' maybe, or 'Watching the River Flow' (8th Nov). The crowd loves it.

[Big River]

In NET Part 3, we heard Dylan do a Dion song, 'The Wanderer', in duet with Paul Simon, I think. Here he does it on his own, and it sounds, to my ear, uncannily like Dion. Clearly Dylan has listened carefully to Dion. This homage to the rogue male, released in 1961, has dated more than Dylan songs have – men are no longer encouraged to boast about their 'two fists of iron' or their rampant womanising, but it's a rocking foot tapper and Dylan has fun with it here.

[The Wanderer]

We're no strangers to 'Stone Walls and Steel Bars', by the Stanley Brothers. Dylan began including the song in 1997, and in an earlier post I suggested that it was, in spirit at least, an ally of 'Cold Irons Bound' (Tony Attwood gives a good account of the song here: bob-dylan.org.uk/archives/11475).

Dylan's performances of the song are remarkable for their power and intensity. This one from the early show at Atlantic City, New Jersey, is no exception. Some gentle acoustic guitar from Mr Guitar Man. It works better for me as a prison song than 'Folsom Prison Blues', but I don't know if the Stanley Brothers ever went to prison either.

[Stone Walls and Steel Bars]

Robert Johnson's 'Crossroads' (1936) is more than just a song. It is a seed that would help inspire and spark the rhythm and blues revolution that underpinned the rock music era. It was covered by Cream in 1966, with Eric Clapton demonstrating his mastery of the blues. The lyrics don't support the myth that the song is about how Johnson met the devil at the crossroads and sold his soul in return for musical genius, but there is the mysterious fact that Johnson suddenly learned how to play the guitar, and play it brilliantly, from being a bad player. Here is Robert Johnson's 1936 original: youtube.com/watch?v=Yd60nI4sa9A

[Crossroads]

The song stands at the crossroads where the folk Dylan and the rock Dylan meet. While Johnson performed alone on an acoustic slide guitar in Delta blues style (the earliest known blues style, featuring slide guitar and harmonica), the song easily lent itself to electric treatment, as the Cream version shows. Dylan learned to convert many of his songs from solo acoustic to electric full band treatment, and it is 'Crossroads' that shows the way.

Here, Dylan is duetting with Eric Clapton, but I'm not sure it was a good idea to put Mr Guitar Man with Clapton. Dylan's obsessive hammering at two or three notes doesn't stand up well against the fleet-fingered, melodic Clapton. (Note: this was not a regular NET performance, but a televised benefit concert with a different backing band.)

[Crossroads]

That's it for my survey of 1999. I think it was not just the band working sweetly together, but Dylan's voice that made this an outstanding year. It is his greatest instrument. He can make it soft, luminous and intimate, or rough and throat torn as he choses. We haven't heard him do that so effectively since 1995, and by 1999 his voice is richer and more full bodied. He hits the high notes when he wants and there's a ton of power.

The performances were more disciplined than previous years, with not so many wandering epics, while two superb lead guitar men seemed to be able to successfully underpin Dylan's own stubbornly unique and problematic guitar style.

Yes, Dylan had reached a peak in his rising curve, but it was not to finish there. While 1999 is lauded as being one of the greatest years of the NET, and I wouldn't argue with that, the following year, 2000, was a triumphant continuation of the 1999 peak with, in my opinion Dylan's best performances ever of certain songs.

That's coming up in the next post. See you then!

Kia Ora

NET song index

By Mike Johnson

Asterix denote songs not written by Dylan.
Co-writers acknowledged in brackets after song title.

2 x 2; 1992 part 1
10,000 Men; 2000 part 3
A Hard Rain's A-Gonna Fall;1988 part 2, 1990 part 1, 1992 part 3, 1994 part 2, 1995 part 5, 1998 part 3, 2001 part 2, 2003 part 5, 2004 part 4, 2005 part 5, 2007 part 1, 2010 part 4, 2011 part 2, 2012 part 3, 2013 part 4, 2014 part 3, 2015 part 3, 2017 part 2
Absolutely Sweet Marie; 1988 part 1, 1994 part 3, 1998 part 1, 2006 part 1
Accidently Like a Martyr*; 2002 part 6
Acoustic Jam; 1991 part 1
Across The Borderline*; 1998 part 2
Ain't Talkin; 2006 part 3, 2007 part 1, 2008 part 1, 2008 part 3, 2009 part 4, 2013 part 1
Alabama Getaway*; 1996 part 1, 1999 part 3
All Along the Watchtower; 1988 part 2, 1992 part 1, 1993 part 5, 1994 part 3, 1995 part 3, 1995 part 6, 1998 part 3, 2001 part 4, 2002 part 5, 2003 part 6, 2004 part 5, 2005 part 2, 2006 part 1, 2007 part 1, 2008 part 4, 2009 part 6, 2010 part 2, 2012 part 4, 2013 part 4, 2014 part 2, 2015 part 4, 2018 part 1
All Or Nothing At All*; 2015 part 2, 2016 part 1, 2017 part 1
Any Way You Want Me*; 1994 part 4
Autumn Leaves*; 2015 part 4, 2016 part 2
Ballad of a Thin Man; 1987, 1989 part 1, 1992 part 4, 1994 part 1, 1995 Part 1, 1996 part 2, 1997 part 4, 1999 part 5, 2004 part 5, 2005 part 3, 2006 part 1, 2008 part 4, 2009 part 1, 2010 part 2, 2011 part 2, 2012 part 2, 2014 part 3, 2015 part 3, 2016 part 2, 2017 part 2, 2019 part 3
Barbara Allen*; 1988 part 1
Beyond Here Lies Nothin' (with Robert Hunter); 2009 part 3, 2010 part 1, 2011 part 5, 2013 part 3,
2014 part 1, 2015 part 2, 2017 part 3, 2019 part 2
Beyond the Horizon; 2007 part 1, 2008 part 2, 2009 part 4

Big River*; 1999 part 6, 2000 part 6

Billy; 2009 part 5

Blind Willie McTell; 1997 part 1, 1998 part 2, 2000 part 3, 2001 part 3, 2002 part 3, 2004 part 1, 2005 part 3, 2006 part 3, 2007 part 3, 2008 part 2, 2009 part 4, 2009 part 6, 2011 part 2, 2011 part 5,
2017 part 3

Blowin' In The Wind; 1991 part 2, 1992 Part 3, 1998 part 3, 1999 part 4, 2000 part 4, 2001 part 2, 2002 part 4, 2003 part 1, 2007 part 4, 2008 part 3, 2009 part 1, 2011 part 2, 2012 part 3, 2013 part 3,
2014 part 2, 2015 part 4, 2018 part 2

Blue-Eyed Jane*; 1994 part 4

Bob Dylan's Dream; 1991 Part 1

Boom Boom Mancini*; 2002 part 6

Boots of Spanish Leather; 1992 Part 3, 1993 part 3, 1995 Part 1, 1999 part 5, 2003 part 4, 2005 part 5, 2006 part 4, 2011 part 4, 2013 part 4

Born in Time; 1994 part 5, 1996 Part 3, 1997 part 2, 1998 part 4, 2003 part 1

Brown Sugar*; 2002 part 6

Bye and Bye; 2002 part 2, 2003 part 1, 2004 part 2, 2005 part 4

Can't Wait; 1997 part 1, 1998 part 1, 1999 part 2, 2000 part 2, 2003 part 1, 2004 part 5, 2009 part 1,
2010 part 1, 2011 part 1, 2012 part 4, 2019 part 1

Carrying A Torch*; 2002 part 6

Cat's in the Well; 1992 part 1, 2001 part 3, 2003 part 6, 2004 part 6, 2005 part 3, 2007 part 3, 2009 part 6, 2010 part 4

Chimes of Freedom; 2000 part 4, 2005 part 5, 2009 part 5

Cold Irons Bound; 1997 part 1, 1998 part 1, 1999 part 2, 2000 part 3, 2001 part 3, 2003 part 1, 2004 part 1, 2005 part 2, 2006 part 3, 2009 part 2, 2010 part 2, 2011 part 3

Come Rain or Come Shine*; 2015 part 1, 2018 part 4

Country Pie; 2000 part 5, 2007 part 1

Crash on the Levee; 1995 part 1

Crossroads*; 1999 part 6

Cry A While; 2001 part 6, 2003 part 4, 2005 part 1, 2007 part 2, 2009 part 4, 2010 part 3, 2014 part 3, 2018 part 1

Dark Eyes; 1995 part 5

Deadman; 1989 part 4

Dear Landlord; 2000 part 2, 2003 part 1

Delia*; 1992 Part 3, 2012 part 2

Desolation Row; 1990 part 2, 1992 part 3, 1993 part 3, 1994 part 1, 1995 part 1, 1995 part 5, 1998 part 3, 1999 part 5, 2000 part 4, 2001 part 1, 2003 part 1, 2005 part 5, 2006 part 4, 2007 part 4, 2008 part 3, 2009 part 1, 2010 part 4, 2011 part 3, 2012 part 4, 2013 part 4, 2014 part 3, 2015 part 4, 2016 part 2, 2017 part 2

Dignity; 1995 part 4, 2000 part 3, 2004 part 6, 2009 part 1

Disease of Conceit; 1990 part 2

Don't Think Twice; 1993 part 3, 1995 part 3, 1996 part 2, 1997 part 3, 1998 part 4, 1999 part 5, 2000 part 4, 2001 part 1, 2002 part 5, 2003 part 5, 2004 part 4, 2005 part 5, 2006 part 4, 2007 part 3, 2009 part 6, 2010 part 1, 2011 part 3, 2013 part 4, 2014 part 3, 2015 part 2, 2016 part 1, 2017 part 2, 2018 part 2

Down Along the Cove; 1999 part 3, 2003 part 4, 2004 part 5

Down In the Flood; 2005 part 4

Drifter's Escape; 1996 part 1, 1996 Part 3, 2000 part 2, 2001 part 4, 2002 part 4, 2003 part 1, 2004 part 3, 2005 part 5

Duncan and Brady*; 2000 part 6, 2002 part 6

Duquesne Whistle; 2013 part 2, 2014 part 1, 2015 part 2, 2015 part 4, 2016 part 2, 2018 part 4

Early Roman Kings; 2012 part 1, 2013 part 3, 2014 part 2, 2015 part 3, 2017 part 3, 2018 part 4

Every Grain of Sand; 1989 part 4, 1991 part 2, 1999 part 5, 2003 part 5, 2005 part 1, 2006 part 4, 2007 part 3, 2009 part 2, 2010 part 1, 2011 part 4, 2013 part 1

Everything is Broken; 1990 part 1, 1992 part 2, 1994 part 5, 1999 part 5

Floater; 2001 part 5, 2002 part 2, 2003 part 1, 2004 part 2, 2005 part 6

Folsom Prison Blues*; 1999 part 6

Forever Young; 1987, 1989 part 3, 1993 part 4, 1998 part 2, 1999 part 5, 2000 part 5, 2002 part 3, 2002 part 5, 2009 part 1, 2010 part 3, 2011 part 3

Forgetful Heart (with Robert Hunter); 2009 part 3, 2010 part 1, 2011 part 4, 2013 part 3, 2014 part 2, 2015 part 1

Fourth Time Around; 1999 part 4, 2000 part 5

Frankie Lee and Judas Priest; 1988 part 1

Friend of the Devil; 1996 Part 3, 1999 part 6, 2007 part 3

Full Moon and Empty Arms*; 2015 part 1, 2017 part 2

Gates of Eden; 1988 part 1, 1989 part 2, 1991 part 2, 1992 Part 3, 1993 part 4, 1995 part 5, 1996 part 4, 2000 part 1

Girl From the North Country; 1991 part 2, 1992 Part 3, 1993 part 3, 1996 part 2, 1998 part 4, 1999 part 4, 2000 part 1, 2001 part 1, 2003 part 1, 2004 part 3, 2004 part 6, 2006 part 1, 2007 part 4, 2008 part 3, 2013 part 4, 2014 part 3, 2019 part 2

God knows; 1993 part 1, 1995 part 3, 1997 part 4, 2004 part 6, 2005 part 6

Gonna Change My Way of Thinking; 2009 part 5, 2010 part 3, 2011 part 3

Gotta Serve Somebody; 1988 part 3

Handy Dandy; 2008 part 3

Hazel; 1994 part 4, 2005 part 4

Hallelujah*; 1988 part 1

Hallelujah I'm Ready to Go*; 2000 part 6

Heavy and a Bottle of Bread; 2002 part 2, 2003 part 6

Heartbreak Hotel*; 2009 part 6

Heartland*; 2004 part 7

High Water(for Charley Patton); 2001 part 5, 2002 part 2, 2002 part 5, 2003 part 1, 2004 part 5, 2005 part 1, 2000 part 6, 2006 part 3, 2007 part 2, 2008 part 2, 2009 part 4, 2010 part 3, 2011 part 5, 2012 part 3, 2013 part 3, 2014 part 2, 2015 part 3, 2016 part 1, 2017 part 1, 2018 part 4

Highway 61 Revisited; 1989 part 4, 1992 part 4, 1994 part 2, 1995 part 6, 1998 part 1, 1999 part 3, 2003 part 5, 2004 part 5, 2005 part 2, 2006 part 1, 2007 part 4, 2008 part 4, 2009 part 6, 2010 part 2, 2011 part 5, 2012 part 2, 2013 part 4, 2016 part 2, 2017 part 2, 2018 part 3, 2019 part 1

Highlands; 1999 part 2, 2000 part 5

Honest With Me; 2001 part 6, 2002 part 1, 2002 part 3, 2003 part 4, 2004 part 5, 2006 part 3, 2007 part 2, 2008 part 2, 2009 part 4, 2010 part 4, 2011 part 3, 2013 part 5, 2017 part 1, 2018 part 3, 2019 part 2

Honky Tonk Blues*; 1999 part 6

Hoochie Coochie Man*; 2000 part 6

House of the Rising Sun*; 2000 part 6, 2007 part 3

I Am The Man, Thomas*; 2000 part 6

I and I; 1987, 1992 part 1, 1993 part 1, 1994 part 5, 1997 part 3, 1998 part 4, 1999 part 5

I Believe In You; 1989 part 4, 1991 part 3, 1993 part 2, 2003 part 1, 2004 part 1, 2004 part 4, 2005 part 6, 2009 part 2

I Could Have Told You*; 2016 part 2

I Don't Believe You; 1994 part 3, 1995 part 3, 2002 part 3, 2010 part 2, 2013 part 1

I Dreamed I Saw St Augustine; 1987, 1989 part 4, 1992 Part 4, 2005 part 5, 2011 part 5

I Feel a Change Coming On (with Robert Hunter); 2009 part 3, 2010 part 3

I Remember You; 2005 part 4

I Shall Be Released; 1988 part 2, 1989 part 2, 1995 part 4, 1998 part 4, 2000 part 5, 2003 part 4,
2005 part 3

I Want You; 1993 part 4, 1994 part 1, 1999 part 5

Idiot Wind; 1987, 1992 part 2

If Dogs Run Free; 2000 part 2, 2001 part 3, 2005 part 4

If Not for You; 1992 Part 4, 1993 part 2, 1995 part 3, 2003 part 6

If You Ever Go to Houston (with Robert Hunter); 2009 part 3, 2010 part 3, 2011 part 2

If You See Her Say Hello; 1994 part 4, 1995 part 4, 1996 part 4, 2004 part 6, 2009 part 5

I'll Be Your Baby Tonight; 1991 part 3, 1998 part 4, 2002 part 1, 2003 part 1, 2004 part 4, 2004 part 6, 2005 part 3, 2006 part 4, 2007 part 3, 2009 part 5, 2010 part 1, 2011 part 2, 2015 part 1

I'll Not Be a Stranger*; 1997 part 2

I'm A Fool To Want You*; 2015 part 2

In The Summertime; 2002 part 3

It Ain't Me, Babe; 1992 Part 3, 1994 part 3, 1995 part 2, 1996 part 2, 1998 part 4, 2000 part 4, 2002 part 4, 2004 part 6, 2006 part 4, 2007 part 3, 2010 part 1, 2012 part 4, 2013 part 4, 2017 part 2, 2018 part 3, 2019 part 2

It Takes a Lot to Laugh, It Takes a Train to Cry; 1988 part 2, 1989 part 4, 1994 part 1, 1997 part 3,
1999 part 5, 2001 part 3, 2003 part 1, 2004 part 4, 2018 part 1, 2019 part 1

It's A Man's World*; 2018 part 4

It's All Good; 2009 part 3

It's All Over Now, Baby Blue; 1989 part 2, 1991 Part 1, 1993 part 3, 1994 part

2, 1995 part 2, 1997 part 4, 2003 part 6, 2004 part 3, 2005 part 5, 2008 part 3, 2009 part 5, 2010 part 1, 2011 part 4, 2012 part 1, 2016 part 2

It's Alright Ma (I'm Only Bleeding); 1989 part 2, 1990 part 1, 1999 part 5, 2000 part 4, 2001 part 2, 2002 part 5, 2004 part 4, 2005 part 1, 2006 part 1, 2007 part 1, 2008 part 3, 2009 part 5, 2013 part 1

It's Not Dark Yet; 1998 part 2, 1999 part 2, 2005 part 6, 2010 part 1, 2011 part 1, 2012 part 3

Jokerman; 1994 part 5, 1995 part 6, 2003 part 4

Joey (with Jacques Levy); 1988 part 1, 1995 part 4, 1997 part 4, 2012 part 1

John Brown; 1987, 1988 part 2, 1989 part 1, 1992 Part 3, 1996 part 2, 1998 part 3, 1999 part 4, 2001 part 2, 2005 part 5, 2006 part 4, 2010 part 4, 2011 part 2, 2012 part 1

Jolene; 2009 part 3, 2010 part 2, 2011 part 2, 2011 part 3

Just Like a Woman; 1991 part 3, 1992 Part 4, 1993 part 2, 1994 part 3, 1995 part 3, 1998 part 2, 2001 part 4, 2003 part 1, 2004 part 1, 2007 part 4, 2008 part 4, 2010 part 4

Just like Tom Thumb's Blues; 1988 part 2, 1993 part 2, 1994 part 2, 2001 part 3, 2002 part 2, 2003 part 1, 2006 part 1, 2007 part 4, 2008 part 1, 2009 part 6, 2010 part 1, 2013 part 4, 2014 part 3

Knockin' On Heaven's Door; 1987, 1989 part 2, 1990 part 2, 1991 part 3, 1994 part 3, 1997 part 4, 1998 part 4, 2001 part 4, 2003 part 1

Lay Lady Lay; 1992 Part 4, 1993 part 2, 1995 Part 1, 2001 part 4, 2002 part 1, 2003 part 1, 2005 part 3, 2006 part 4, 2007 part 4, 2008 part 1, 2009 part 5, 2010 part 4

Lenny Bruce; 1994 part 5, 2005 part 6, 2019 part 2

Learning to Fly*; 2017 part 2

Leopard-Skin Pill-Box Hat; 1999 part 3, 2000 part 3, 2009 part 6, 2010 part 2, 2011 part 5, 2013 part 1

License to Kill; 1995 part 2

Like A Rolling Stone; 1988 part 1, 1995 part 3, 1998 part 4, 2000 part 3, 2001 part 4, 2002 part 5, 2003 part 1, 2004 part 1, 2006 part 1, 2007 part 4, 2008 part 4, 2009 part 6, 2010 part 2, 2011 part 3,
2012 part 2, 2013 part 4, 2016 part 2, 2018 part 1

Lonesome Day Blues; 2001 part 6, 2002 part 3, 2004 part 5, 2006 part 3, 2008 part 3, 2014 part 3, 2016 part 2

Long and Wasted Years; 2013 part 2, 2014 part 2, 2015 part 3, 2017 part 3, 2018 part 4, 2019 part 3

Long Black Veil*; 1997 part 2

Love Minus Zero No Limit; 1988 part 2, 1989 part 2, 1992 Part 3, 1996 Part 3, 1997 part 4, 2002 part 1, 2002 part 2, 2003 part 1, 2005 part 5, 2008 part 1, 2012 part 1

Love Sick; 1997 part 1, 1999 part 2, 2000 part 3, 2001 part 3, 2004 part 1, 2004 part 5, 2006 part 3, 2007 part 3, 2009 part 2, 2010 part 3, 2011 part 1, 2013 part 5, 2014 part 1, 2015 part 2, 2016 part 2, 2017 part 3, 2018 part 3

Lucky Old Sun*; 1991 part 2

Maggie's Farm; 1988 part 2, 1995 part 3, 1996 part 2, 1997 part 3, 1999 part 1, 2002 part 3, 2004 part 5, 2005 part 2, 2006 part 4, 2009 part 6

Mamma, You Been On My Mind; 1994 part 1, 1995 part 5, 2000 part 4, 2001 part 1

Man Gave Names to All the Animals; 1991 Part 1

Man in the Long Black Coat; 1989 part 1, 1990 part 2, 1991 part 3, 1992 part 2, 1994 part 5, 1995 part 2, 1996 part 1, 1999 part 5, 2002 part 3, 2004 part 6, 2009 part 5, 2011 part 2, 2013 part 1

Man of Constant Sorrow*; 1988 part 3

Man of Peace; 1989 part 3, 1991 part 3

Masters of War; 1988 part 2, 1994 part 1, 1995 part 4, 1996 part 1, 1998 part 2, 1999 part 4, 2000 part 4, 2001 part 2, 2002 part 4, 2003 part 6, 2004 part 6, 2005 part 5, 2006 part 4, 2007 part 3, 2008 part 3, 2010 part 2, 2010 part 4

Melancholy Mood*; 2015 part 1, 2016 part 2, 2017 part 3

Milk Cow Blues*; 2004 part 7

Million Dollar Bash; 2005 part 4

Million Miles; 1998 part 1, 2003 part 1, 2004 part 2, 2005 part 6, 2008 part 3, 2009 part 4

Mississippi; 2001 part 6, 2005 part 6, 2008 part 2, 2011 part 2, 2012 part 1

Moon River*; 2018 part 1

Moonlight; 2001 part 5, 2002 part 3, 2003 part 4, 2004 part 2, 2005 part 3, 2007 part 1, 2008 part 2

Money Honey*; 1999 part 3

Most Likely You Go Your Way (and I'll Go Mine); 1999 part 3, 2001 part 3, 2003 part 4, 2004 part 3, 2005 part 3, 2009 part 6, 2010 part 4, 2013 part 4

Most of the Time; 1989 part 1, 1992 part 2

More and More*; 1998 part 4

Mr Tambourine Man; 1989 part 2, 1992 part 3, 1993 part 3, 1994 part 1, 1995

Part 1, 1995 part 5, 1996 part 2, 1997 part 4, 2001 part 1, 2003 part 6, 2004 part 3, 2005 part 3, 2006 part 1, 2006 part 4, 2009 part 2

Mutineer*; 2002 part 6

My Back Pages; 1994 part 3, 1996 part 2, 1996 part 4, 1997 part 4, 1998 part 4, 2000 part 5, 2001 part 2, 2003 part 6, 2008 part 4, 2009 part 6

My Wife's Home Town (with Robert Hunter); 2009 part 3, 2010 part 1, 2011 part 2, 2011 part 3

Nettie Moore; 2006 part 2, 2007 part 2, 2008 part 2

Never Gonna Be the Same Again; 2005 part 4

New Morning; 1991 part 1

Newry Highway Man*; 2000 part 6

No One More Time*; 2004 part 7

Not Dark Yet; 1998 part 2, 2000 part 2, 2004 part 1, 2005 part 6, 2004 part 1, 2009 part 4, 2010 part 3, 2019 part 4

Not Fade Away*; 1997 part 2, 1999 part 3, 2000 part 6

Oh Babe, It Ain't No Lie*; 1999 part 6

Old Man*; 2002 part 6

Once Upon A Time*; 2017 part 2

One of Us Must Know (Sooner or Later); 1997 part 2

One Too Many Mornings; 1989 part 2, 1990 part 2, 1991 part 2, 1993 part 4, 1994 part 1, 1995 part 5, 1997 part 3, 1998 part 3, 2001 part 1, 2002 part 5, 2003 part 5

One More Cup of Coffee; 1993 part 2, 1993 part 4, 2009 part 1

Oxford Town; 1990 part 1

Pancho & Lefty*; 2004 part 7

Pass Me Not, Oh Gentle Stranger*; 1999 part 6, 2000 part 6

Pay in Blood; 2013 part 2, 2014 part 1, 2015 part 2, 2016 part 1, 2017 part 3, 2018 part 3, 2019 part 2

Pledging my Time; 1995 part 6, 1997 part 2

Po Boy; 2002 part 2, 2004 part 2, 2005 part 6, 2009 part 2

Political World; 1990 part 1

Positively 4ᵗʰ Street; 1994 part 2, 1996 part 1, 1996 Part 3, 1997 part 4, 2004 part 6, 2006 part 4

Pretty Peggy-O*; 1996 part 4

Queen Jane Approximately; 1989 part 1, 1993 part 4, 1996 Part 3, 1997 part 3, 2003 part 1, 2005 part 3, 2005 part 6, 2013 part 1

Rainy Day Woman #12 & 35; 1992 Part 4, 1995 part 6, 1996 part 4, 1998 part

1, 2001 part 4, 2004 part 6, 2008 part 1, 2009 part 6, 2013 part 4

Rank Strangers*; 1988 part 3

Restless Farewell; 1998 part 3

Ring Them Bells; 1993 part 4, 1994 part 5, 2001 part 4, 2004 part 3, 2005 part 4

Rollin' and Tumblin'; 2006 part 2, 2007 part 2, 2008 part 2, 2009 part 4, 2010 part 3, 2011 part 5

Roll On John; 2013 part 2

Romance in Durango (with Jacques Levy); 2003 part 1

Roving Gambler*; 1997 part 4, 1999 part 4, 2000 part 6

Sad Songs and Waltzes*; 2015 part 3

Samson and Delilah*; 2004 part 7

Satisfied Mind*; 1999 part 6

Saving Grace; 2003 part 3, 2004 part 6, 2005 part 6, 2012 part 1

Scarlet Town; 2012 part 1, 2013 part 3, 2014 part 2, 2015 part 3, 2016 part 1, 2017 part 3, 2018 part 3

Searching for a Soldier's Grave*; 2000 part 6, 2002 part 6

Seeing the Real You at Last; 1989 part 3, 1992 part 2, 1996 Part 3, 1999 part 3, 2003 part 6

Senor; 1987, 1991 part 3, 1994 part 4, 1995 part 4, 1998 part 4, 1999 part 1, 2002 part 3, 2003 part 1

2005 part 6, 2006 part 1, 2008 part 1, 2009 part 5, 2010 part 4

Serve Somebody; 1998 part 2, 1999 part 5, 2000 part 3, 2001 part 3, 2008 part 1, 2009 part 5, 2018 part 1, 2019 part 3

Seven Days; 1996 part 1

Shadows*; 2012 part 2

Shake Sugaree*; 1997 part 2

She Belongs to Me; 1988 part 2, 1990 part 2, 1992 Part 4, 1993 part 2, 1994 part 1, 1995 part 4, 1996 part 1, 1999 part 5, 2000 part 5, 2002 part 5, 2006 part 1, 2007 part 1, 2013 part 1, 2014 part 1, 2015 part 2, 2016 part 1

She's About A Mover*; 2000 part 6

Shelter From the Storm; 1989 part 3, 1991 part 3, 1994 part 4, 1995 Part 1, 1996 part 4, 1997 part 3, 1999 part 5, 2001 part 4, 2005 part 1, 2007 part 1, 2014 part 3, 2015 part 4

Shooting Star; 1991 part 2, 1997 part 3, 2003 part 1, 2004 part 3, 2005 part 6, 2007 part 3, 2009 part 2, 2011 part 5, 2013 part 1

Simple Twist of Fate; 1989 part 3, 1991 part 3, 1992 part 2, 1993 part 4, 1994 part 4, 1998 part 4, 2003 part 6, 2010 part 3, 2011 part 3, 2012 part 4, 2013 part 3, 2014 part 2, 2015 part 2, 2016 part 2,

2017 part 2, 2018 part 2, 2019 part 2

Silvio (with Robert Hunter); 1996 part 1, 1998 part 1

Sing Me Back Home*; 2004 part 7

Solid Rock; 2002 part 1

Something*; 2002 part 6

Song to Woody; 1999 part 4, 2000 part 5, 2001 part 2

Soon After Midnight; 2012 part 2, 2013 part 3, 2014 part 2, 2015 part 3, 2017 part 3, 2018 part 4, 2019 part 3

Spirit on the Water; 2006 part 2, 2007 part 2, 2008 part 1, 2009 part 4, 2010 part 3, 2011 part 3, 2013 part 3, 2014 part 2, 2015 part 3, 2016 part 1

Standing In The Doorway; 2000 part 1, 2002 part 5, 2004 part 1, 2017 part 1

Stay With Me*; 2014 part 2, 2015 part 4

Stone Walls and Steel Bars*; 1997 part 2, 1999 part 6

Stormy Weather*; 2017 part 1

Stuck Inside of Mobile with the Memphis Blues Again; 1992 part 4, 1995 part 6, 2001 part 4, 2004 part 5, 2005 part 2, 2007 part 4, 2008 part 4, 2009 part 2, 2010 part 4

Subterranean Homesick Blues; 2002 part 4

Sugar Baby; 2001 part 6, 2002 part 4, 2004 part 4, 2005 part 3, 2008 part 2, 2009 part 4, 2011 part 3, 2012 part 1

Summer Days; 2001 part 5, 2002 part 3, 2003 part 4, 2004 part 2, 2004 part 4, 2005 part 2, 2006 part 3, 2007 part 2, 2008 part 2, 2009 part 4, 2010 part 3, 2011 part 5, 2012 part 4, 2013 part 3, 2014 part 3, 2017 part 1, 2018 part 4

Suzie Baby*; 2013 part 5

Tangled Up in Blue; 1988 part 3, 1989 part 1, 1990 part 2, 1992 part 1, 1993 part 1, 1994 part 4,

1995 part 2, 1995 part 5, 1996 part 2, 1996 Part 3, 1997 part 3, 1998 part 2, 1999 part 5, 2000 part 5, 2001 part 1, 2002 part 5, 2003 part 1, 2004 part 6, 2005 part 6, 2006 part 4, 2007 part 3, 2008 part 4,

2009 part 1, 2010 part 1, 2010 part 2, 2011 part 1, 2011 part 3, 2012 part 2, 2013 part 5, 2014 part 1,

2015 part 2, 2016 part 1, 2017 part 1

Tears of Rage; 1989 part 4, 1994 part 1, 1996 part 4, 1998 part 3, 2001 part 3,

2005 part 5, 2006 part 1, 2007 part 3, 2008 part 4

Tell Me That It Isn't True; 2002 part 5, 2005 part 3

That'll be the Day/The Wanderer*; 1999 part 3

That Old Black Magic*; 2016 part 1

The Ballad of Frankie Lee and Judas Priest; 2000 part 2

The Ballad of Hollis Brown; 1998 part 2, 1990 part 2, 1996 Part 3, 1997 part 2, 1998 part 3, 2005 part 5, 2009 part 5, 2010 part 4

The Disease of Conceit; 1989 part 1, 1993 part 4, 1995 part

The End of Innocence*; 2002 part 6

The Levee's Gonna Break; 2006 part 2, 2007 part 2, 2008 part 2, 2010 part 2, 2011 part 5, 2013 part 5, 2014 part 3, 2015 part 2

The Lonesome Death of Hattie Carroll; 2003 part 5, 2005 part 5, 2006 part 1, 2008 part 3, 2009 part 6, 2010 part 4

The Man in Me; 1988 part 1, 1991 Part 1, 1995 part 6, 1998 part 2, 2005 part 3, 2009 part 5, 2010 part 2, 2011 part 5

The Mighty Quinn; 2002 part 4, 2003 part 4

The Night We Called It A Day*; 2015 part 1

The Sounds of Silence*; 1999 part 1

The Times They Are A-changin'; 1987, 1988 part 1, 1995 Part 1, 1995 part 5, 1996 part 4, 1999 part 5, 2001 part 2, 2005 part 5, 2006 part 4, 2007 part 4, 2009 part 2

The Wanderer*; 1999 part 6

The Water Is Wide*; 1989 part 3

Things Have Changed; 2000 part 1, 2001 part 4, 2002 part 4, 2003 part 4, 2005 part 6, 2006 part 3, 2007 part 3, 2008 part 3, 2009 part 1, 2011 part 1, 2012 part 3, 2013 part 3, 2014 part 1, 2015 part 2, 2016 part 2, 2017 part 2, 2018 part 3, 2019 part 2

This Dream of You; 2009 part 3, 2012 part 4

This Wheel's On Fire; 1996 Part 3, 1997 part 2, 1998 part 2, 2000 part 3, 2001 part 4, 2004 part 3, 2006 part 1, 2010 part 1

This World Can't Stand Long*; 2000 part 6, 2001 part 2, 2002 part 6

Thunder on the Mountain; 2006 part 2, 2007 part 2, 2008 part 1, 2009 part 4, 2010 part 2, 2011 part 5, 2012 part 2, 2013 part 5, 2014 part 3, 2017 part 1, 2018 part 1, 2019 part 3

Tight Connection to my Heart; 1993 part 4

Till I Fell In Love With You; 1997 part 1, 1998 part 1, 1999 part 2, 2001 part 3, 2005 part 6, 2006 part 3, 2007 part 1, 2008 part 1, 2009 part 4, 2011 part

5, 2015 part 3

To Be Alone With You; 1996 part 4, 1998 part 4, 2001 part 3, 2002 part 2, 2003 part 1, 2004 part 4, 2005 part 4

To Make You Feel My Love; 1998 part 1, 1999 part 2, 2003 part 5, 2004 part 2, 2006 part 3, 2008 part 3, 2009 part 2, 2011 part 4, 2013 part 5, 2016 part 1, 2017 part 3, 2018 part 2, 2019 part 1

To Ramona; 1989 part 2, 1989 part 4, 1992 Part 3, 1993 part 3, 1996 part 1, 1996 Part 3, 1997 part 4,

2000 part 3, 2001 part 1, 2003 part 1, 2005 part 5, 2006 part 4, 2007 part 4, 2009 part 2, 2011 part 2, 2014 part 3, 2015 part 1

Tombstone Blues; 1995 part 4, 1997 part 3, 1999 part 3, 2002 part 1, 2003 part 5, 2005 part 5

Tonight I'll Be Staying Here With You; 1990 part 2, 1998 part 4

Tomorrow is a Long Time; 1999 part 4, 2001 part 1, 2005 part 6

Tough Mama; 1997 part 2, 2001 part 4, 2003 part 5, 2009 part 2

Trail of the Buffalo*; 1989 part 3

Tryin' to Get to Heaven; 1999 part 2, 2000 part 1, 2003 part 1, 2004 part 6, 2005 part 6, 2008 part 3, 2009 part 4, 2010 part 3, 2011 part 1, 2012 part 3, 2017 part 1, 2018 part 1, 2019 part 2

Tweedle Dum & Tweedle Dee; 2001 part 6, 2003 part 4, 2004 part 6, 2006 part 3, 2008 part 2, 2009 part 4, 2010 part 1, 2013 part 5, 2014 part 3

TV Talking Song; 1990 part 1

Under The Red Sky; 1990 part 1, 1991 part 3, 1993 part 2, 1996 part 2, 2003 part 6, 2004 part 3, 2007 part 3, 2010 part 2, 2013 part 1

Under Your Spell; 1987

Union Sundown; 1992 part 1

Viola Lee Blues*; 1997 part 2

Visions of Johanna; 1989 part 4, 1991 part 3, 1995 part 5, 1999 part 5, 2002 part 2, 2003 part 1, 2005 part 1, 2010 part 4, 2011 part 4, 2012 part 4, 2013 part 4, 2015 part 4, 2018 part 1

Waiting For You; 2005 part 4, 2013 part 3, 2014 part 1

What Good Am I?; 1989 part 1, 1991 part 2, 1992 part 2, 1994 part 5, 1996 part 4, 2010 part 3, 2013 part 3, 2014 part 1

What'll I do?*; 2015 part 4, 2016 part 2

What Was It You Wanted?; 1995 part 4

Watching the River Flow; 1991 part 2, 1995 part 3, 1996 part 1, 1996 Part 3, 2000 part 3, 2003 part 1, 2004 part 5, 2005 part 3, 2007 part 4, 2008 part

3, 2009 part 5, 2010 part 4, 2011 part 2, 2013 part 4, 2014 part 3

We'd Better Talk This Over; 2000 part 3

When I Paint My Masterpiece; 1991 part 2, 1995 part 6, 1996 part 2, 2007 part 4, 2011 part 5, 2018 part 2, 2019 part 1

When the Deal Goes Down; 2006 part 2, 2007 part 2, 2008 part 1, 2009 part 1, 2012 part 3

When you Gonna Wake Up?; 1989 part 1

Where Are You*; 2015 part 3

Where Teardrops Fall; 1990 part 1

Why Try To Change Me Now*; 2015 part 3

Wicked Messenger; 1987, 1997 part 2, 2000 part 2, 2001 part 4, 2004 part 5, 2005 part 5, 2009 part 5

Wiggle Wiggle; 1990 part 1, 1992 part 1

With God on our Side; 1988 part 1, 1994 part 1

Working Man's Blues; 2006 part 2, 2007 part 2, 2008 part 1, 2009 part 4, 2010 part 2, 2011 part 4, 2013 part 5, 2014 part 1, 2015 part 2

You Ain't Going Nowhere; 1997 part 3, 2002 part 4, 2003 part 1, 2012 part 1

You Angel You; 1990 part 2

You Win Again*; 2004 part 7

You're A Big Girl Now; 1988 part 3, 1989 part 3, 1990 part 2, 1991 part 2, 1992 part 2, 1997 part 3, 1998 part 4, 2001 part 4, 2002 part 2, 2003 part 4

You're Gonna Quit Me*; 1999 part 4

You're Too Late*; 1999 part 6

About the Author

Mike Johnson, fiction writer and poet, is recognised as one of New Zealand's leading, innovative writers. He lives on Waiheke Island and has taught creative writing at AUT University and the University of Auckland. In 2002 he received The University of Auckland's Literary Fellowship, having been Literary Fellow at Canterbury University in 1987. His first novel, Lear, the Shakespeare Company Plays Lear at Babylon was short listed for the New Zealand Book Awards in 1986, his novel Dumb Show won the Buckland Memorial Award for Literary Excellence in 1995, and he won the Frances Kean Award for his short story, 'Magic Strings' in 1999. His first book of poetry, The Palanquin Ropes, (1983) was co-winner of the John Cowie Reed Memorial Competition. His non-fiction, Angel of Compassion, was shortlisted for the Ashton Whyle Award in 2014, and a poem from Vertical Harp, The selected poems of Li He (2006) has been anthologised in the Essential New Zealand Poems: Facing the Empty Page (Random House, 2015). Critic Martin Edmond described the 2020 novel, Driftdead, as 'a masterpiece.' Mike Johnson is the author of thirty-five books including ten novels, fourteen books of poetry, four of shorter fiction, one non fiction, and three children's books.

Mike Johnson –Publishing history

Novels

2025 – Speechless, Lasavia Publishing: Auckland

2020 – Driftdead, Lasavia Publishing: Auckland

2016 – Zombie in a Spacesuit, Lasavia Publishing: Auckland

2014 – Hold my Teeth While I Teach you to Dance: Lasavia Publishing Ltd: Auckland.

2011 – Travesty, Titus Books: Auckland.

2004 – Stench, Hazard Press: Christchurch. (Republished by Lasavia Publishing, 2016)

2001 – Counterpart, Harper Collins: Sydney. (Republished by Lasavia Publishing, 2021)

1996 – Dumb Show, Longacre Press: Dunedin. (Won the Buckland Memorial Literary Award for fiction in 1997. Republished by Lasavia Publishing, 2016)

1991 – Lethal Dose, Hard Echo Press: Auckland. (Republished by Lasavia Publishing, 2019)

1987 – Antibody Positive, Hard Echo Press: Auckland.

1986 – Lear: The Shakespeare Company Plays Lear at Babylon, Hard Echo Press: Auckland. (Shortlisted for the NZ Book Awards)

Short fiction

2023 – Afterworld, A novella. Lasavia Publishing: Auckland

2017 – Confessions of a Cockroach/Headstone, two novellas, Lasavia Publishing: Auckland

2016 – Back in the Day, short stories. Lasavia Publishing: Auckland

Lasavia Publishing: Auckland.

1991 – Foreigners, three novellas. Penguin Books: Auckland.

Poetry

2025 – Wheeling South, Lasavia Publishing: Auckland

2024 – The Nine Lives of Willa the cat, Lasavia Publishing: Auckland. (Graphics by Frances Ryder. To be published in November, 2024)

2024 – Love In The Age of Unreason, Lasavia Publishing: Auckland.

2023 – Selected Poems, Mike Johnson, edited by Jack Ross, Lasavia Publishing: Auckland.

2023 – Sketches (Graphics by Leila Lees), Lasavia Publishing: Auckland.

2020 – The Raising Light Trilogy, Lasavia Publishing: Auckland.

2020 – The Raising Light Trilogy published as separate volumes: The Toy Box, Hide Your Eyes and Extinction Rebellion, Lasavia Publishing. Auckland.

2017 – Ladder with No Rungs, (Graphics by Leila Lees), Lasavia Publishing: Auckland.

2016 – Two Lines and a Garden, (Graphics by Leila Lees), Lasavia Publishing: Auckland.

2011 - To Beatrice Where We Crossed The Line, Second Avenue Press: Auckland. (Graphics by Simon Oosterdijk)

2009 – The vertical Harp, Titus Books: Auckland.

1996 – Treasure Hunt, Auckland University Press: Auckland.

1985 – Standing Wave, Hard Echo Press: Auckland.

1984 – From a Woman in Mt Eden Prison & Drawing Lessons, Hard Echo Press: Auckland.

1983 – The Palanquin Ropes, Voice Press: Wellington. (Co-winner of the John Cowie Reid Memorial Competition for a long poem or sequence of poems)

Non Fiction

2014 – The Angel of Compassion, Lasavia Publishing Ltd: Auckland. (Shortlisted for the Aston Wylie Awards, manuscript section)

1973 – Dialogue, Whitcomb and Tombs: Christchurch: a text for senior English, (Co-author with A.T. Johnson).

Children

2019 – Flippity Fluppity Flop (graphics by Daniela Gast), Lasavia Publishing: Auckland.

2016 – Kenni and the Roof Slide (Graphics by Jennifer Rackham), Lasavia Publishing: Auckland.

2015 – Taniwha (Graphics by Jennifer Rackham), Lasavia Publishing: Auckland. Bilingual: English and Te Reo.

www.ingramcontent.com/pod-product-compliance
Lightning Source LLC
Chambersburg PA
CBHW061556120626
46550CB00004B/1507